MYLESTONES

"How Mice Become Men"

Best Wishes

Gary Ian Braxton

MYLESTONES

"How Mice Become Men"

CHAPTER ONE
HOTSHOT

The closest I ever came to being an angel was back when my mind had not yet been defiled by sex, pride or fear. You could say I was a virgin in every sense of the word. The only things that held any significance to me were eating, sleeping and my mother. She was as essential to my existence as the air I was breathing.

I remember waking one night to the sound of her slippers sliding across the floor and the moans of the old wood planks underneath each of her steps. Curiosity, an affliction I still can't seem to get rid of, caused me to roll over my older brother, Adrian and climb out of bed. My other two elder brothers, Leon and Ambus were still sleeping soundly. I pulled back the sheet that served as our door and saw my mother, a pale woman with deep red hair that fell just over her ears. She was standing at the front door gripping the knob and bracing her body against it, as if a strong wind was about to force it open.

The door was old and fragile. The top half had a huge area for a window, but the glass had been broken out long ago. My uncle thought it more cost effective to replace it with a thin sheet of plywood. It had been his mother's house some years back and had more leaks in the roof than we had pots. There were towels and rags stuffed in all the nooks and crannies to keep out the cold of winter and the cockroaches of summer. This ghetto ingenuity was not very effective on either front.

Potbellied and wiping the sleep from my eyes, I heard my mother say in her girlish voice, "Go away. Please go away."

There was a loud crack and the thin sheet of plywood was

reduced to an implosion of splinters that rained down upon her. If that had not shocked me into an immediate state of awareness, her high pitched screams would have. The intensity of them was paralyzing; I have never heard a sound so horrifying.

His dark arms reached out at her until he managed to grab hold of her hair. The door no longer an obstacle, he groped at her nightgown, ripping it into shreds and exposing her bare breasts. Keeping him out of the house was a task beyond a woman of her stature.

I didn't utter a single sound the entire time. As a matter of fact, the only reaction I remember having was at the sight of the blood on her hands. This encouraged a warm trickle of urine to seep down my inner thigh. I must have been in a mild state of shock because it was her screams that brought my other siblings rushing toward what was left of the front door. Leon, the man of the house at twelve, picked up the only weapon we possessed the straw broom in the corner next to the door, and began wildly swiping and poking at the intruder. My sister Resa, the eldest by a year, grabbed hold of my mother's arm and pried her free of his grip. A butcher's knife fell to the floor and Leon picked it up. It had a chipped, wood handle; rusted screws and a tarnished stained blade, but by the time Leon could return to an upright position, the intruder was retreating.

I don't remember if or when the police came, but my mild state of shock lasted less than six minutes. The splintered door, the gash in my mother's hand and the fact that I was standing in a puddle of my own urine, were the only visible signs that he had ever been there.

That night I came to realize that I was not safe and as strong as she was, my mother could not protect me. It was a horrifying reality, but she was a living breathing woman who could be taken away at any moment. An overwhelming sense of vulnerability came over me and stayed. From that moment on night brought nothing, but fear and uncertainty. When it was time for bed and my mother came to tuck me in, I pretended to be already asleep. Once the lights were out and all my brothers had fallen asleep, I would sit up in bed and look out the window. I stayed up for hours waiting on the intruder to return. Even though sleep eventually prevailed, I woke at the slightest noise. I looked forward to sunrise, but it no longer brought with it the brilliance and luster it once did.

There was a sense of unrest during that time and it wasn't just me. Sometimes I put off going to bed by begging my mother to let me stay up just until the nightly news went off. Cuddled underneath her arm, I would be immersed in the images of the small black and white television propped up on her dresser. By the block, cities were being swallowed by fire, policemen swung nightsticks with evil intent, dogs attacked people and firemen pinned men and women against brickwalls with their high-pressure hoses. I saw soldiers shooting in a jungle, but didn't know who or what they were shooting. When the helicopters landed, I liked watching how the tall blades of grass bent over toward the ground from the spinning blades. And the puff of smoke coming out of Charles Whitman's rifle as he shot students from the University of Texas tower, looked as harmless as a magician's trick. Everyone seemed angry, but about what I had no idea. The angriest person of all was my older brother Leon.

Maybe it was the pressure of having to be the man of the house. If so, his prayer was answered when our mother herded all of us into the girls' room to introduce Mr. Jerome. He stooped in through the bedroom door and stood there wearing a deceivingly gentle smile on his dark face. He stood six foot six, weighed three hundred and twenty pounds and wore a size sixteen shoe. I don't believe any of us had ever seen a man so large.

When he walked over to greet us, the wood planks quivered underneath his feet and I clung closer to Leon.

For some reason he immediately took a liking to me, maybe because my fear of him was obvious. He hoisted my little chubby stump off the ground and started laughing. I was forty pounds of baby fat with a head that looked to have been plopped on by an ice cream scooper. When he was done being amused at the sight of me, he set me down and called me Hotshot.

Though he and my mother had been seeing each other I had never seen him before that night. He took on the role of our father like a duck to water. He had three children of his own living across town, which he saw often. He requested we call him Daddy Jerome and Leon was the only one who had a problem with that.

I just called him Daddy and deservedly so. My mother had barely been able to keep us fed and clothed, so he immediately had a huge freezer brought in, stocked it with meat and bought our clothes for school. In the summer he took us to a public pool so we could swim and afterward we always stopped downtown at the ice cream parlor to buy two huge drums of chocolate and vanilla. Mom went from skipping meals to going to a Chinese restaurant once a month and even though Daddy Jerome had a bad knee from an old football injury, they still dressed up occasionally and went dancing.

On several occasions all six of us piled into his brown Buick and went to the movies. He was a John Wayne fan and took us to see *True*

Grit and *Big Jake*. He had a thing for horror movies as well and took us to see some flick called *The Equinox*. Halfway through the movie, he heard this sniffling behind him and when he looked back, it was me and my younger sister Paulette with tears running down our faces. We were scared to death so he reached over the seat, picked me up by the back of my shirt and hoisted me over the seat and onto his lap. Resa gave Paulette to my mother and there we both sat in the protected arms of our parents. I never felt safer in my life.

We even went horseback riding once. I was too small to ride alone, so he took me galloping around in circles; I think my older brothers enjoyed it most, especially Leon. Once Daddy Jerome showed him how to take command of the horse, he trotted around the park like John Wayne.

Daddy Jerome let him have as much time on the horse as he wanted, but when Leon began running the horse a bit, Daddy Jerome cautioned him. "Be careful, Leon." No sooner had he said it, Leon kicked the horse too hard and it took off into a full gallop right under the swing, knocking him off.

The next day he was fine other than the knot on his head and my brothers never let him live it down.

I basked in the idea of having a man in the house. A son watching his father shave seems like a cliché, but that was exactly what I did. He would get severe razor bumps, so instead of a blade he used Magic Shave which had the most offensive odor. It stunk up the whole house and no one understood how I could sit there with him while he used that stuff. It was interesting to me because he didn't shave like the white men on television. He'd mix the foul powder in a cup with water, stirred it until it liquefied and then he would spread the white icing on his face with a small wooden spatula. It needed to stay on for about five minutes to work and when he scrapped it off, so went the hair or most of it. What was left my mother would patiently pick from his chin with tweezers.

My mother was happy, and that alone brightened all our days. On Sundays, after dinner was cooked, they would lie in bed hugged together, watching football. His favorite team was the Dallas Cowboys, but he also liked watching the Buffalo Bills because O.J. Simpson was the best runner in the league. To some it would seem a woman's worst nightmare, but after each play he would take a moment to explain the rules and what had happened. It wasn't long before I started to hear her cursing the quarterback for not hitting the open receiver.

I was his favorite so when he assigned me my first chore I was eager to please. Prior to that, my only responsibility had been hitting the toilet when I went to the bathroom. On the floor, next to his side of the bed, he kept a two pound size Folgers coffee can. It was red with white lettering and looked much the same as they do now. The purpose of the can was to keep him from having to walk down the hall to the bathroom to urinate. I was assigned the honorable task of emptying it.

I heard somewhere this was a common practice in the old days, but I'm pretty sure they probably had outhouses then too. But to tell you the truth it didn't bother me all that much. Only when it was filled to the rim and still warm did I feel the chore a bit unbecoming. Otherwise I actually took pride in the responsibility and emptied it most times without his asking.

I was grateful that he shared my mother's bed. The break-ins ceased immediately and I was no longer frightened to go to sleep. I knew as long as he was there, no one would dare try to hurt us. These were selfish reasons, I know, but the days seemed brighter and more optimistic after he came. Having a man brought a sense of security, but having a father in the house brought me peace of mind. His presence was overwhelming and in one way or another we all felt it. Sometimes those who didn't live in our house felt it too.

One day Resa got a visit from two male friends from school, who asked her if she wanted to take a ride to her best friend's. She was hesitant, but wanted to go, and when she asked Daddy Jerome he drilled her about the curfew, but eventually gave his consent. She grabbed her coat and met her friends outside on the porch.

Daddy Jerome took a brief look out the window at the two guys, then sprang from the bed. Bursting out of the screen door, he yelled, "Resa!" In just boxer shorts and brown slippers, he came down off the porch like a king from his throne. Without breaking a stride he told Resa to go into the house and he proceeded toward the boys. She watched through the screen door as he put his huge claws on their shoulders. There was no way of knowing what he said, but the young men were held captive by his words, as sure as they were by his clutch. When he was finished they repeatedly thanked him as if he had enlightened them somehow, and they quickly drove away. He went back into the bedroom and never mentioned it, nor did she ask. Today she believes he saw something she did not and in doing so he might have done her a huge favor.

Daddy Jerome was very protective and more so of my mother than any of us. For the first time I knew what it meant to have a father. There was no question that what he was doing for us our own fathers were not. Since he accepted the responsibility of feeding and clothing us why should he not have the right to discipline us as well? I don't know if my mother and he ever actually had that conversation or if he just assumed the privilege was his. Regardless, he believed that respect could not be obtained without the element of fear.

CHAPTER TWO

THE SESSIONS

Leon refused to call him Daddy Jerome and even tagged him with the nickname Toad, ridiculing his enormous hands and feet. Of course no one dared call him that to his face, but I have to admit it was appropriately funny. It still makes me laugh when I think of it.

Leon was thirteen and rebellious. Even before the arrival of Daddy Jerome he was becoming more difficult for our mother to handle and blamed her for not staying with his father A.J. who he still caught the bus to visit if he had the bus fare. He fought at school, fought with us at home and constantly got into shoving and shouting matches with Resa.

Knowing he was supposed to come home after school, he hung out with his buddies and went to see his girlfriend. He knew exactly when our mother would be home and could slip in, grab the broom in the corner and pretend to sweep as she walked through the door. As long as he got in before she did, Resa never told.

One evening after school, Resa warned him and as usual he did exactly what he wanted. By then he had gotten his timing down to an art, but this time when he reached for his prop in the corner, it wasn't there. When he turned around there was the straw part of the broom coming down on his head. After a few swats he yanked it out of my mother's hand, threw it to the floor and raised his hand to hit her.

"If you lay a hand on me mutherfucker, it'll be the last thing you ever do! I'll kill you myself!" She rarely cursed, but when she did it was always pretty explicit.

Bluffing or not Leon lowered his hand more out of respect than fear.

Mom never really hit us outside of a spanking or quick swat on the lips for saying something bad. That was before Daddy Jerome; when he came; a few more rules were added. For instance, after school the older kids liked stopping by the icehouse to get a chunk of ice to suck on during the walk home. The owner had no problem with it, but Daddy Jerome said it was unsanitary and he was probably right. We were not allowed outside without shoes on our feet (which our mother didn't permit either) and by nine o'clock everyone had to be in bed with the lights out. There was one more infraction we were warned of that was right up there with lying, cheating and stealing. Daddy Jerome made it perfectly clear that under no circumstances were we to eat any of his sausage. It was strictly for his lunch.

Leon broke every rule at one time or another, except for the sausage rule. He lied, cheated and stole and the more Daddy Jerome chastised him, the more he resisted. I remember the time Leon got paid for his paper route and bought his girlfriend a watch. My mother and Daddy Jerome were lying in bed watching television when he came in and politely asked permission to take it to her. Daddy Jerome told him it was too dangerous for him to ride his bike that far at night. He offered to give him a ride in the morning. Leon agreed and politely excused himself, but when my mother entered our room to check on us before going to bed he was not there.

I'm not sure what time he climbed back into his rickety bed, but the light came on as soon as he did. Seething in anger, Daddy Jerome thundered toward him with a rope doubled several times over and dripping water from its looped ends. He began thrashing Leon and we could feel the sting of the water pellets coming off the rope as it went back and forth across Leon's flailing body. Adrian and I tried getting as far away from the rampage as possible by embedding ourselves in the corner, and I'm sure Ambus was doing the same.

The agonizing screams of pain and the familiarity of it sent chills down my spine, but the screams were soon muffled when Daddy Jerome shoved Leon's face into the pillow. To me, that sound was just as ghastly as Leon's floundering changed from one of self-defense to panic and survival. Daddy Jerome was just too big and strong; even as an adult, Leon would never weigh half as much as he did.

Even after the rope had gone dry and Leon's body had withered into a fetal position, Daddy Jerome continued the assault. To him Leon represented the counterculture of the time, for he was as angry and defiant as the hippies and beatniks on television. He fought against my mother's and Daddy Jerome's authority as if they were the Establishment themselves and Daddy Jerome beat him for it. He beat Leon as if he were doing it for the betterment of mankind. I cried for Leon and held on tight to Adrian as I prayed to God to make him stop. The light finally went off symbolizing the beating was over.

We meandered back to our places in bed, while Leon whimpered in the darkness. As horrible as it was to hear my eldest brother crying, it was also encouraging to know that he was still alive. I wanted to tell him that I loved him and tomorrow everything would be fine, but I felt like my existence was nothing more than a nuisance to him. He was the eldest boy and I saw him through a younger brother's eyes. When he spoke to me, he always had a captive audience even if it was ridicule. I literally wanted to imitate everything he did and in many instances I would.

When he eased out of bed, I could see he was hurting. My eyes followed his wounded silhouette across the room. He cautiously opened the dresser and pulled out some clothes and got dressed standing up.

"Where you going Leon?"

"Shut up Beanhead," he responded angrily. He crept out of the room and out the front door.

He ran away to his father's and that hurt my mother even though around us she showed no visible outpouring of sadness. He was her eldest son and having his allegiance was important to her, but there were still six other children to worry about. I was divided between the safety Daddy Jerome provided and Leon's free spiritedness and it was that very spirit that he wanted to beat out of Leon.

Daddy Jerome had a good job loading trucks for Coca Cola and was a very proud man, but it was the sixties and he knew his place in society. Times were changing, but slowly. For the surrendering of his pride, it would be Leon and his generation that would benefit. But regardless of what was happening outside our home, Daddy Jerome, made sure that within those walls, we all knew who was king.

Adrian was nine or ten during this time and was a pretty good artist. He dragged his sketchpad around with him like a security blanket and sketched landscapes or anything else that stood still long enough for him to get a mental snapshot of it. In school the teachers complained that he stared out of the window too much instead of studying his lesson. When he wasn't he was doodling in his pad. He made high marks in art, but got Ds in almost every other subject and his conduct was always unsatisfactory. This was one of Daddy Jerome's pet peeves. He used to say that an idiot could sit down and shut up, and like Leon he beat Adrian for the betterment of society. He would try to prove this point by giving money for As and Bs, nothing for Cs and an ass whipping for anything less.

Jo and Ambus usually got the most money while Adrian would get a savage beating. He would be summoned into my mother's room and I could hear the "idiot" line coming from Daddy Jerome and soon the beating would follow. Adrian didn't have the spirit Leon did so the screaming didn't last as long. This played out every report card day. Daddy Jerome would start soaking the rope even before he saw the grades. The day after was just as predictable. My mother would get a call at work from the school's nurse that Adrian was being sent home because he was unable to sit down.

She didn't agree with Daddy Jerome's degree of discipline, but she didn't intervene either. She thought, as we all did, that he was doing what needed to be done. When he took it upon himself to cure me of stuttering, even then I felt that his heart was in the right place.

I entered their bedroom to empty his can while they watched television. He asked me something and I don't remember what it was, but I responded with a mumble that probably only another four-year old could understand.

"Slow down!" he shouted and told me to repeat myself.

I did and he whipped his belt from around the bedpost and told me to say it again, but say it slower. I didn't know what I was doing wrong, but figured I better get this one right. I did as he asked, but still I felt the sting of his leather belt across my bare legs.

"Say it again!" he shouted, "but slower."

My body tightened, as well as my throat. I was trying to do what he asked even though I still didn't know exactly what I was doing wrong, but every attempt resulted in the same thing. The more frustrated he got, the less he waited between the licks. He demanded that I repeat myself and by that time all I could do was cry uncontrollably and mutter. Nothing coherent could rise from my vocal cords so he stopped and gave me a moment to collect myself. He told me to stop crying. Sniffling, I wiped the tears away. I just wanted to grab the can and get the hell out of there. I sniffled a few more times and he told me to stop crying again and by his tone he meant immediately. With one swipe of my forearm, I wiped the tears from my eyes and held on to that last sniffle as he adjusted himself at the edge of the bed and we began again.

My mother eventually intervened, telling him that it was time for me to go to bed. He allowed me to leave, but I would never be off the hook. He was devoted to curing me of what he saw as a speech impediment that could be alleviated by simply taking my time when I spoke. It was not like making me eat green peas, even now the smell of them curdles my stomach, but everyone else ate them so to prevent a butt whipping I would force them down, and held most of it. But I had no idea what to do when it came to my speech. I didn't think I was speaking any differently than anyone else. How was I to correct that?

On into my kindergarten year we continued to have our speech therapy sessions. We had them quite regularly, usually right after school when Paulette and I took our mandatory nap. While we were supposed to be sleeping, Daddy Jerome would sit up close to the record player and replay one song over and over. It was *I Stand Accused* by Isaac Hayes. The song began with a five-minute narrative, and his voice was hoarse and hypnotic, like Daddy Jerome's. The piano was as constant as raindrops tapping against a window pain. When it was over I could hear the cracking of the arm of the record player lifting up and moving over for another repeat. The song put me to sleep quicker than any lullaby. I could never stay awake long enough to know how many times he repeated it.

Well into my nap, he would awaken me by yelling out, "Hotshot!"

Though he usually woke me under the pretense of emptying his can, the end result would be to have one of our sessions. They weren't much different than the first; except my mother was no longer present and sometimes he swapped the belt for one of his shoes. Both were equally painful, both were equally ineffective as an antidote for the stuttering.

Very seldom did he put a hand on the girls, or Ambus, for that matter. Ambus was seven years older than I was, the most responsible of all us boys. His fair skin and short height made him a target at school, but he was smart and on the honor roll. He played the tuba in his high school and was teaching himself how to play the bass guitar. Because he avoided confrontational sports, like basketball or football, Daddy Jerome thought he was soft and wouldn't get picked on so much if he was a little tougher.

One summer during one of our customary visits to a public pool an older boy was bullying Ambus by holding him under water. When Ambus broke free, he came to the surface gasping for air and saw Daddy Jerome standing on the bank with a disgusted look on his face. He shook his head with disapproval and walked away. Later on he went so far as to tell Ambus the whole experience was good for him. He would do things like that, but as much as we wanted to hate him he would extend a show of love that our fathers never would.

Leon ended up in a juvenile detention center for assault and robbery. His father never went to visit him, but our mother and Daddy Jerome took turns so he could have someone there everyday. When he was released he came back home to live with us. That pleased my mother.

When my father came by "skinning and grinning," as my mother called it, in his brand new car it was usually under the pretense of wanting to see Paulette and me. But most of his time was devoted in trying to persuade my mother into having sex with him. Daddy Jerome would ask her if he had given her anything for us. If he did, it was never more than ten or twenty dollars. The next time he came by, Daddy Jerome waited until our visit was over and told him that he had no problem with his coming by if his intent was to support his kids, but if he wasn't going to, then there was no reason for him to come back anymore. He must have gotten his point across because I didn't see my father for a very long time after that. I can't say that I missed him though.

What little comprehension I had of a live-in father, was Daddy Jerome and being his favorite was like having the status of a trustee in a prison. Two years had gone by and there were few perks. Emptying his can surely wasn't one of them, but it was expected of me, like taking out the trash. I tried being as meek and unnoticeable as a piece of furniture, hoping to avoid any run-ins with him. It was Leon's disobedience and Adrian's grades that kept the rope soaking in the bathtub, but all that came to an abrupt end when one afternoon while loading trucks for Coca Cola, he suffered a serious back injury.

For months he could do nothing, but lay around the house

recovering and collecting disability. My mother rubbed his back down every night with alcohol so it wouldn't stiffen up. Sometimes Paulette and I walked on his back and we always found that amusing. While he hibernated in the bedroom, a tainted sense of liberty invaded the house like an old and welcomed acquaintance. By this time I had already developed a great fear of him and while the other inmates rejoiced in the yard, I still had to venture into the warden's quarters to retrieve his can. Watching him grimace with pain as he attempted to adjust himself in bed, did give me pleasure. He wasn't even agile enough to get out of bed without great effort or strain, but his resourcefulness would surprise me.

One afternoon he yelled, "Hotshot!" ripping me from my nap. I woke immediately but didn't crawl out of bed right away. "Hotshot, come in here!" he demanded.

I hopped out of bed and hurried into the room while he still had his penis in the can. That was the first time I had seen one other than my own and it was proportionate with everything else on his immense frame. He shook the last droplets off and wrestled it back into his boxers. He handed me the can and I grabbed the warm sides with both hands and prudently walked down the hall. As I poured his dark yellow urine into the toilet it comforted me to know that he was still unable to put any strain on his back. I returned to the room as he was cautiously positioning himself at the edge of the bed. I put the can in its place on the floor next to the bed and went for an expeditious exit.

"Come here," he said, stopping me cold.

"Yes sir," I said.

Sitting up he rested his forearms on his thirty-four inch thighs and said, "So how is school coming?" Bait obviously.

"Fine" I said.

His face was about two feet from mine and he asked, "So what did you learn today at school?"

What my exact response was or how I articulated it I can't remember, but I do remember his middle finger feeling like a roll of quarters when he thumped me on the forehead with enough force to push me back three or four feet. *What the hell was this?* I was stupefied.

"Get up and come here," he said casually.

I got up and stood in front of him with a pain echoing in the center of my skull. He told me to take my time when I spoke and to repeat myself. Apparently, not once did I say it correctly because he popped me on the forehead several more times. He never laughed right out, but by his expression, I think he found it amusing. This made it more demeaning. I actually preferred his belt or shoe over his thumping. Eventually the waterworks came on and he told me to stop crying or he'd give me something to really cry about.

During those years I hated coming home after school, I hated the sessions and I was learning to hate him as well.

CHAPTER THREE
NEEDS OF THE MANY

The national average for unemployment was about six percent so Daddy Jerome was not the only one out of work. His disability checks stopped coming before he could fully recover so he started helping his brother, Albert, at his barbecue restaurant. Albert was a bit smaller than Daddy Jerome, but still a large man in his own right. Business at the restaurant was good, but hardly enough to support a woman and seven children, so he gambled a little on the side.

Every morning my mother got up at four-thirty to fix Daddy Jerome's lunch before going to work herself. His lunch was always the same; two fried sausage sandwiches, one with mustard and one with mayonnaise. Once I realized her routine, I was always awake before her alarm clock went off. She always hit the snooze button at least once before I heard her slippers sliding across the hall floor on the way to the bathroom.

The first couple of times she was surprised to see me up that early, but it quickly became something regular. While the sausage sizzled in the frying pan, we sat at the table and talked. My idea of a conversation was asking a million and one questions; when she got tired of them, she'd shut me up by shoving a small piece of meat in my mouth. Even with Daddy Jerome it was still hard making ends meet, and I think it saddened her when there wasn't enough to give me. She would force me back to bed and be annoyed that I had gotten up at all.

I don't know if she knew, but I was never getting up for the sausage. With six brothers and sisters and a man all demanding their share of her, it was a rare moment for me to have her alone to myself and this was my only opportunity. For a few minutes every morning, I felt like I was her only child.

As Daddy Jerome's back got better, my stuttering got worse, so much so that others began to notice. They started poking fun at me on the playground, and though I hated them for mocking me, I hid it by laughing along, knowing that would take some of the fun out of it. My strategy usually worked—they moved on to the fat kid in the class—but I made sure to get my revenge when we played dodgeball.

I wasn't as concerned with them as I was with making sure my teachers never made an issue of it. Mrs. Edwards, my third grade teacher, used to have us stand up at the black board and read aloud. Reading aloud was difficult enough, though somehow I managed with nothing more than a few giggles from a classmate or two. But always my heart raced, my palms sweated, and my knees shook as Mrs. Edwards thumbed down the attendance roster searching for the next victim. I would practice saying the next couple of sentences, just in case. When she called someone else's name, my relief was short-lived, because I'd skip down to the next paragraph and practice those first words.

Once when she did call my name, the paragraph began with the word "The." I had practiced it a couple of times while the kid ahead of me was reading, but now that it was my turn, the capital T stared back at me, almost daring me to pronounce it. The pause started to draw attention.

I started slowly, as Daddy Jerome had taught me. It seemed effortless, coming up from my belly. I even became a little excited at the ease of it. Then, without warning, my jaws froze. With my tongue stuck between the T and the H, a moronic audible came spewing from my mouth. The children laughed; Mrs. Edwards took notice.

Determined to get it out, I pushed harder, hoping to force my jaws to work the way everyone else's did—but it wasn't only my jaws, it was my whole body. My stomach was knotted, as well as my fist. My throat veined and my tongue stuck to the roof of my mouth. I could stop any time, but I was committed and determined to say it on one attempt. My classmates laughed at the difficulty I was having, trying to do something as simple as talking, but this was not the playground and there was nothing else to divert their attention.

"Be quiet!" Mrs. Edwards told them and she began writing a note. She called me over to her desk and told me to take the note to Ms. Crabb, the Special Education teacher.

If you've never stuttered, you cannot understand the frustration and humiliation of knowing exactly what you want to say but being unable to say it. I divided people into two groups; those who finished my sentences for me and those who waited patiently for me to get out what they already knew I was going to say. As I got older I adapted by changing my words around and substituting other words for words I felt were about to give me trouble. The whole objective was to conceal the fact that I had a speech impediment. So when someone took the liberty of verbally finishing one of my thoughts I found it extremely offensive. It was like throwing me a life jacket in shallow water.

When I walked into Ms. Crabb's classroom I took a moment to look around at the other students. By their different sizes I knew that some of them had been left back. After reading the note, Mrs. Crabb looked at me for a moment, maybe searching for some visible sign of my ignorance, then picked up what looked like one of my old kindergarten books. She asked me to read the first couple of pages. I opened it, took a short breath, and spoke the words crisply, clearly, and without pause. She picked up another book and asked me to read it. Again I read through it cleanly until she told me to stop. I put the book into her outstretched hand and she just looked at me. She gave me another book, the same as the book I had in my desk. She opened it to some arbitrary page and pointed to a paragraph.

"Read this," she said.

As fate would have it, the first word was *the*. Without hesitation or rehearsal I read it cleanly and without a bit of difficulty. When I was finished I gave the book back to her, looking as baffled as she was as to why I was there. She gave me a couple more things to read and I did so with ease. Finally, she sent me back to my regular class with a note of her own. I walked into class with my head up as if I had single-handedly conquered some evil demon. Mrs. Edwards read the note and shrugged her shoulders, as if to say, "I tried," then told me to sit down.

I was able to avoid severe attacks like that either by luck or fate. Despite occasional setbacks, I saw school as a reprieve, a time away from the anxiety at home. I felt more highly thought of there than I did at home. My teachers praised my behavior, my grades were good, and at recess I excelled. I was among one or two other boys that the teacher would strategically place on a team to make sure the other team had competition. I was also among those the teacher would call on to run errands. I felt special at school; more importantly, no one knew about Hotshot.

At home everything was just the opposite. I was pushed around, made fun of, and yelled at for being in the way. Emptying Daddy

Jerome's can wasn't doing much for my self-esteem, either. As honorable as I had once taken it to be, it was now a chore. I hated being the youngest boy and being labeled as Daddy Jerome's favorite.

Payoff day finally arrived when Daddy Jerome came home with two puppies. They were Pit Terriers and he named them Chico and Gringo. That night we were all beside ourselves with joy. Even Leon let his guard down long enough to hold one. Chico was a cream color and Gringo was darker and everyone seemed to dote over Chico, including Daddy Jerome, but I was partial to Gringo—so much so that everyone referred to him as Gary's dog. After school, if Daddy Jerome was gone, I would put him in bed with me while I napped.

My mother put up with the dogs for a few months, but they became too destructive. The last straw came when my little sister and I returned from school and found what looked like a murder scene. The two dogs met us at the door with bloody bites all over their bodies and their ears chipped and bleeding. In the boy's room, the sheets on the beds were pulled off, the pillowcases were ripped, and there was blood in the beds—from biting on each other.

Daddy Jerome gathered all seven of us in one room and we took a vote for which dog to keep. It was five to two because Paulette voted with me. We were the youngest and I convinced her we had to stick together. He saw how quickly I had become attached to Gringo so he didn't take him away immediately. He told me that one day, when I got home from school, Gringo would not be there and I needed to start getting used to that idea.

It was all done fair and square and I appreciated how he handled it, so I made the best of the time I had with Gringo. As long as Adrian didn't mind, my mother agreed to allow him to sleep with me.

When the day finally came, Daddy Jerome stepped into the room before school that morning and told me to say goodbye to Gringo. I hugged him while the others watched. They said their goodbyes as well, and I went to school. The whole day I dreaded going home and not having Gringo greet me.

I unlocked the door with the key that was tied around my neck with a shoestring and out jumped Gringo. Daddy Jerome had taken Chico instead.

I used to wonder why he did that. Was it because he knew I had already prepared for the worst and accepted it like a man? Was it guilt? Or was it just a display of power, to show me that being the favorite did have its perks? Regardless, I never got any false hope that things would get better between us—but it did make emptying his can a bit more bearable.

Daddy Jerome's job at the barbecue place and even his winnings at poker were not enough to replace what he made loading trucks. And when he had a bad night at the table he would come home looking for a reason to exalt his frustration. Some nights he'd park down the street so we wouldn't hear him driving up and he'd sneak up to the window, hoping to catch someone out of bed after curfew. He even resorted to driving around the neighborhood after school, hoping to catch one of us at the icehouse. One day Jo and Ambus walked home sucking on chunks of ice and he drove by very slowly, making sure they saw him. He whipped Jo, the only time he ever did so, but he was harder on the boys. While he whipped Ambus with the belt, he yelled out, "I finally gotcha! You thought you were going to get away, didn't you."

And remember the sausage rule? Late one night after work he started rifling through the refrigerator, looking for his sausage. When he found none, he stormed into the boys' room and woke us up. With the wet rope dangling from his fist, he asked who had eaten his last sausage. No one owned up to it so he asked again but this time added, "If someone don't tell me, I'm whipping *all* y'all."

We looked at each other hoping someone would confess, but no one did. He started on Leon. Leon resisted as much as possible, which only infuriated him. He grabbed Leon by the neck and held him up against the wall like a rag doll before throwing him into the corner. Leon threw his hands and feet into the swiping blows of the rope, but Daddy Jerome lashed at him without regard to where it landed. As Leon's welt-riddled body flopped around like a dying fish, Daddy Jerome turned to the three of us huddled together. "Who's next?" he barked.

Adrian reluctantly stepped up. He had been at the receiving end of the rope so often that he regarded it as just bad medicine that postponing only made worse.

"Did you eat my sausage?"

"No, sir," Adrian responded. I think Daddy Jerome believed him because he didn't beat him as long as he had Leon.

After Ambus had been beaten, my mother stepped into the room as if she had been around the corner the whole time. I hastened over and clung to her nightgown. Wounded and angry, Ambus crawled into bed. The rope was dry by then and it was my turn. As Daddy Jerome approached me, my mother pushed me behind her and held me there.

"Jerome, he's too young."

I wished to be invisible, but I settled for standing behind her so he couldn't see any parts of my body. The silence forced me to poke my head out, and I saw him rolling up the rope as if he agreed with her. I wasn't fooled by this, though. He could get me whenever he wanted. We still had our sessions; the fact that I knew that, was good enough for him.

Leon was gone by the time everyone woke up. I think he had been planning it for sometime, and I guess that was as good a night as any. Before leaving he walked over and knelt down next to my bed.

"Beanhead," he whispered.

I watched him get out of bed and move about in the darkness, but didn't say anything. He opened his pillowcase stuffed with clothing, and there, on top, I saw the rope. "Tell Ambus and Adrian."

He closed the pillowcase and I wanted to ask him not to leave, but I felt in some way it was best for him. I thought if he stayed, Daddy Jerome would really hurt him one day, so when he crept out I didn't cry. I laid my head back down on my pillow, envying Leon for being old enough and brave enough to leave.

Leon and his best friend Dana decided to hitchhike to San Francisco, as many their age did in the early seventies. Catching a ride was the easy part; surviving would be much more difficult. The first night they arrived they went to a shelter near Haight and Ashbury, where all the hippies hung out. While Leon was taking a shower, a couple of naked guys came in and offered to wash his back. After he politely declined, they started having sex right there in front of him. He and Dana, both shy of their seventeenth birthdays, decided to take their chances on the street.

At home, Daddy Jerome remembered that he himself had eaten the last of his sausage, but offered no apologies. Instead on report card day, when he found out his rope was missing, he gave Adrian a rain check. He was amused at the gall of it and didn't even ask who took it, though I'm pretty sure he knew. He didn't replace the rope right away, but he put us on notice that eventually he would find a suitable replacement.

Leon used to tell us that Daddy Jerome was insane, and my brothers laughed at how seriously he said it. He was so convinced of his insanity that he even went as far as to warn our mother of it. It was the ridiculous ravings of an adolescent boy who bore great resentment toward the man who was trying to take his father's place.

But one day, during one of our sessions after school, I started to believe that Leon was onto something. Daddy Jerome had smoked his last Winston and was extremely frustrated with me and my lack of progress, so we walked down to the corner store for another pack. On the way back, on top of some boxes he spotted a yellow cargo strap that truckers use to tighten their load down on flatbed trailers. It was made of that durable seatbelt material. He doubled it over and holding both ends together, raised it to eye level and yanked his hands apart, forcing the strap to make a loud crack. The sound frightened me. So did the Grinch-like smile he had stretched across his face. He had found a suitable replacement for the rope, and guess who was going to be the first Guinea pig?

By the time we got back home, I had come to the realization that whatever I was doing wrong when I spoke was beyond my control and I could do nothing to change it. I could be speaking perfectly one moment and in an instant, not be able to get out anything more than a syllable. He could not understand how I could do that, and quite honestly, neither could I.

When we continued our session, I was doing no better than before his cigarette break. At the peak of his frustration he told me to lie across the bed and he grabbed "the Querk." That's what he named it; somehow that seemed appropriate. He started striking me with it across my backside. My flesh was on fire. It seemed I could feel every blood vessel beneath the surface of my skin exploding with each lick. I tried putting my hands back to ease the blows to my legs, but nothing abated the pain. I twisted and turned, hoping that my panic would cause him concern, but it only agitated him. To keep from putting too much strain on his back, he put his foot on my neck to hold me down as he whaled away at will.

Afterward, while I whimpered, Paulette quietly rolled out of Leon's bed and crawled into mine. We clasped our hands together and shut our eyes tight as we both tried convincing God to strike him dead right then and there.

To this day I don't think I've ever prayed harder.

When Adrian came home from school that evening, Daddy Jerome collected on the rain check he had given him for the unsatisfactory report card. I felt fear when I heard Leon and Ambus screaming, but Adrian's screams saddened me. We all liked attention, but none of us could hold an audience as Adrian could. At home he was our class clown. He used to make quick little rhymes out of stupid things we had done so we could never forget it. He was not confrontational and never would be. He found humor in some of the worst situations, but there was no humor to be found in the beating he was receiving from Daddy Jerome.

Our mother went outside and stood on the porch to distance herself from his sounds of agony. Paulette followed unnoticed and watched her stare out into the night. Listening to her muffled whimpers, she asked, "Why are you crying, Mom?"

She never answered.

I knew that after the break-in, she felt as frightened and vulnerable as I had, and our prayers happened to manifest in the coming of Daddy Jerome. For me it was a love of last resort—meaning he was the only one volunteering to play the role of my father, so who was I to be choosy? He didn't have to be there; knowing that only made my love for him stronger. He was everything I longed for as a little boy—and everything I hated. Sometimes I felt this gluttony of love for him, and he would drain every single drop with just one of our sessions. Then he would do things like keeping Gringo and the well would be full again. I thanked God for his being there and also prayed that He strike him dead. My affection for him teetered back and forth like that.

I was learning a great deal from him, though, very little of it as tangible as throwing a baseball or learning how to tie my shoes. It was more a lesson in philosophy, like learning that all things good come with considerable consequences.

That lesson was being pounded into my skull by more than just him. I didn't understand ideas like Civil Rights, but I grasped the pain and suffering it was causing. It seems that every time I heard the word, it was always accompanied by images of rioting, marching, and fighting. I was told that Vietnam was a bad thing, but Civil Rights were a good thing. They didn't look that different from the images I saw, especially after the assassination of Martin Luther King. My most vivid memories of that day are the rioting, and my mother crying as if there were no tomorrow.

I was frustrated and confused because I could not grasp the

significance of what was going on around me. When man took his first walk on the moon, I was making mud pies in the front yard, and when Charlie Manson smiled at me during the evening news, he looked like a nice enough guy. The only thing I could wrap my mind around was whether or not my mother was happy, and she was happier after Daddy Jerome came.

I never mentioned the sessions to her, not that I wanted to hide them; I just didn't think she could do anything about it. The needs of the many outweighed the needs of the few. Leon could not understand that, but I did. She had suffered severe beatings at the fists of A.J., the father of all my older siblings. In the span of eleven and a half years she had ten children, not counting one miscarriage. Daddy Jerome was very gentle toward her and genuinely had her best interest at heart. It must have been a blissful experience, after so many years of being misled and abused by the men she loved. For the first time since she was a little girl, she was happy more than she was sad. There was a price for that. Since she was ten years old, love and happiness had always come at a steep price.

CHAPTER FOUR
PAPA'S WHISTLE

My mother's eyes still light up like a child when she talks about her father, Will Henderson Montgomery, whom she reverently refers to as Papa. He was a tall, thin half-breed in the original sense of the word. His mother was an Apache and his father was a white judge, and that was all we knew about them. He married Olivia Melonson, a mulatto, and they settled in the small black community of Ames, Texas. All we knew of my grandmother was that to marry him she had to elope. She had ten children for him, my mother being the youngest. She died not long after my mother's birth. My mother inherited her pale skin, big ears, and long brown hair, but she had not even the vaguest memory of her mother. She has no recollection of her mother, at all.

She had one black and white photograph and a lock of brown hair she kept of her mother's in a small box, in her underwear drawer. When I was younger, it fascinated me and I would ask to see it. The lock of brown silk was suspended above a cloud of cotton and glistened under the bedroom light. It hadn't aged since the day it was cut. The picture was frayed and tattered, but that didn't keep me from staring at it, hoping to learn more about my grandmother than my mother was able to tell me.

She hardly knew anything because Papa didn't talk about her. He never really got over her death but dealt with it as men did in those days and never allowed his children to see him break down. He was a mechanic and his automotive shop was in town. Though he had several vehicles at his disposal, he preferred to walk. Everyone knew how much he had loved Olivia, but he never brought his depression home; the long walk home seemed to be his way of dealing with it. The walk took about an hour, and when an acquaintance who didn't know his routine offered him a ride, he would politely refuse.

Most of his sons had joined the service and his two eldest daughters were married, so that left only my mother and her two sisters, Rita and Edna, to be raised. According to her, people came from miles around—doctors, lawyers, and politicians—just to have him work on their automobiles. She might have seen it through the eyes of Daddy's little girl, but he made enough to allow all his girls to go to the local Catholic school.

If he wasn't home by the time the sun went down, the girls had specific instructions to go to their Aunt Altha, who lived less than a quarter mile down the dirt road. The girls helped Aunt Altha clean the house; my mother saved the back porch for last so she could have a jump on her sisters when Papa got home. When he got there, he'd light a coal oil lamp, open the kitchen window by pulling back the wood shutters, and whistle for his girls. When my mother heard that whistle, she would drop the broom and start running home as fast as she could, even if it meant running through the cow pasture that she'd been warned about. Her sisters were three and four years older, and it never dawned on her that they didn't share the same zeal to be the first to get to Papa. She'd burst into the kitchen and grab him around the waist in her handmade cotton dress, taking no notice of the dirt and oil that soiled his clothes.

One evening when she was about seven years old, she heard his whistle as she swept Aunt Altha's back porch, and she darted off home. Running through the pasture, she met the old ornery cow that her father had warned her of; it stood right in her path. She tried shooing it away, but instead it started charging toward her. When she tried running away, the soft dirt slowed her down, so she started to scream as she ran. The ornery cow's horns ripped through her dress and suddenly, with a single thrust, tossed her in the air. When she came down, she landed in the cradling arms of Papa.

He would scold her, but never once laid a hand on her and made sure no one else did either. Knowing this, she got into her share of trouble. One time she insisted on watching her brothers mend a section of the fence after they told her to go back into the house. She refused, and wound up disturbing a nest of bees. She ran into the house screaming and hollering leaving her brothers with the feeling that justice had been served. Papa put ointment on the stings and went outside and gave the boys a chastising.

Not even the nuns could lay a finger on Papa's daughters. Sister Claudia used to punish her students by making them ball their fists and smacking them on the knuckles with a ruler. When my mother and her sister complained to him about it he went to the school and told Sister Claudia never to touch his girls again.

Growing up with Papa was a time of splendor for her. She felt safe and secure. She wanted to be around him all the time and would even crawl into bed with him while he slept. By the time the sun rose, he was at the edge of the bed with her foot in his back, but he never complained.

For Christmas he would go into the woods, cut down a tree, and set it up in the hallway before whistling for his girls to come home. My mother wanted to be the first one in the house to show Papa the decorations she'd made in school. By coal oil lamps, the girls would decorate the tree with popcorn and colored construction paper, while Papa supervised from his own father's cane back chair, embracing a mason jar of white lightning. Their gifts were rag dolls and Papa being home for a full day. It was everything she could ask for.

A couple of weeks before Christmas in 1944 Rita met Papa in town after he had gotten off work. He gave her a few dollars to go shopping for her two sisters, and while they were talking, a white man came out of the store and took notice of the sixteen-year-old beauty.

"Henderson," he commanded, "who you got there?"

"That's my daughter," Papa countered, but the man seemed not to care, looking at her lustfully.

Taking offense at the crude inquiry, Papa stepped away with the man, out of hearing range of Rita. She watched as he reprimanded the man as much as he could without being arrested. Visibly annoyed at the nerve of him, the man stormed over to his tractor-trailer and climbed into the cab. Papa returned to Rita and told her he would be home in a few hours.

As they always did, the girls went to their aunt's home once it got dark. My mother was ten years old and was eager for Papa to return so she and Edna could snoop around the house to see where he had hidden the gifts. It wasn't until they crawled into their aunt's bed to go to sleep that night that they began to worry.

They remained awake for more than an hour before hearing a man's voice in the hallway. My mother recognized it as the husband of one of their aunts. His tone was low and disturbing as he described seeing a truck hit a man as he walked alongside the road. His voice lowered even more when he said, "I can't be sure, but I think it was Henderson."

"Oh, my God!" her aunt screamed, then remembered that the girls were in the next room.

He confessed to seeing the whole thing. The girls overheard him say, "It was done on purpose. I was afraid to go see."

There was silence after that and while Edna and Rita prayed that it wasn't their father, my mother began silently crying. In her heart she knew it was. He had never been away from them that long before.

A stranger found him and called an ambulance. The first hospital he was taken to refused to attend to his injuries because he was only half white, so he was transported to Liberty County Hospital where he lay on a gurney, with broken bones and a gaping hole in his right side. By the time my mother's eighteen-year-old brother Coy got there, the doctors had just begun to work on him.

His last words to Coy were to make sure the girls were taken care of. Coy assured him that they would be. Coy would later tell Rita that the hole in their father's side was big enough for him to put his head through.

Her aunt's husband never reported what he saw, so the closest thing to an investigation was a small article in the rear of the local newspaper titled, "Negro Victim of Hit, Run Driver."

I believe we guide our futures with decisions, but our lives are determined by two or three major events in a lifetime. Like a gust of wind to a sail, an event can divert us from a course or unerringly propel us forward. Papa's death was one of these major events in my mother's life. That night she was wounded in places that never healed. When she asked her brother Coy about their father and why God had taken him, he told her that God needed another angel in Heaven. As she grew into a woman, in some ways she remained that ten-year-old girl still waiting for her father to come home.

The girls were separated and sent to live with different members of the family. Rita stayed with Aunt Altha, but was married a year or so later and moved to Louisiana. Edna went to live with their brother Alex in Houston.

It was difficult to find a place for my mother because no one wanted a young girl on the cusp of her teens living in the same house with their husbands and sons. There was talk of her going to California and passing for white, but she refused. Most of her brothers were in the service during WWII and the only one that could take her lived in Seattle. She wanted to go, but her Aunt Louise stepped in at the last minute and decided to keep her. Coy boarded up the house after the funeral and joined the Army.

Aunt Louise's decision to keep her was based more on necessity than love. She needed someone to cook and clean for her husband, their son, his wife, and their three children. For years to come, their son Richard would sneak up behind my mother and grab her breasts when no one was around. When she told her aunt, of course she didn't believe her and my mother didn't want to make things any worse than they were. It was bound to get that way on its own.

In the ninth grade my mother started going to public school and enjoyed it. She became a cheerleader and the boys paid her a great deal of attention. Their girlfriends retaliated by yanking on her ponytail, but she wasn't interested in dating at that time. That didn't come until she met a dark older boy everyone called A.J. When I asked her about the day they met, it was her eyes that captured my attention. They became youthful and exuberant as she started to speak. She reminded me of a fifteen-year-old, talking about some hunk she met at the mall. I couldn't help but enjoy the moment because I was actually getting a glimpse of my mother at that tender age. After a minute, I don't think she even realized that I was there anymore because she had gone to that place.

He was standing at the counter of a neighborhood café when she walked in to get a hamburger. He was eighteen and she thought he had the prettiest lips God had ever blessed a man with. His dark brown face was smooth and his mahogany eyes attracted her, but it was his lips that drew her like a bug to a windshield. He wore a white dress shirt with freshly pressed Khakis and black low-cut work boots that weren't for working. He had another pair for that.

After a brief introduction he wanted her phone number, but she knew Aunt Louise wouldn't allow him to call so she told him where she went to school. After school the next day she noticed him a block away, waiting next to his car. He wasn't allowed on campus because he wasn't a student, so she went over and talked to him. They spoke for a minute, then she hurried back to catch the bus. From that day on, he'd be there waiting for her and each day she noticed that he would park closer to the school.

At home, Richard started getting more aggressive despite her feeble threats to tell his wife. When he was around he watched her every move. One afternoon he noticed her walking into the woods. He followed her, but stayed out of hearing distance. She stopped at the end of the property while he lurked from tree to tree. When she was alone and out of screaming range of the house, he must have salivated at such an opportune moment, but all his hopes were doused when A.J. appeared. They sat down and talked, and when she returned home, Richard was indignant toward her and accused her of having sex. She denied it and left, hoping he wouldn't tell Aunt Louise.

Ames, Texas is still a small town and was even smaller then, so it wasn't long before it got around that she and A.J. were seeing each other. Everyone in town knew him or knew of him—especially the police. He dropped out of school in the third grade, but didn't steal or vandalize. He had a reputation for fighting. He was the boy all mothers warned their daughters about and yet the one all daughters were attracted to. Around my mother, he was kind and reserved until someone tried getting in between them. She saw it as an act of chivalry. He made her feel protected, as she had felt when Papa was alive.

One day as she walked through the hall after a class, a girl by the name of Gussie came up and pushed her down.

"White bitch, you better leave my man alone!"

It was during segregation and they knew she wasn't all white, but with her pale skin tone she might as well have been.

Gathering her books, she responded, "What are you talking about, Gussie?"

"A.J. He's my boyfriend."

"We're just friends, and even if we weren't, I'm not going to fight you over him."

After school she told A.J. what happened. The very next day, Gussie came up behind her while she was standing at her locker. "You can have that nigger!" she shouted.

My mother turned around and saw that Gussie had two black eyes. Alarms should have gone off, but instead she saw it as a sign of affection, of how much he cared about her.

During gym class she sprained her ankle and wasn't able to walk down to his car to meet him before getting on the bus, so she asked one of her girlfriends to tell him why she couldn't come. He didn't believe her but wanted to see for himself. When he attempted to get on the bus, the principal grabbed him by the shirt and pulled him off. A.J., who hated being touched, jerked free of the grip. As the bus drove off, my mother and the rest of the school watched as A.J. and the principal began tussling on the sidewalk. Mom believed his insane jealousy was an expression of love; the more enraged he got, the more she believed he loved her.

Aunt Louise hated him, probably more for the darkness of his skin than for his reputation. She would tell my mother to stay away from that black nigger. It's a shame she couldn't offer any better reason for her disdain. I'm sure there were a few.

Richard continued his pursuit and eventually graduated to getting into bed with my mother one night while she slept. He put his hand over her mouth, but she sprang from the bed and began yelling. Afraid that she would wake everyone in the house, he left, but she remained awake for the rest of the night and no longer had a peaceful night's rest under that roof. Aunt Louise and her husband were sickly and frequently had stays in the hospital, so my mother knew Richard was just patiently waiting for the right opportunity. If that ever came, she had no doubt that her virginity would be taken.

Summer approached and she anxiously accepted the invitation to go to New Braunsfels for a two-week vacation with an older couple whose house she cleaned. New Braunsfels was about four hours away, and after a week without any contact, A.J. became impatient and started asking around for directions. She returned before he could leave and when they met in town, he proposed right there on the street.

She loved him and wanted to marry him, but she thought he was bluffing so she called it. Then he suggested they go take their blood tests right away. That caught her by surprise. She came up with some excuse about having to get back home and she would do it tomorrow. When she saw him the next day he had already had his blood test done, and then she knew that he was for real. When they got to the doctor's office, Richard happened to be there. A.J. warned him not to tell Aunt Louise and he didn't, but like I said they lived in a small town, and it wasn't long before Aunt Louise began throwing my mother's things into the dirt road in front of the house.

She got wind of what was happening and A.J. brought her back home to collect the things that had been thrown in the street. Enraged that she had married A.J. against her advice, Aunt Louise came outside as my mother collected her things and began beating her with a wooden sandal. A.J. started to intervene, but his grandfather held him back, telling him to stay out of it. That was between her and her aunt.

Everything that wasn't thrown in the street was burned the next day, including pictures of her father and cards and letters from her brothers and sisters. They stayed with his grandparents until A.J. and his grandfather finished the two-room house they built next door.

CHAPTER FIVE

THREE GIFTS

Being left alone in Liberty, my mother still held some resentment, but Houston was only a half-hour's drive. Her sister Edna lived there with her husband Charlie who was thirty years older. She wrote Edna and saw her, but rarely had any contact with her sister Rita. Rita married quickly after their father's death and moved to Louisiana. Her sisters wanted badly to have a family, but neither of them was having any success. My Uncle Charlie was already well into his fifties, and Rita's husband had been rendered sterile from a venereal disease.

My mother must've been about eight weeks into her pregnancy with Resa when she started writing another letter to Edna. A.J. wanted to see it, but she refused, knowing there were a few choice words about his grandmother, who was never happy with how she cooked or cleaned. He attempted to grab the letter and she started running. He chased her around the room, groping for it, and she laughed. To her it was only horseplay—until he knocked her to the floor with a slap across the face.

That was the first time she had ever been hit. No man had ever laid a finger on her. Papa wouldn't allow that to happen, and if any man had struck one of his girls, he would have surely killed them on the spot.

It took a while for the initial shock to wear off as A.J. hovered over her, enraged, screaming for her to never refuse him anything. When he left, the letter sat on the floor; he never picked it up or read it.

The beatings continued and so did the babies. After Leon was born, Mom was pregnant again three months later with her next son, Riley. She cooked and cleaned to make extra money, while A.J. took whatever job he could find in Liberty and the surrounding counties. After having been fired from almost all of them, the odds of his finding another was getting very slim. He was a heavy drinker, and when he did get a paycheck, most of it went on liquor and women. Whatever was left when he stumbled through the door the next afternoon was for food and clothes. Mom recalls once his stumbling in and throwing three cents on the bed and having the nerve to ask why the babies were crying.

"They're hungry. All we have in the house is cornmeal and a half quart of milk."

He replied, "Then go find some nigger that'll feed'em steak every day!"

She laughed when she told me this, because that's almost exactly what she had done. She was, of course, referring to Daddy Jerome, but there were more fights and more children to come before he would enter our lives.

Edna knew about the beatings and how difficult things were. She brought food and clothes, and when she found out that my mother was going to have her third child, she wanted to adopt it. Edna and Charlie were doing well. He was about to retire from the railroad with a good pension, and they were living in the home once owned by his mother.

When my mother asked A.J. how he felt about Edna's adopting Riley he said it didn't matter to him and to do whatever she wanted. A.J. found a job in Houston and that made the difficult decision a little easier because Riley could still be raised with Leon and Resa. They adopted him right after birth and he would live in their home and take their name, but they made sure he always knew who his biological parents were.

In Houston, my mother was able to find enough work cooking

and cleaning in between pregnancies to keep a little food on the table. A.J. continued his old habits of drinking, getting fired, and coming home with lipstick on his collar. She dared not question him about it. When she did, she ended up with a black eye or busted lip, sometimes both. But she never left him until after she had Ambus Jr., the fourth child. A.J. took a special interest in naming Ambus, which was unusual because he had never cared before. If it was a boy, he insisted on his being named after him. My mother didn't know why, but would soon find out.

Ambus Jr. was only six weeks old and my mother had taken him to the hospital for a checkup. One of the nurses walked over to her and asked if she wanted to see her stepson. Confused, she followed her to the newborn unit and she pointed out a boy that had been born premature a couple of days earlier. As soon as she saw those lips and eyes, the woman didn't have to say anything else, it was A.J.'s son. He sang in a quartet and the mother was an eighteen-year-old choir singer he had met at one of his church gigs. She was planning to name the child after him, but was forced to change her plans after my mother named her child Ambus.

My mother went to the apartment and packed what little they had and asked Edna to come pick them up. The separation didn't last long. He called every day; begging her to come back and telling her things were going to be different. After two months she and the kids returned. She admits that she knew he would not change, but she loved him, and that was never going to change either.

She became pregnant again, but this time she would lose the baby trying to empty a washtub after bathing the three kids. She didn't want to have any more children, but there wasn't much she could do about it. Refusing to have sex or suggesting that he use protection meant she was having sex with another man and that led to a beating.

She became pregnant again. Jo was her fifth child and second daughter. Adrian became the sixth child and her fourth son. While she was pregnant with her seventh, her sister Edna came calling again. Barely able to raise the five she had, she agreed to another adoption. Edna named the baby after her brother, Madison. He would be raised in the same house as our brother Riley.

In Louisiana, Rita's husband was a womanizer and a heavy drinker too. She contracted his venereal disease and it left her unable to bear children. She fell into a deep depression. Alone in the house most of the time, she only ventured out for necessities; the other twenty-five days of the month she stayed in bed with the shades pulled down. Her husband left a small .22 automatic in the drawer of the nightstand for protection, but she began to see it as a way out of a miserable existence.

While Rita contemplated suicide, my mother was getting more concerned about Leon. He had been witnessing his father's violence towards her and was getting more hostile. For almost seven years he watched her being beaten by the man he adored. The older he got, the more difficult it was for him to stay huddled in the room with Resa until it was over. She started to believe that if A.J. didn't kill her first, Leon would eventually grow up and kill him.

It was a near-death experience that finally convinced my mother to leave A.J. for good.

After a night of drinking, he came in accusing her of being with another man. He grabbed her around the throat and began choking her.

44

When she started losing consciousness she remembers thinking what was going to happen to her babies if she died. She lashed out with the long, red nails that he liked so much and when he let go to grab his bleeding face, she ran out the door. The children were already spending the night at Edna's, and when she got there she promised my Uncle Charlie that if he let them stay, it would be just until she was able to get on her feet. Edna wanted her to stay and my uncle was too old and feeble to object anyway. But A.J. wouldn't take it lying down, and that was his only concern.

He called every day threatening to kill her if she was seeing another man. At the time she didn't know that she was pregnant with her eighth child. It was a girl and very early into her pregnancy, Rita asked if she could adopt her. She initially refused because Rita lived in Louisiana and she wouldn't be as involved in her child's upbringing as she was with Madison and Riley. A few days later she called Rita and agreed, then turned around and refused again. That's how it went until she found out it was a girl, at which point she totally rejected the idea.

She was as protective of her girls as Papa had been of his. She had given up two of her sons, hoping that they would have a better life than she could offer. She had to make drastic decisions in drastic times, and if you asked her, she'd tell you she was learning to be a mother by the seat of her pants. She didn't want any of her daughters to make the same mistakes.

Even though she was visibly pregnant, a friend of hers who had been admiring her from afar invited her out. She refused several times, but Edna urged her to go. She needed it. After they'd had a bite to eat, he let her out of the car—a block from the house because of A.J.'s spying.

As she walked along the sidewalk, A.J. came out of the bushes carrying a pistol. He walked straight up to her and hit her in the mouth with the butt of it, sending her and her front teeth crumbling to the cement. He stood over her cursing while blood and teeth seeped between her fingers. He lifted her from the ground by her hair, and just then Uncle Charlie came out with his double-barreled shotgun. A.J. dared him to pull the trigger so Uncle Charlie did, but the gun misfired. A.J. shouted and cursed liked he owned the world then left her on the sidewalk.

After that incident, she reluctantly agreed to her sister Rita raising Renee', but she wouldn't agree to an adoption. When Rita took the newborn home, my mother had no clue what she had done for her sister. Ironically, instead of bringing them closer together it would pull them farther apart, for later my mother became very critical of how her daughter was being raised and envied the allegiance Renee' had for Rita.

My Aunt Edna became pregnant, which was a surprise to everyone because she didn't think she could have children either. But no one was more surprised than my Uncle Charlie, who, like Aunt Edna, was very light skinned, her newly born son Patrick was darker than both of them—not to mention the fact that Uncle Charlie was impotent. Their marriage had been one of convenience. He was well into his sixties and she was barely into her thirties, which had become very inconvenient for her. She went out to the clubs whenever she wanted and there was nothing he could do to stop her. She was six feet tall and robust. He was thin and frail and she would argue him into submission every time he tried expressing any dissatisfaction about anything.

I would like to say that my mother never saw A.J. again, but she did. She even flirted with the idea of getting back with him. After a couple of meetings that ended with her pleading for her life, she stopped taking his calls and eventually refused to see him. He finally let her go when she became pregnant with me.

She had no intentions of having another child. Feeding and clothing the five she had was nearly impossible without assistance from friends and family. Regardless, she would meet the meek and mild wolf that would become my father.

CHAPTER SIX

WHERE'S THE MEAT

Right here I'm supposed to boast about how much my parents loved each other. In reality, my mother was looking for a good time and he was looking to plant his seed. She was a maid in River Oaks, the wealthiest neighborhood in Houston. It was always easy for her to get work there because everyone had big houses and nice cars, but not very many had white maids. Though legally she was not white, she looked close enough. She was able to move out of Edna's and rent a house a few blocks away. My father would sit across the street at a café and watch her get off the bus, then strike up a conversation when she passed. She thought he was cute with his youthful demeanor and sense of humor. He appeared harmless, and that, more than anything else, appealed to her. He admitted freely to being in the proverbial unhappy marriage, but she didn't fall for it. It was the lie about his being sterile that she fell for.

With eight children by 1963 my mother had already made a significant contribution to the baby boom. In January Martin Luther King delivered his "I Have a Dream" speech to millions. Many were not opposed to what he was saying; they just didn't want it to come at their expense. The passionate speech eased some of the tension the country was experiencing at the time. However, it reminds me of how my mother described her brother's slaughtering a pig for dinner. She said he would walk up to the pig with a butcher's knife hidden behind his back, kneel down and tickle the pig behind the ears, then stroke his underbelly. When he thought the pig was totally at ease, he would thrust the knife into the pig's throat.

The calm after Dr. King's speech ended when the country received its own knife to the throat with the assassination of President Kennedy. Dallas was only a few hundred miles from Houston, and like most Americans, my mother saw Kennedy as the answer to all the civil unrest. The brutality of his death was more than her feeble body could handle. Three days later she gave birth to a premature baby boy.

Even then I was a spitting image of the wolf. He couldn't have denied me even if his lie had been true. He came by often during that time and always left before dawn. Despite his marital status, he tried being possessive of my mother. Full of Jack Daniels, he'd lose his temper when she didn't give him what he wanted. His rages weren't as lethal as A.J.'s, but he did throw a glass ashtray at her once and it hit her in the temple. It didn't knock her unconscious, but it gave her a nasty black eye. Usually, before he caused too much trouble, my elder siblings would gang up on him and toss him out of the house.

My mother justified her actions at that time by saying that women had affairs with *her* husband, so why should she play fair? That changed when she came face to face with Mrs. Mary Lee, my father's wife. The affair lasted barely eighteen months—long enough for Mom to defy all logic and get pregnant with her last child. My mother had broken off the affair months earlier, so he didn't believe the child was his until a couple of weeks after Paulette was born. There was a knock at the door and when she answered, it was my father's wife. My mother had never seen her before, but by the vibe she knew who she was and also why she had come.

She politely asked to come in and Mom humbly invited her. Mrs. Mary Lee told her that she wanted to see her newborn because there were rumors that it was also my father's child. When Resa brought the baby girl in, Mrs. Mary Lee immediately knew that she was his. She divulged that she was unable to offer my father any children and thanked my mother for the hospitality.

When Mrs. Mary Lee left, my mother admits that she felt so low that if she had been under a rug she wouldn't have even made a hump.

He still refused to claim my little sister even after his wife told him the child was his. Paulette had learned to walk by the time he did come to see her. His acceptance of his children or A.J.'s didn't matter to my mother. Her main concern was that the children not be divided, so Paulette and I didn't take our father's name, we took A.J.'s. My father never protested that.

I think I was in my teens when I asked her why she never filed for child support and she told me that a real man shouldn't be forced to take care of his own children. I understood and admired her philosophy, but that was short-lived when I looked down at my tattered Chuck Taylor's and my friends were wearing their new Dr. Js.

By the time my mother was thirty-one, she had ten children, seven of whom she was raising. The little money she made was barely enough to feed us. We ate beans quite frequently and if the people Mom was working for had ham, she would save the bone, bring it home, and put it in the pot with the beans—but the holidays were always worth looking forward to. She needed help and wasn't getting it from our fathers. For Christmas the church would donate a box of used toys. She borrowed and practically stole to make sure we had a grand meal on Christmas and Thanksgiving. On a couple of occasions, while cooking for her employer, she would purposely drop a ham or turkey on the floor.

Since it was then "unfit to be consumed," she would be given the money to walk down the street and get another one. She would apologize for her clumsiness and as soon as their backs were turned, she would pull it out of the trash, clean it off, and bring it home.

She tried lessening her dependence on Edna and Charlie by calling for assistance only if one of the kids needed to go the hospital— and even then sometimes she took the bus. My aunt and uncle moved out of the home his mother left him and bought a home in an affluent neighborhood that was predominately black. Their old house had a couple of renters and eventually we moved into it. By then it was rundown and in bad need of repair. There were holes in the roof and holes in the floor; the wood floor was so weak that getting a splinter was inevitable if you walked around in your bare feet. I remember running to my mother a few times, crying for her to pull one out. The house was so overrun with rats that when my mother turned on the oven, the aroma of burning rat flesh consumed the house. She paid rent, but when my uncle failed to make repairs she started paying him what she could afford.

When Mom felt the walls closing in around her, she would go outside and sit at the edge of the cement porch. I'm sure she wondered how she got herself into such a mess. With A.J., she was looking for the loving protection that Papa had given her, but Papa died before Mom matured enough to know that no one ever would do that. When she met my father, I believe she was still in this state of naiveté, looking for protection wherever she could find it.

But although Mom searched in all the wrong places, she did eventually find what she was searching for.

One night out with Edna, Mom sat at a table having a few drinks when she kept feeling this bump against her chair. She turned around and it was this enormous Mandingo warrior wearing a beige fedora, rocking back and forth in his chair. Finding the bumping not all that annoying anymore, she turned back around. She looked at Edna giddily and when the bumping continued, she turned to him and said, "If you keep doing that, you're going to put me to sleep."

He apologized and introduced himself as Jerome.

None of the children knew about it when they started seeing each other, for she usually met him at the café. The first time she allowed him to pick her up at the house; he found his way into the kitchen while Resa was preparing beans and rice for dinner.

"Where's the meat?" he asked. Resa responded with a perplexed expression. "Shorty!" he shouted. That's what he called her because of her height.

Mom burst into the kitchen. "What happened?" she asked, looking us over to see which one needed to be rushed to the county hospital.

"Where's the meat?" he asked, pointing at the plates.

Breathing a sigh of relief, Mom explained that meat was for Sunday dinner or special occasions. He commandeered Leon, and within an hour the house was filled with the sweet aroma of fried pork chops.

On weekends I would be the first one awake, and instead of waiting for him to yell out for me to empty his can, I wanted to get in and out before he awoke. Mildly, I would knock on their bedroom door and wait. On occasion he would yell out, "Go back to bed, Hotshot!" and I did, with great haste, but if I heard nothing, that meant they were still asleep.

He slept closest to the door, with his arm stretched across the other side of the bed. He appeared to be the only person there until Mom's pale face would peek from behind his hulking shoulder and smile at me.

His girth alone could make a hard woman feel feminine, but it took more than his size to make her feel safe. He had a coveting generosity and gentility that was both affectionate and cocky. In his presence, my mother felt an immunity she hadn't felt since she was a child.

For a while, I bathed in the same certainty. After the break-in, I felt susceptible to my environment, like a wounded gazelle in a lion's den. But when Daddy Jerome came, the theoretical fear of being hurt by some stranger was quickly replaced by a more relative fear; the fear of being hurt by him. I think all the boys shared this fear, though it affected us in different ways, depending upon our stage of development.

Leon was almost seventeen and approaching adulthood. The Haight Ashbury District was a bit much for the two sixteen-year-olds from Houston. Leon and Dana hitchhiked back home, and when her prodigal son walked through the door, my mother was overjoyed that he had returned safely, but shocked at his appearance. He had an afro that was napped and matted. He was filthy, unshaven, and had a body odor that could compete with a boiling pot of chitterlings. She peeled off his clothes and disposed of them in a trash bag and ran him a hot bath.

Daddy Jerome stood in the doorway and never said a word. That was worse than some speech about what Leon should have learned from the cross-country tantrum he had thrown.

That journey, hitching rides with truckers and hippies, was a sort of rite of passage for Leon. He had matured in ways that neither he nor

Daddy Jerome would fully understand. He fascinated us for hours telling how it had been to cross the Sahara Desert on foot. How the biting cold and the sound of howling wolves kept them awake at night.

Daddy Jerome hated the attention Leon was getting, especially from me. Next to Daddy Jerome, I looked to him for guidance. He was almost seventeen and had been under the warden's reign for almost five years.

When Leon saw Daddy Jerome cuddled up in his car with another woman, he hoped to put an end to it by rushing home and telling my mother. Her response to him was that his father had done the same thing. That must've enraged Leon, but not as much as her doing nothing about it. He packed his things and he was gone again.

As soon as he came of age, Leon married his high school girlfriend and moved in with her parents. She was a year older and the relationship was doomed from the beginning. They quarreled all the time, and if he knew anything about conflict resolution, it was what his father taught him. He slapped her around, giving her several black eyes before she became pregnant. When she miscarried he saw it as his way out.

He enlisted in the Marines. Daddy Jerome thought it was a great idea, but our mother strongly disagreed with his decision to enlist. He lacked the discipline to come straight home from school, how was he going to survive a crucible like the Marine Corps? She told him he was making a huge mistake, but Leon wanted to get away, as far as he could.

Ambus was the most dependable son. He kept his grades up and knew how to fly under Daddy Jerome's radar most of the time. That left me and Adrian to focus on. Noticing my shoestrings weren't tied late one evening, Daddy Jerome told me to tie them. Right away by my confused expression he knew I had not learned yet, so he bent over and told me to watch. He tied one of my shoes, then the other, then told me to untie them and tie them back. I squatted and untied them, but tying them back was another thing. He reached for the "Querk" that seemed to always be hanging on the bedpost.

"I said tie your shoes," he demanded.

Now speed had become an element in the equation, and after a few seconds I felt that familiar but unwelcome burning sensation across my hip. "I said tie your shoe!" I don't know how many times he repeated those words, but a lash followed each time. It took a while, but I did learn and felt proud that I had. It was late in the evening and I remember showing whoever gave me the time of day that I could tie my shoe.

Unfortunately, our sessions didn't go as well, despite his variety of stimuli to cure me of the stuttering. The method by which he would punish me depended on how much time and patience he had that day. When his back gave him trouble, he would lie in bed and make me stand on one leg while he watched television. I would wobble back and forth, and inevitably when I fell over he'd sit up and give me a battery of lashes across my legs with the "Querk."

He'd settle me down by asking, "Hotshot, are you a man or a mouse?"

He'd repeat the question until I muttered, "A man," which neither one of us believed.

"A man, then stop that crying." When I did, the sequence repeated itself until he got tired.

No matter where I was in the house I could feel his Jurassic movement vibrating under my feet, and the closer he got the thinner the air seemed, like a great weight pressing down upon my chest. At all times I knew I was only a "Hotshot!" away from a session, and that put me in a sort of suspended anxiety, the kind that comes with the sound of squealing tires trying to avoid a collision. I constantly carried around with me that unrest before impact, until the wreck finally came. That took more out of me than anything physical he could do.

I would become a stuttering fool by simply being in his presence so when he left to go to work, gamble, or do whatever he did, I was jubilant. The lewd aroma of Magic Shave and Old Spice were pleasant indications of his departure; it was difficult containing my enthusiasm. Being able to express myself freely without fear of being corrected, even if just for a few hours, was liberating. It was like a prisoner being let out in the yard for a few moments to stretch his legs.

Daddy Jerome's departures became more frequent, a sign that he and Mom were having problems. He was seen again with his other woman, but this time it was by my Aunt Edna, who told my mother where she could find them. Now, Mom accepted everything a man could dish out, but she was still a very jealous woman. Though she wasn't a smoker, she took a couple of hits off the cigarette my aunt was smoking, then walked a quarter of a mile to the Allen Parkway Housing Project and waited next to his Buick.

The only thing shorter than Mom's stature was her temper. When Daddy Jerome and his other woman came out arm in arm, she stormed toward them. Seeing her short, fiery red hair pulled back by the wind, the woman must have thought she was a crazed demon and made a hasty retreat into her apartment. Daddy Jerome stood there. Putting all the force her five-foot-three romp could muster, she swung at his chin, which was a lofty goal for a woman of her height, and when she lost her footing, he caught her before she could make the humiliating fall to the black asphalt.

She asked, "So what are you going to do, Jerome?"

"I'm tired of struggling, Shorty. I love you and want us to have something, but I don't think I can wait until all the kids are grown and out the house."

"I see," she said, putting her weight down on her own two feet. "Well, I have kids to raise."

He had been seeing the woman for more than a year, and nothing was truly keeping him and my mother together. She was still legally married to A.J. and none of us were his children. He returned home that night anyway, but the end was near. It came on an Ash Wednesday that my family and I will never forget.

My Aunt Edna was cooking dinner for us while we were at church, when Daddy Jerome came home. There was no love lost between him and my Aunt Edna anyway, but this time they got into an argument and he told her to leave. She reminded him that it was *her* house that he was staying in, and he stormed out, almost ripping the screen door from its hinges.

We were a couple of blocks away, making our way toward the house, when his car whipped around the corner and sped toward us. He slid to a stop and sprang from the car in an outburst of rage that surprised all of us. Nostrils flaring with anger, he demanded my mother get into the car.

Unlike A.J. and my father, he had never laid a hand on her, but she was frightened anyway, and as she hesitantly began to comply, Resa shouted out, "Mom, don't go!"

That was all the confirmation she needed to change her mind, which only stoked his anger. He slammed the car into park, grabbed my mother by the arm, and started pushing her into the front seat.

Resa, the frailest of all my mother's children, who had an appendectomy and developed hypothyroidism, a goiter, and arthritis, all before her twenty-first birthday, jumped on his back. It took nothing more than a shrug of his shoulder and she went crashing to the sidewalk. She was visibly hurt by the plunge, and my mother shouted for Adrian to go get Ambus. With Leon in the Marines, he would be the man of the house by default, a responsibility he would not embrace.

Spectators gathered on their porches. One of them, a classmate of mine, watched as Jo went to our wounded sister's aid. My mother jerked loose of Daddy Jerome's grip, and in doing so, she fell too.

Seeing her crumpled in the gutter in her Sunday dress rendered us all motionless for a moment. It must've had a sobering effect on him too. While we converged around her, he remained standing behind his car door, as if the purpose for his behavior had drained out of him. He then sped off just as Ambus came running around the corner with the broom. We were all pretty stunned, because the casualties of his rage were Resa and our mother, the two we least expected.

When we got home, we catered to Resa's and our mother's scrapes and bruises. My mother stayed in bed the rest of the day—until we got a knock at the front door. It was Daddy Jerome returning to collect his things. While he packed his things, we huddled in the rear room where she had introduced him to us five years earlier. We were satisfied that he was leaving—all of us except Mom. Her verdict was still undecided.

Once everything he owned was piled into the car, he walked in to say goodbye. His sarcasm was angry and he used big words and overly exaggerated his movements to accent the fact that he was talking down to us, but I could see that he was genuinely hurt. She would have taken him back in a heartbeat, but it was we who no longer wanted him there. For our mother, he had been doing for us what no man in his right mind would, and despite that brief moment of insanity, he adored her more than any man since her father.

I avoided his eyes like Medusa's. It was apparent that he expected me, more than anyone, to walk over and say goodbye. The three years before he entered my life had been summed up in the brief moments of my mother's attacked. It frightened me to think that he wouldn't be there anymore, but my fear was eclipsed by the beatings, the sessions, and the emptying of his can. Standing paralyzed like a stone soldier, I was more than willing to take my chances with the monsters outside the house rather than continue to deal with the one inside.

Still, knowing all that, today I wish I had gone over and said goodbye.

That night he literally bowed out of the door and out of our lives. At the time, I hoped forever. The deep purple bruises that stained my mother's pale flesh helped to persuade her that she had done the right thing. She cried for days from well-deserved self-pity. When it came to men, she had made some bad decisions in her time. Daddy Jerome was as close as she would ever come to having the love and protection she longed for, and he was as close as I would come to having a father.

She never would admit to it, but I wonder if she ever felt that her biggest mistake was not going to California and passing for white.

CHAPTER SEVEN

WHITE TRASH

They surrounded us like starved and salivating wolves. The only female of the pack blocked our path. She snarled and taunted, while the males maneuvered their way behind us, eliminating any possibility of escape. Brandishing her fangs, it was obvious she was the leader and they were waiting on her to make the first move. Upon smelling our fear, she made her move and went for the jugular.

"Yo momma's white! Yo momma's white!" Diane accused. *How stupid,* I thought, *my mother's as black as yours. Why can't you see that?* "Yo Momma's white," she badgered.

"No, she's not!" I shouted back. "My momma's not white!"

They started pushing us around in their small circle, hoping to get one of us to throw a punch or at least break down and cry. Our mother, who hated violence, told us it was better to run than to fight, unless there was nowhere to run. All Paulette and I needed was a seam, and we found one. We blew by Diane, almost spinning her around. They chased us within a block of our home before giving up their pursuit.

Only a few hundred feet from where we lived was Gregory Elementary. If I was in the front yard, I could literally throw a rock and it would fall in the school's playground. Wharton Elementary was almost a mile away from our home, in a predominately white and liberal neighborhood referred to as the Montrose Area. During that time, it was where the beatniks and hippies hung out and the only place racially mixed couples and gays felt safe. Resa and Leon had gone to Gregory, but as soon as desegregation became law, Mom sent Ambus, Jo, and Adrian to Wharton because the books were two grades behind at Gregory. Our getting a good education was very important to her; unless we were bleeding profusely or unconscious, there was no excuse to miss a day of school.

Being the youngest, Paulette and I had always gone to Wharton; so did Diane and her mob. Getting home was like being trapped behind enemy lines. Our objective was to make it across Taft Street undetected. We would be pretty much home free once we did, but there were only two routes we could take, and they couldn't cover both.

Knowing the enemy had lookouts, we had to become well versed in the art of evasion. We took cover behind buildings, trees, and mailboxes; if spotted from afar, we would pretend to walk drunk to disguise our identity. That never worked, and I can't imagine why, but as soon as our covers were blown there would be this mad dash to cut us off before we could get to our house. No matter what plan we devised to avoid the inevitable confrontation, we knew never to split up. Though they had us outnumbered, they always remained cautious of us. Maybe they didn't think two against four were good enough odds.

We were treated differently in the neighborhood and didn't really know why. Like most in the neighborhood, when the bologna was about to spoil, we washed the sticky mold off and put it in the frying pan. When rats got into the bread, we'd throw away the slices they had eaten off and keep the rest. When roaches got into the bread we'd just pull off the area where they ate, then toast it. When there was absolutely nothing in the house to eat, we had Cush-Cush, a bowl of fried cornmeal served with cold milk and a sprinkle of sugar. Most of the people we lived around got by the same way we did.

As a family we stuck close to the house and played with each other, mostly—that was one of the advantages of having a large family. There was Hide-N-Go Seek; Red Light, Green Light; Momma, May I; Tag; and personally I loved the Chinaberry wars and rolling old tires down the street with my brother Adrian. When we went to the movies, we went as a pack until we actually got into the theater. Paulette and I were bought tickets to see movies like *Young Frankenstein*, *The Towering Inferno*, and *Willy Wonka and the Chocolate Factory*, while the older kids saw stuff like *The Groove Tube*, *Midnight Cowboy*, and *The Exorcist*. When we could, my little sister and I would sneak into the R rated movies—and most of the time we wished we hadn't. *The Texas Chainsaw Massacre* scared the hell out of us, and we were too young to grasp *Cabaret* or *Taxi Driver*. I didn't get a chance to see blacksploitation films like *Superfly*, *Shaft*, *Foxy Brown*, *Claudine* or *Cooley High* because the only theatre in the vicinity that showed them had only one screen and they wouldn't sell us a ticket because of our age.

On weekends we walked down to Buffalo Bayou and played in the murky water. Our mother disapproved, but she knew the older kids would watch out for the youngest. When she could, she tried leading by example, but it was *Do as I say and not as I do,* mostly. She tried instilling a kind of attitude, as if we were the upper crust of the ghetto, and for the most part it worked.

She wanted that kind of influence over all her children, though.

Renee' and my Aunt Rita had moved from Louisiana to Houston a couple of years earlier, after her husband died. Renee' was seven and my mother was delighted to have an opportunity to develop their mother-daughter relationship. She wanted to have the same kind of bond she had with Resa, Jo, and Paulette, and hoped that being Renee's birth mother would somehow supercede who was raising her. That was not rightfully hers, though when it came to Renee', and she would sour patiently, waiting for it.

She was very critical and judgmental of how her children were being raised by her sisters, but neither of them took great offense at her condemnation. Rita was very grateful for being allowed to raise Renee', for it saved her life; Edna raised Riley and Madison as her own. That aside, on Saturday nights the three sisters went dancing at the Continental Lounge, a hole-in-the-wall beer joint on the north side of town that played Zydeco music. Resa was of age and went with them sometimes, leaving Jo and Ambus in charge. We would play music and dance until we were all exhausted. The ladies would stroll in about three in the morning.

Sometimes Paulette would spend a night at Renee's and I would spend a night at Riley and Madison's. It took spending a night there for me to know the meaning of envy. Their neighborhood smelled like pine trees, and in the morning I could hear birds chirping. I can't remember once waking to the sound of birds chirping in the Fourth Ward, though I know they must have been there. When the train's horn blew around six-thirty in the morning, I was already up, pouring myself a box of Capt N Crunch while everyone else was still asleep. Riley was a senior in high school and I rarely saw him, so I spent most of my time playing with my cousin Patrick, my Aunt Edna's only birth son. Madison didn't like playing the rough and tumble games we played, so he resorted to helping my Aunt Edna clean the house or he played with his Ken and Barbie dolls.

On Saturday mornings my aunt and uncle went to K-Mart to

shop. Patrick got a pellet gun, which was like giving an arsonist a box of matches. They bought a target, but the bull's-eye didn't hold the same attraction as shooting at cans, trees, cats, or dogs. Madison, who was eleven at the time, got the Barbie Camper to go with his Ken and Barbie. Actually, I thought the camper was cool. It was bigger than the Tonka truck I got for Christmas.

On the way home, my aunt stopped to get gas and the line was wrapped halfway around the block. The country was in the middle of the gas shortage; it was going to be at least forty minutes before she could get to a pump. It was hot and my aunt and uncle did what they did best when they were together, argue. In the rear of the station wagon with me was Patrick, pointing his pellet gun at people walking down the street. Madison sat alone in the back seat, positioning his dolls in their new RV. My mother, who suggested counseling, had been telling her sister since he was three that she suspected he would be gay, but my aunt refused to believe it.

The days moved at a slower pace and with Daddy Jerome out of my life, I was happy again. The nightmare was finally over; no one called me Hotshot. It had been a label symbolizing weakness, degradation, and cowardice. I never confessed that to anyone until now, but my siblings just seemed to know. I could never accept it as an endearment. I wanted Hotshot to be dead. As far as I was concerned, he was.

For us, at home things were getting better. Mom started working at a bag factory for minimum wage, which was more than she had been getting cleaning homes in River Oaks, but standing up all day and turning 15,000 burlap bags sent her home exhausted. Resa ran interference, keeping us away from her with our petty needs for affection.

Resa ran a tight ship. The only person who could overrule her decisions was our mother. To get Adrian and Ambus out of bed for school she poured cold water on them. No one was more lethal with a large, wooden soupspoon than she was. On Saturdays she delegated the chores. After our rooms were clean, Jo and Ambus went to the Laundromat with our mother to wash clothes; Adrian and I cleaned the yard; and Paulette helped Resa clean the rest of the house, while she cooked the traditional pot of pinto beans.

Mom suffered with wicked migraines, sometimes so bad she could not hold any food down or lift her head off the pillow. It was one such time that I whined outside her door to get in, but Resa kept me at bay with a belt dangling over her shoulder from her cocked elbow. From the room, I could hear my mother's strained voice, trying to reach a peak where she could be heard. She was telling my sister to allow me in. Resa opened the door but gave me an evil stare before allowing me to enter. Slowly, Mom pivoted her head toward me, as if her brains might spill out if she did it any faster. She made several attempts before opening her eyes, and even then it was just a glare.

"Look, Mom," I said, raising a picture of a red dragster I had drawn with crayon. "Tonka should make one like that."

She took a deep breath and released it as she replied, "You should tell them that." She then laid her arm across her forehead and slowly pivoted her head away from me.

I was old enough to recognize a good idea when I heard one. Soliciting help from Jo, I was able to get the address, and a day later, before she left to go to work, I handed Mom the letter. Even on her pale, sickly face, I could tell she was surprised that I had followed through with it. The only thing missing was a stamp. She slid the letter into her purse and kissed me goodbye.

What Mom lacked in encouragement she made up in indulgence. Resa, on the other hand, had no interest in encouragement or indulgence. After school no one was to leave the house until our mother came home. One afternoon a half hour before she was to arrive, I walked to the bus stop to meet her. I knew Resa would be looking for me, and if I didn't have my mother there by my side when I returned, she would beat me silly.

The next bus rolled up and my heart fluttered when I saw her red hair pressed up against the window. She was tired, but when she saw me standing there waiting for her, a smile came to her face and she seemed to forget about her hard day at work. She stepped off the bus and gave me a sloppy kiss on my chubby cheeks as I grabbed her hand and we walked home.

When we walked through the front door, Resa went right at me with the belt. I hid behind my mother while she calmed Resa down. Resa pleaded her case, explaining that she had been looking for me for more than an hour, and Jo and Ambus were out right now looking for me. My mother pulled me from around her and told me that I should have told Resa where I was going, but I knew if I had she would have never let me go.

I accepted the scolding and every day after that, unless it was bad weather, I would wait for her at the bus stop. If she was late, I waited as long as it took. I got the first hug, which is important when you have other siblings also vying for your mother's time. There was no more getting up to fix Daddy Jerome's lunches, so by bending the rules I managed to find other ways to have her all to myself.

I hardly noticed, but the times were changing, and even slowing down the speed limit to fifty-five couldn't slow the changes. Vietnam was finally over and Hank Aaron broke Babe Ruth's record. I made my own personal contribution by rejecting the metric system, with failing grades, as most of my classmates did during the mid-seventies. My siblings went to a high school with a well-balanced racial mix, and that influenced me too. Ambus preferred Rock-n-Roll and listened to Chicago, Kiss, Three Dog Night, Blood Sweat and Tears, Blue Oyster Cult, Crème, Bad Company, and Deep Purple. The Average White Band was as far as he went when it came to R&B.

Jo had a Hispanic boyfriend and Adrian, who was about fourteen, started dating Lillian, a petite white girl. Our neighbors stared and whispered as they did when my mother sat on the porch with a male friend.

Diane happened to be walking by while Adrian was outside with his girlfriend; I was on the ground digging holes for a solo game of marbles. She returned a few minutes later with two older boys that I had never seen. I figured they were relatives. She called for me to come across the street, but knowing she was up to no good, I ignored her and continued practicing my shots.

"Gary, come here!" she called again.

I looked at Adrian and Lillian as he prepared to walk her home. It was warm and the attic fan was not working, so Resa had come out to sit on the porch.

"Gary!" Diane called again.

I got off my knees and walked across the street. "What?"

"Ask him," one of the guys urged the other.

Diane watched hungrily.

"Is your momma white?" he asked.

"No, my momma ain't white. That's my momma right there." I pointed at my nineteen-year-old sister, Resa, who was only ten years older than I was. They laughed at the absurdity of it.

"My momma said your momma was white trash," Diane said.

I swiped back, "My momma ain't no white trash. Yo momma's the one that's white trash."

They laughed at the absurdity of that, too.

The next day at school we were at recess and the game was dodgeball. I was on one of the ends throwing the ball; unfortunately, Diane was already out. She was hanging on the fence behind me making snide remarks, as I took aim at my next casualty.

"Gary's momma's white trash," she said aloud, enough for most of the kids to hear, but not loud enough for the teacher, who was sitting in her chair reading. "Gary's momma is white trash." She repeated it several more times, while the anger started burning a hole in my stomach. The victims that remained in the game were absorbing the brunt of my frustration and flinched every time I had the ball.

Just before they could start complaining to Mrs. Prim, Diane began singing this chant of ridicule, "Whitetrash, whitetrash, whitetrash, Gary's momma will do anything for cash. Whitetrash, whitetrash, whitetrash, Gary's momma will do anything for cash."

For a brief moment, my anger overcame my mother's expectations of me, and I did exactly what my seething heart desired.

Without a glance or even an aim, instinctively I seemed to know exactly where Diane was along the fence. With pure malice in my heart, I cocked the ball behind my head. The children in the game began scattering like roaches. I whipped around like a pitcher when the runner is trying to steal second and released the ball at the precise moment that would ensure it reached peak velocity. That smug look of self-approval Diane flaunted completely transformed into a state of shock by the time the rubber ball hit her in the stomach. The impact pushed her against the fence in a concave sort of way, then she crumpled to the ground, holding her stomach as one of the girls screamed out for Mrs. Prim. She sprang from her seat and went to Diane's aid. I was still in the position of a spent pitcher, savoring the last pitch of a perfect game, but my satisfaction was quickly doused by the look of disappointment on Mrs. Prim's wrinkled old face.

Everyone knew how Diane taunted me and my sister, but for some reason that didn't matter. What I had done was sacrilegious, and they stared at me as if I were the son of Satan. My satisfaction turned into embarrassment as Diane's withered body was being helped up and dragged off to the nurse's office.

For the rest of the day I was forced to stand outside the room. I was always a good student, so some of the other teachers were curious to know what I could have done that would force Mrs. Prim to send me outside the room to stand. After a brief discussion with her they would come out shaking their heads in disappointment. I pouted, visibly trying to show remorse, but inside I was still reeling with excitement.

My mother found out what happened at school and told me that I was not supposed to hit girls. She knew we were having problems with some of the kids and just left it at that, but there was something else on her mind. It was hidden behind her back and her smile.

"Guess who's got some mail?" she said, holding a package in front of me. "It's a response from Tonka."

I was amazed for a moment, staring at the box that was about three inches high and seven inches long. It had been months since I wrote the letter. I had forgotten all about it.

I ripped the brown paper off like Christmas wrapping, and there it was—a shiny red dragster. Almost like the one I had drawn. I rolled it on the floor once and set it down. It spun off and began popping wheelies down the hallway.

I was so overjoyed my knees were wobbly. I was delighted and confused all at the same time. What kind of person would take the time to send me anything, a kid they didn't even know? Until then the confines of my small world consisted of my family, my classmates, and the teacher that happened to be teaching my grade level at the time. All of a sudden the world seemed a little larger.

We were all happier, everyone except Leon. Just as he had resisted Daddy Jerome's authority, he resisted the military. When he showed up at the door one afternoon, my mother was hesitant to be joyful, but he told her he was on leave. Since he was staying with his wife, Carol, in the Westend near his father, she had no reason to doubt him . . . until a week or so later when he got a job at a printing company. Before he enlisted, he had applied for that position of apprentice at least eight times but was never hired, so when he came over to tell our mother the good news, she asked, "What are you still doing home?"

"I went AWOL," he admitted, then tried curbing her worry. "It's not that serious Mom. Vietnam is over. They don't care. If anything, they're trying to kick guys out."

Two weeks later, while he was taking a bath, his wife opened the bathroom door and two MPs stepped in. "Braxton, Leon Henderson?" one asked, looking down at his pad.

Leon got dressed and they took him to the county jail, where he stayed for three days before being taken to the airport and placed on a 747. Standing in the aisle, he realized the whole plane was filled with men from different branches of the service who had also gone AWOL.

He continued going over the fence, as they call it, and after a few weeks in Carlsbad, California, bingeing on angel dust, Valium, and alcohol, he'd turn himself in. But it was drug-sniffing dogs and an ounce of weed in his footlocker that got him six months in the brig.

Mom knew going to the Marines was a bad idea. All her brothers had gone to the service, and none of them was the better for it. When Ambus, for whom she had the highest expectations, decided to enlist in the Army, she was broken-hearted. (Ambus had applied for a music scholarship to the University of Houston, but did not get it so the military was his ticket out.) And while Ambus was leaving Leon was being discharged.

Divorced from his high school sweet heart, Leon was living with a friend and with Resa working we could finally afford to move out of our uncle's dilapidated house and into a less dilapidated one three blocks over. Adrian and I were excited about having a room to ourselves. He asked my mother if he could decorate it. I don't know if she had any concerns about his decorum, but she probably should have. He kicked me out of the room one Saturday afternoon and instructed me not to come back until he called.

I had developed a good friendship with a boy next door, Willie, who was my age. His older brother, Marvin, was about Leon's age and mentally disabled. Marvin's small afro was always nappy; so was the sparse hair on his chin. Willie was sensitive about his brother's illness, but boys being boys, of course, I picked on him about it as he did about my mother's light complexion. We pushed each other around and pretended to fight, but we liked each other too much to do any harm. Besides, he was the only one I could beat in marbles.

Marvin had severe schizophrenia and carried on conversations among three or four different personalities within him. One moment he would be sitting on the sofa talking in a low tone and laughing at his own jokes; the next moment he would detonate into a violent argument, spewing out profanities while everyone watched television and ate dinner. Unlike his family, his outbursts were impossible for me to ignore. Every so often, he would look me right in the eye and start spitting profanities at me. When I moved he continued cursing as if I were still standing there. It was eerie, when his eyes did follow me though.

No matter what, Willie adored his older brother and believed him to be benign. I understood how he felt because I adored my older brother too, but I was frightened of Marvin. Apparently others were, as well, because I was the only friend that came over to play with Willie.

One day as we were out playing catch, Marvin came out to watch. Leon was visiting and standing in the doorway keeping watch over the red Porsche his friend let him borrow. Marvin came over to me and asked for the ball. I looked at Willie and he offered nothing, but behind the screen door Leon did.

"Don't give it to him, Gary," Leon shouted.

"Give me the ball!" Marvin demanded.

Not seeing any harm in it, I tossed him the ball. He tossed it in the air a couple of times, then flung it deep into the empty lot across the street and began laughing. Leon came out of the house and put his face into Marvin's.

"Go and get it!" Leon demanded.

Marvin refused and a fight quickly ensued. Marvin had Leon by about twenty pounds, but Leon managed to get him in a headlock. To shake him loose, Marvin picked him up and slammed him to the ground, but Leon held on. They rolled around the front yard and Leon was able to get to his feet first, with Marvin's head still in tow.

"I'll break your fucking neck," Leon threatened and squeezed a little tighter. Marvin relaxed as if to concede and Leon let go. Marvin then grabbed hold of Leon and drove his head into the cement steps, chipping his front tooth, then tried digging his fingers into Leon's eye sockets. Leon fought to get loose and darted into the house to arm himself. Resa tried stopping him, but he shoved her aside, while Marvin stood in our front yard taunting him to come back out, laughing and stomping the ground with glee, as if he, too, had found someone to play with.

Armed with a knife, Leon bolted toward the door as Resa picked up the phone to call the police. That brought Leon to a sliding halt, because he had a few warrants out. He told her to put down the phone, upon which she gave him an ultimatum. With his chest heaving in anger, resentfully he lowered our mother's carving knife. At that, Resa went over to him to tend to his cuts.

I came from the bathroom with a wet rag and offered it to Leon. He didn't take it but gave me a nasty stare, making me feel like the bastard I was. In the bedroom I lay across the bed on my back, feeling totally useless to him. I wanted him to like me, but instead he hated me—and with a chipped tooth as a permanent reminder, he always would.

To rescue me, a beautiful woman, naked, with portly breasts, seemed to descend and pull me from my stupor of self-pity. I rose from my bed and looked around the room; Adrian had pulled out pictures from his nude magazines and pinned them on all four walls and some parts of the ceiling too. I was embarrassed by it, but being new to masturbation, I found some redeeming value in it. Our mother had the last word though, and when Adrian opened the door, she was shocked. There was nothing but naked women wall to wall, in very compromising positions, but she must have been grateful that it wasn't men, because she told him he could leave them up as long as he kept the door closed.

Like most boys after their first successful attempt at masturbation, I thought I had stumbled across something that no man knew about. Waking up every morning to a woman's vagina staring me in the face, masturbation became pretty frequent. Feeling guilty for the detestable thing I was taking part in, I decided to tell the priest at confession. I had never confessed before in my life, but I was compelled to tell someone, hoping to find out if this was something that could keep me out of Heaven. I decided to tell Father Nicholas; he was a well-respected priest despite the rumors that the wine he drank during mass wasn't the only wine of which he partook.

The Catholic Church we attended was downtown and as crazy as it sounds, Adrian and I were altar boys. After mass I rushed to beat him out, and after sneaking past my mother I waited at the occupied confession booth. An elderly woman came out and I entered.

"How have you sinned, my son?"

I kept my head down and didn't know how to begin. I stumbled over my words. The priest said nothing. I wanted to peer through the screen to see if he had fallen asleep, as he did during mass, but if he hadn't recognized me I didn't want to take that chance. "How have you sinned, my son?" he inquired again.

Unable to bring myself to tell him what I had been doing, I burst out of the door—to encounter my mother and Adrian standing there waiting. Adrian wanted to laugh, and my mother was a little surprised because she wanted to know what I had done that was worth confessing. Normally she would have had to drag me to confession, but thankfully she didn't ask.

To deal with the guilt, I made a pact with myself that I wouldn't do it on Sundays, but undergoing the torment of not knowing if I was normal or some freak of nature, I decided to tell Mom anyway. She was the one person that always had the right answers.

I strolled into her room while she watched television, but found it difficult to begin. "What is it, honey?" she asked. Seeing my continued hesitation, she prompted, "What is it? You can tell me."

"I'm having these funny feelings," I said.

"Funny feelings?" she asked and it sounded worse when she said it. With my reluctance to speak another word, the light bulb finally came on but she wasn't sure what to say. That's when I figured this might not have been the best idea. Mom told me everything was normal, but later that night, while lying in bed, Adrian asked if I wanted to tell him about those funny feelings I was having. He was poking fun at me, so I went over and punched him a few times, while he laughed. There are only a few times I can remember ever really missing the presence of a man in the house and that was one of them.

My father did come to the house from time to time. He was good-natured and my mother loved his company. She was always the focus of his visits, since he came just late enough that after about an hour into his visit, it was our bedtime. If Paulette and I wanted to see him, we'd have to be on the lookout for his car at the café he hung out at. It was three blocks from the house and if we saw his yellow and black Torino from the corner, we walked down to see him. He never turned us away, but would give us five dollars to share and ten dollars for our mother. He did pick us up at the prodding of his wife, Mrs. Mary Lee, and bought us bikes and school clothes once.

It must have been around Father's Day, when he decided to drop by again because I gave him a card that I made in class. When I gave him the card, I watched as he carefully opened it. He glanced over it as I waited patiently for his response. He looked bewildered and passed it to my mother, who was sitting on his lap, and she read it for him. He gave me a dollar or two and sent me to bed. The next morning I asked her why she had to read it to him and she told me he was illiterate, knowing I had no earthly idea what the word meant.

"Ma'am?"

"Illiterate means your daddy can't read."

I was floored by the news. I thought all adults could read,

especially my father. He was a custodian for the city and hauled scarp metal on the weekends to make extra money. He had a home in a middle class black neighborhood, wore fancy clothes, and drove brand-new cars. On his fingers he wore diamond and gold rings, one of which he always let me wear until the next morning when he got up to leave. In spite of all that, I felt sorry that he couldn't read.

We enjoyed his visits and wished he could come by more. He was a bit of a ham; I think Mom enjoyed his humor the most. I would inherit a little of that also.

Once a year an old guy would come to school and put on a puppet show. At the end he would ask a sixth-grade teacher to pick one of her students to come on stage and play the saxophone. It was actually a toy instrument, and he would play music from his synthesizer while the child pretended to be playing the saxophone. The only problem was that every year some insipid kid would be chosen who would stand in one place suffering from stage fright. For years I watched this and yearned to have a shot at it, but it was unlikely, since there were three sixth-grade teachers and about a hundred students I was competing with. When he chose Mrs. Prim, that narrowed the field quite a bit and I threw my hand up. She had to have seen the excitement in my eyes.

I got on stage and did the Funky Chicken and played that sax like it was a real instrument. The audience was blurry to me and everything seemed to rush by, but there was a roar of applause while most of the students and teachers doubled over in laughter. Paulette rushed home to tell everyone how crazy her big brother was.

I was speaking well, I assume, because no one made an issue of it, which meant I was enjoying being a kid again. It was wonderful to be out of the shackles of Hotshot. He was dead to me. Leon was the only one who called me that from time to time, and he did it only as a point of ridicule.

My new fame at school didn't help the relationship with Diane and her goons. They hadn't chased us home since the dodgeball incident, but I knew it wasn't over between us. I went to Paulette's class, where her teacher was holding her over for some reason. Seeing a few of my friends playing football on the playground, I joined in. Maybe thirty minutes passed before I went back to the classroom. I figured if I was a little late Paulette would wait on me, but when I got to the class her teacher told me she had already left.

Immediately I got a horrible feeling in the pit of my stomach. I jumped the stairs and took off running toward the house. I saw a few schoolmates and asked if they had seen Paulette. They pointed toward the house and said that she was being chased by Diane and her gang.

As I ran home I imagined what horrible things they were doing to my little sister—like pulling her fingernails off with a pair of pliers and pouring alcohol over them. I jumped up on the porch and burst through the door. There she was crying, with Adrian and Resa consoling her.

Feeling defeated and unworthy to be called a big brother, I had to do something. Adrian knew I was going to explode if I didn't. He took me outside and just followed me to make sure I didn't get in too far over my head.

My first stop was Diane's house. I called her out, but no one answered. Then I saw her brother and most loyal henchman, across the street at the high school. Adrian and I jumped the fence and I went up to him.

"Did you chase my sister home?"

He started to say something, but it wouldn't have made a difference anyway. With a tackle, I took him to the ground and unleashed a battery of punches to his chest and face. None of them had any real malice behind them, just frustration. Adrian watched us for a minute or so, laughing until an older boy came and pulled us apart.

My adversary hopped the chain link fence and ran into his house; I was right behind him, because I knew the one I really wanted was inside. Adrian grabbed me by the collar to keep me from running into their house.

At the curb I screamed for Diane to come out. She never did, but her brother came out wielding a butter knife. I dared him to come off the porch, but he wouldn't. Another one of her sidekicks lived a half block up and I went to his house and called him out. His mother came to the door and told us she was going to call the police if we didn't leave.

During class the next week Mrs. Prim forced Diane and me to work together on posters for the Bicentennial celebration in the auditorium. We lay on the floor with each other for hours, drawing and coloring. After an accidental bumping of the arms, I noticed her skin didn't feel amphibious, despite her clammy exterior. And even that seemed to change when she smiled and insisted that I share her crayons.

We were getting along fine, but it was too late, my family was moving closer to my mother's job. I liked the Fourth Ward, but I looked forward to leaving. Willie had moved earlier that summer to Waco with his family. I was ready to see something different and experience different things.

Summer came, and so did the day for us to leave. By dusk, when we had the last load piled on my uncle's truck, I saw Diane standing across the street. She was alone and maybe wanted to make one last poke at me before I left. She didn't call me over; she just stood there and watched, so I decided to walk over to see what she wanted.

"You're moving?"

"Yeah."

"Where?"

"Fifth Ward."

Neither of us knew where that was, other than it was farther than walking distance. Briefly our eyes caught one another's—and suddenly she wasn't as evil as I had once thought. Actually, she was kind of cute.

"Guess I'll see ya' round," she said, breaking the lingering silence.

"Yeah, I'll see ya' round, Diane."

I was twelve when I climbed into the bed of my uncle's truck and waved goodbye to Diane and the Fourth Ward forever.

It was a period of transition. I was moving into adolescence as well as a new neighborhood. The country was two hundred years old and seemed to be going through the same hormonal change as I was. Like acne, ten years of civil unrest left physical scars and the Vietnam War and Watergate had taken the country's virginity. Luckily, I still had mine and the innocence that came with it.

PART II

CHAPTER EIGHT

THE VIRGIN

With Leon and Ambus out of the house and Jo and Resa working, we moved up from poverty to low income. In the Fourth Ward, everyone was too poor to have anything worth stealing or dying for, but the Fifth Ward was different. I found out there were two levels of low income. There were those that lived like the middle class, which usually meant a father living in the home or a single parent with only one or two children; the others were families like my own that didn't go hungry anymore, but still saw boxed cereal as a luxury.

We moved into a house at the end of Schwakhardt Street across from a rice mill that gave off an awful stench at times and the P-N-C Drive Inn. It was a black truckers' bar where every weekend there was the customary beating, stabbing, or shooting. Most of the men took notice of my pale-skinned mother and her beautiful daughters. They also took notice of how big her sons were.

Adrian was a six-foot high school sophomore and playing on the football team. Sometimes Riley came by to visit; he was six foot four. I was a few months shy of my thirteenth birthday and weighed about a hundred and seventy pounds.

Leon lived just down the street with a girlfriend and Ambus had returned home from the Army. As my mother feared, he had changed. He resisted the temptation of drugs, avoiding the vampires in the neighborhood that peddled it. Even Leon and Riley tried getting him to take a hit of marijuana, but he refused. Like Leon, he became discontent with the military and began having problems with his superiors. He had traded his tuba for a bass guitar and during a jam session with a friend on base he decided to take his first hit. After that, he began experimenting with other drugs and getting into more trouble. He received several Article Thirteens, which is a mild form of court-martial, for insubordination. When he was offered a General Discharge he took it and returned home bitter and angry.

It was post-Vietnam, and the public's attitude toward veterans wasn't as patriotic as it is now. Ambus applied for everything from a bus driver to a waiter and ended up taking the first job offered; sweeping floors in an office building. At home he was verbally abusive and our mother told him to leave if he couldn't get along with the rest of us. He moved into an apartment in the Montrose Area and began bartending at a comedy club. Mom was very disappointed. She had higher hopes for Ambus and expected him to be the first to go to college.

In the Fifth Ward, as I entered the seventh grade and adolescence, the boys seemed harder and the girls more experienced. On my first day in gym class the guys were pitching nickels against the wall and Bigfoot; literally the big man on campus, standing six-two at the age of thirteen, invited me to join the game. It was an invitation coming from the Godfather of my grade level, so graciously I complied. I figured the worst that could happen was I wouldn't have any lunch money—but I started to win. When Bigfoot ran out of money, he said, "I'm gone," and grabbed a handful of my winnings. That was cool; I still had more than I came there with and also I saw how he acted between classes.

Bigfoot liked starting fights with the Hispanic students. Once I actually watched him beat his own head against the wall until he bled. I figured he was just trying to impress us, but it would take our becoming

88

good friends before I would find out that it went much deeper than that.

The only other person in gym class that I noticed was Toni, a lovely dark-skinned girl who was a year older. She was a woman and made all the other females appear juvenile. It got around that I liked her. I was a little relieved because at least I would know if she felt the same. Her friend pointed me out while I watched, and when she saw who her admirer was, she started to laugh. From more than ten feet away, I could hear her say, "That little boy? Please."

Bigger than most of my peers, most of it was pudge. I couldn't even play basketball, and that was expected. I couldn't dribble the ball without looking down at it and would get picked second to last, just before the nerd. That was humiliating. I hadn't made any real friends, so I looked forward to seeing Madison and Renee' in between classes. I wasn't as aggressive or as socially advanced as the other students, so I went through most of the school year pretty much dismissed and unnoticed.

All that changed on a beautiful spring morning during gym. The coach lined all the boys up on the track and blew his whistle for us to make one lap around. Bigfoot took the lead, as he did in everything, and I just stayed behind him. About halfway around, the other boys fell back and I could see Bigfoot looking over his shoulder, surprised that I was still there. He sped up and so did I. I was content with coming in second until he started to slow down and I still had another gear. I pulled alongside of him and he told me to stay beside him. I did as he said as we came around the last curve . . . then something inside of me kicked in. I began pulling ahead.

"Hold up, man!" he demanded, but it was too late. I could taste victory and didn't look back.

I could hear the students cheering and I saw the coach taking notice. When I came in, everyone was patting me on the back and the coach pulled me aside.

"What's your name, son?" he asked, scanning his attendance roster.

"Braxton, sir. Gary," I said, trying to catch my breath.

"You want to run track?"

"Sure."

That evening I walked onto the field and went up to the coach while he was attending to his other athletes. I got his attention but he barely recognized me. Had he forgotten already? Feeling out of place, I began wondering if I had made the right decision.

As I stood there, a thin boy with hair already growing out of his chin walked over and introduced himself as William. We struck up a friendship that would last a lifetime. William lived just across the railroad tracks and took care of his grandparents after practice. Afterward, he came over to the house and ate dinner. Later on we took a walk with no particular place to go. We took our time and talked about how we wanted our lives to be when we got older. He was going to be a famous artist; I hadn't really decided yet. Whatever it was, I wanted to make enough money to buy my mother a house.

I was on the track team, but by no means was I part of the in-crowd. The few friends I had were all having sex. I figured maybe it was time for me also, but I didn't know anything about it other than I needed a female partner. There was a pretty girl who sat behind me and the rumor was that she had a little experience in that area, so I chose her. At some point during class I decided it was time to let her know my plans, so I turned around and whispered, "Felicia, can I get you?"

It was bad enough that she laughed out loud, but to make matters worse, she turned around and told the girl behind her. With my last name starting with B, I watched the ripple of laughter as it went from student to student, up one row and down the other.

I vowed not to ever try having sex again.

After class, William and I walked home. Sympathetically he said, "I heard what happened in English." He really wanted to laugh, but he held it back and I appreciated that. The only females I associated with, outside of my sisters, were a couple of girls on the track team. Eva was one of them and we spoke on the phone almost every night. She was a virgin too, and I think she knew I was, though I never said it.

I made up my mind to learn to play basketball. The closest place to practice was Finnegan Park, across the street from the Coke Street Housing Projects. Hanging at the home of one of his football buddies, Adrian saw me bouncing a partially deflated volleyball down the street and called me over.

"Where you going?" he asked, sitting on the porch with his friend Dale, his brother Barry, and their cousin Steve.

"To the park to shoot some hoops."

"With a volleyball?" He laughed and so did they. "Boy, you're going to get your ass kicked."

"We got a goal behind the house," Dale suggested. "Let's air it up and play."

We played several games, switching partners several times trying to make it more competitive, but Adrian and I sucked. The only score I managed to make was purely accidental.

Our new friends were great athletes; I was determined to be as good as they were. On the weekends, the first thing I did when I got up was put on my Chuck Taylor's and go down to Dale and Barry's to practice. It never entered my mind how annoying it must have been to hear that basketball banging against the backboard at eight on a Saturday morning.

Barry would come out yawning and putting on his sneakers. We'd shoot around and Dale would come out and eventually Adrian and Steve would show up. Barry and I were the same age and shared the same tribulations that younger brothers do. Steve was a year older and about a hundred pounds overweight, but very agile for his size. Dale had a couple of years on me and could outdo all of us in everything. He was a couple of seasons away from a football scholarship. He was faster, smarter, and better-looking. His girlfriends were prettier. He also had a physique like a Greek god—and an ego to match.

Every Friday and Saturday night around ten-thirty, we went to Finnegan Park and played ball. No one played that late, so we had the court to ourselves. The goals didn't have nets so we brought our own and took them when we left. The floor was smooth cement and unmerciful when you came down on it. But the court had a covering. Only slanted rain or close gunfire could keep us from playing.

We quickly became a clique. That summer we got a basketball goal of our own and I practiced every day. Otis, one of the drunks from the bar across the street, liked coming over to play. He always bragged about how good he had been in school. I could tell he wasn't lying—the old man had game, but the smoking and drinking between shots kept us from ever finishing one. Bigfoot lived two blocks away, so he came over to play regularly. He had the height advantage, but I developed a wicked

92

twenty-footer.

When school started I was a few months from my fourteenth birthday and feeling less like an outcast. I knew how much my mother liked watching football so I entered the coach's office to inquire as to how I could get on the team. He looked at me dreamy-eyed as if his season had been saved. His best running back was entering high school and the coach had no one to replace him. He thought it could be me, but the first day of practice he discovered, to his dismay, that I knew very little about the game. When I saw the guys huddled on television, I thought they were devising a plan like we did in street ball. I had no idea that they had preconceived plays that had to be remembered.

To improve my learning curve, the coach had me play on both the junior varsity and the varsity football teams. Thursdays I would play with the eighth-graders; Friday mornings I played with the ninth-graders. Sometimes I played in both games on the same day. As the season progressed, I was pretty much a disappointment on both teams. The only thing that kept me from quitting was Adrian. I knew he would give me a hard time if I did. In the final game of the season, we were playing the sorriest team in our district; the only team we could beat. I ran my first touchdown and he was there to see it. When the quarterback handed me the ball, no one wanted to hit me so I just kept running until I got into the endzone. I was so thankful that I took a knee and said a prayer. That same year I improved so much in basketball that not only did I make the team, but I was also a starter.

My popularity began to grow, but some things remained the same. I was still a closet virgin and had no qualms with it. I wanted to have sex like any other natural male, but was content with going at my own pace. Toni ignored me most of the year and despite her having had a baby the previous year for some older guy, I still fantasized about her constantly.

Listening to this kind of stupidity officially made William my best friend, but Barry ran a close second. Will was a dreamer like me. We enjoyed the long walks plotting out our futures down to the finest detail. Barry was an outlet when it came to athletics, he liked lifting weights, playing basketball, and playing football, and we were evenly matched. I could use him to get better, though the gold cup was his brother Dale.

Dale was cocky and could back up everything he said. I had secretly admired him until I realized my sister Renee' was in the crosshairs of one of his sexual conquests. I knew how much of a playboy he was and how badly he spoke of girls once he had sex with them. I didn't want that for my sister Renee'. Not being raised in the same home, we were not as close as I think she would have liked us to be, but I wouldn't realize that for some time to come.

Dale would visit Renee' and stay long after my Aunt Rita had gone to bed. Renee' wore huge shirts all the time so we didn't find that unusual, but soon my mother became suspicious. She was still bitter that Renee' had not come around like Madison and Riley, who were being raised by my Aunt Edna. Renee' saw Aunt Rita as her mother and that never set well with our mother. She had warned my aunt of Dale, and yet the very thing my mother tried preventing her daughters from doing, Renee' had gone and done.

When Mom told my Aunt Rita that she thought Renee' was pregnant, she didn't believe it. A week or so later they took her to the gynecologist, and of course she was. Mom was so upset that when the baby was born it was a couple of days before she was able to walk down the block to see her grandson. I was worse. It was months before I saw my nephew Christian. When I did, I could not deny how pretty he was or that he was Dale's son.

Dale denied the baby was his; so did Barry and their mother. Adrian didn't want to get involved; he said it was Renee's problem. The pregnancy widened the wedge between her and our mother, so she didn't come around too often. One afternoon when she did venture down the block to visit, she sat down in the living room while I was watching television and tried striking up a conversation. Without a word, I left the room and went outside to shoot some hoops. I was upset that she allowed herself to get pregnant in the first place, and knowing the father was Dale ate away at me like gangrene. From that moment on, I made a conscious decision to live and breathe Dale. I wanted to beat him in everything he did and saw no reason why I couldn't. Though Dale was older, we weighed about the same. The two years he had on me wasn't going to make a difference. It was just a matter of practice.

Fist to fist he could beat me—not that I wasn't willing to try, but in basketball I could get at least a little revenge. That weekend I decided to check Dale for the first time and told Adrian to get Barry. He refused, knowing my motives and my temper. As much as I tried hiding it, everyone knew my discontent with him, including Dale. Adrian felt that if I wanted an ass-kicking that bad, then why should he stand in my way, so he reluctantly agreed.

Condescendingly, "Oh, you think you can handle this," he said.

He blew past me and dunked the ball, which wasn't easy for his height. I began playing very aggressively and he did too. I slammed him to the ground, disguising it as a foul; he retaliated in kind. We usually helped each other up, but not that night. When I finally had enough, I just tackled him to the ground and we tussled until Adrian came over and broke us up. Dale laughed it off, as if I were nothing more than a flea on an elephant's ass, but he didn't know that there was a war on and that was just the first battle.

I felt I had to defend our Braxton name, though it really wasn't mine to defend. I wanted to make them respect us because I believed they didn't. Adrian was cutting class and smoking dope. He had been held back one year and was on the verge of failing again. I felt sandwiched between my brother, whom they thought of as a dope-smoking clown, and my beautiful sister, who only a few months ago was a virgin, and at school was now being labeled easy.

It was just the opposite for me. To protect my reputation I had to lie about having sex. Bigfoot had a girlfriend and Will was dating Bigfoot's sister Cynthia. I knew both girls and they were definitely having sex, so I had to invent a girl who was conveniently from the old neighborhood to show that I was too. Bigfoot and Will never questioned my ruse. Only Eva knew the truth and my secret was safe with her.

I even lied to my mother about having sex, but it was Michelle, a new girl in school, who would force me to prove my sexual prowess. She followed me to all my classes and met me outside of them when the bell rang, while Eva and others took notice. After school, Paulette and I walked Will home and Michelle started tagging along. When I got home she watched Otis and me shoot around. She was cute and I liked her and it was obvious she liked me too. It was even more obvious that she was hanging around for more than just my company.

One rainy afternoon she came over after school and Adrian left us alone in the room. We started kissing and I helped her pull off her panties. I dropped my pants and underwear to my ankles, and it hurt as I tried inserting myself inside of her. The more excited I got, the greater the pain. At first I figured that was normal so I continued, but the pain became too much to bear. None of the boys my mother raised were circumcised and I would eventually have to be, but at that moment I was more concerned about what Michelle would say tomorrow at school.

I made it to homeroom early the next day, but the word was already out that Michelle and I had sex. When I saw her she smiled at me and I was grateful that she gave me credit for it, but technically I was still a virgin. Regardless, she felt that she owned a piece of me now and held my hand on the way to my classes and kissed me goodbye. Eva was angry at me for selling out, and I wasn't about to tell her that I hadn't. She refused to talk to me, and when she did accept my calls she had nothing to say. She wrote me off as one of *them*. If things had worked out the way I had hoped, I would have been. Michelle and I never officially dated so there was no breakup. I just began to see less of her.

I had a serious problem and I had to tell my mother. It wasn't as difficult as you would imagine. I guess after virtually admitting to her that I was masturbating, I could pretty much tell her anything. As I feared, she found it humorous and didn't take the situation as seriously as I'd hoped. She soothed me by saying that she would schedule a doctor's appointment as soon as she could. I left her bedroom relieved; now all I had to do in the meantime was avoid sex. That should have been easy.

Months later, lying in bed in the darkness, waiting to doze off, Adrian and I were talking. He asked me if I had a girlfriend. I told him no and he replied, "Boy, you better get you a girlfriend or somebody's going to think you're a faggot, like Madison."

"You better not let Mom hear you say that. She'll kick your ass."

He was right, though. How much longer could I keep up the charade? I was fifteen and my mother was taking her time about setting a doctor's appointment and started to become angry when I mentioned it. It wasn't that I was so eager to have sex, even though everyone else seemed to be; I just wanted to be ready if the opportunity presented itself.

In the meantime, I was introduced to the sister of one of Madison's friends. Tess was a year younger than I and going to Our Mother of Mercy Catholic School. She was a pretty, light-skinned girl who lived with her mother, grandmother, and two sisters. When we began seeing each other her grandmother never let us out of her sight. She only left us alone just before it was time for me to leave so we could say goodbye. In our kiss we both knew we wanted each other. As far as Tess was concerned, her grandmother was the only thing standing in our way, but I knew better.

CHAPTER NINE
ADOLESCENCE

Returning home after school one evening, I saw an ambulance on the corner and a crowd of spectators around it. I walked up and asked what happened, and someone told me that Otis had gotten into a fight. I don't know what the fight was about or how it began, but he shot someone and his throat was cut. I peeped into the back of the ambulance and saw Otis and the paramedics working on him. I didn't expect to see Otis ever again, but months later he showed up with a seven-inch scar on the side of his throat. He didn't play, he just watched me shoot around. He came around less and less after that, until I no longer saw him again.

Mom didn't really care for Otis coming around, but I didn't care much for her companions, either. She dated a couple of truckers from across the street. Johnny Huston was one of them. He was younger than she by about six or seven years and reminded me of a youthful A.J. Their relationship was brief.

Mom had another gentleman caller that summer, and when I saw him it was like seeing a ghost. The corners of his mouth were tightly tucked away into his high cheeks. He wore the same Grinch-like smile and a fedora that looked too small for his head; it was Daddy Jerome looking deceivingly gentle. When my nerves settled, I was actually glad to see him. It had been more than five years and it was time that he saw the man I had grown into. I was nervous and fidgety and hid it by inspecting the threads of the football I carried around with me all the time. My scheme was just to nod as much as I could and give yes and no responses, that way I could limit the risk of stuttering.

"You play football, Hotshot?"

I hadn't been called that since he left. Surrendering to my pride, I boasted about being the starting running back of my ninth-grade team. I could hear myself stuttering, which made me cringe, but I remembered how much he loved the game and I thought that would impress him.

While I masticated my words, he masticated a piece of stew meat. When I was done, he smiled and shook his head from side to side, letting me know that it was a shame that my speech hadn't improved. Sitting across from him was Hotshot again. That turned my stomach. I hoped Hotshot had died, but he was alive and well inside of me. I was his benefactor, nourishing him with my insecurities.

After a brief and unpleasant moment of silence, Daddy Jerome asked, "You don't run through the line with your eyes closed, do you?"

"Sir?"

"I said, you don't run through the line with your eyes closed, do you?"

What the hell kind of question is that? It amazes me, to this day, that out of all the questions he could ask, he asked that one. I stuttered a denial while wondering what was wrong with running through the line with my eyes closed. As soon as I expected contact, I closed my eyes waiting for it; didn't the other guys do the same? That was how I had been playing for two seasons and scored a touchdown or two. Daddy Jerome continued eating, while I went back to inspecting the strings on my football and contemplating this revelation of keeping my eyes open.

Unexpectedly, Ambus walked in. He came over once or twice a week to visit Mom. Ambus and Daddy Jerome were both shocked to see one another and stiffened when it came to addressing the other. Ambus wore a small afro and a goatee. He had a black pullover sweatshirt underneath his worn blue jean jacket. The jacket had Army patches and rock band names sewn into it and had military pins and ribbons all over the front of it. That was the style back then. They shook hands only out of politeness and as Ambus turned to leave, Daddy Jerome grunted, "Hippy," then went back to eating. Ambus left the room as if he hadn't heard him. It was the late seventies and I guess there might have been a couple of hippies left, but Ambus wasn't one of them. Terms like hippy, groovy, Black Power and ya' dig had all played out, but our fear of Daddy Jerome seemed to linger.

With nothing left to say, I pushed away from the dinner table as he laid his huge hand across my forearm. His fingernails were long, thick, and hard, like an eagle's claw. "The world is a harsh, cruel place, Hotshot. You're dealt a hand from the day you're born, and it's up to you to improve that hand." Taking a puff from his cigarette, he continued, "You improve your hand by making good decisions, from choosing to smoke cigarettes to choosing a girlfriend." He then bent and twisted the cigarette into a huge glass ashtray my aunts used on the weekends.

He looked somewhat despondent, as if accepting the idea that all the years of politely waiting to get what was rightfully his was never going to pay off. It was going to be Leon and Ambus who would benefit. He looked tired and almost broken.

He spent the night in my mother's room, which I didn't particularly like. Unlike other boyfriends, Daddy Jerome left behind debris. For all the good he had done, he also did a great deal of damage, and I was coming of an age where I could see that. I made sure by the time he got up the next morning that I was at the park shooting hoops. I didn't want to see my mother serve him breakfast in bed or listen to any more of his philosophy.

When football season started I was looking forward to playing at the high school level and trying out the tidbit of advice he gave me. With my eyes open, my performance didn't change right away, but it improved with every practice. By the time we played our first game I was a starter on the junior varsity team. By the third game I broke a long run for touchdown, then all of a sudden I was scoring two and three touchdowns a game. I was almost scoring at will, which caught the attention of the head coach for the varsity team, Coach Hendricks.

The coach was huge, dark, and ornery as a snake. We all were deathly afraid of Coach Hendricks. I didn't look forward to playing for him the next year. The rumor was that Sam Huff had ended his professional football career with a vicious hit that left him with a steel plate in his head. And the lone student that ever dared to mention Sam Huff's name in the coach's presence was thrown off the football team after being slammed against the lockers.

The more I scored, the more popular I became. Things began to change quicker than I could absorb. Girls, who initially didn't know I existed, were now giving me lengthy stares and accidental bumps, as I stood at my locker. A couple of juniors even flirted with me. Teachers became more approachable also, one in particular; Mr. Howard.

He was an English teacher and modern dance instructor. He asked me to come by one morning to see his dance troupe practice and consider joining. I told him I would check it out, but never did. Mr. Howard wasn't pushy, but he was persistent. He was the students' favorite teacher because he cut corners and didn't always play by the rules. He was in his early thirties and by his demeanor probably took part in the free love and peace movement ten years earlier. I dismissed dance completely. What did I need with a dance class? I was a football player.

Though I was going with Tess, I still felt for Toni. I wondered if my mediocre rise from obscurity impressed her at all. She left school early for work and I rarely saw her, until one morning when I spotted her coming down the hall. I heard she and her baby's father had broken up and this might be the best opportunity I would have, but I didn't know how to approach her. Even if it was just in silent passing, I wanted her to know that I was different. I shoved my head in my locker to collect my bearing and when I thought she was near, I shut my locker and turned around. To my surprise, she was walking right towards me.

We greeted each other and talked for a moment. She was calm and spoke with confidence. I admired that about her. She was just a year older, but it felt like ten. I guess having a child when you're a child can do that. After having our longest conversation, she left for her next class. I knew we were right for each other; it would just take a little time for her to see that.

Suddenly a fear came over me. Did I stutter? In a mild panic, I asked myself that question over and over. If so, I knew she would never give me the time of day. That haunted me until Will and I went to a house party uninvited. Party crashing was acceptable as long you weren't there to cause trouble. The living room was set up like a club, complete with a disco ball spinning from the ceiling. Most of the guys hung on the wall, waiting to make their move.

Disco was at its peak and I liked dancing. That went back to all those Friday and Saturday nights in the living room with my brothers and sisters while the ladies were out. I knew the popular dances like the Freak and the Rock and they played songs by Rod Stewart, Stevie Wonder, Donna Summer, Prince, Parliament and The Bee Gees. I was having a ball and in the corner looking at me was Toni.

I went over to her and we began talking. She reminded me of how shy I had been during our first year of junior high. We talked about how different things were in high school and how much I had changed. Because of sports and weight-lifting, I had developed a decent physique, but my affection for her hadn't changed at all. I still wanted her as badly, as I had then. My girlfriend Tess came to mind, but she had always been a consolation when it came to Toni.

They began playing "Get Off" by Foxy and I asked her to dance. We danced for a while, and when we got off the floor another older guy asked her to dance. She accepted and I figured that was it, but she continued to stare at me almost constantly.

When they played "Please Don't Go" by K.C. and The Sunshine Band, the lights dimmed and everyone began slow-dragging so I asked her if she wanted to. The room was dark, except for the flickering strobe light. Her arms were clasped around my neck and I gently held her waist. With her head on my chest, I could smell the sweet aroma of curl activator. She seemed so at peace and I never felt so honored to be a male. She was a young mother but I didn't care. All I wanted at that moment was to protect her from all the cruelties and injustices life would bring.

She grabbed my hand and we disappeared into a back bedroom. The streetlight filtering through the shaded window provided our sensual setting. I don't know whose room we were in, or if the house was even hers. I didn't care all that much, either. We sat on the bed and began to kiss. Ultimately I found myself on top of her as we kissed and kissed and kissed some more. I prayed that would be enough for her, at least for now. But by the way she moved her tongue in my mouth and the way she moved her hips against mine she was giving me the green light. I was excited and she could tell that through my jeans. I was also in pain.

I was on the fringes of popularity and had the girl I desired most in my arms. What was a little pain? Maybe this was how it was supposed to be. None of the guys had ever mentioned such a torment, but they were probably keeping it to themselves, as I was. Girls had pain and after a couple of tries it went away. Maybe it was the same for boys—but what if it wasn't? This was a pinnacle moment in my adolescence; I would have to live with this night forever. I made the decision not to go for it.

She stopped kissing me and pulled back, sinking her head deeper into the pillow to get a better look at me. I smiled, but she didn't. She knew something was wrong and it looked as though she was trying to find it hidden behind my eyes. I could explain that it was just a tiny matter of surgery, but the results of that could be detrimental. What if she told? I could never show my face in school again, so it was better off that she didn't know.

I was a virgin and I didn't want her to know that either, but not being able to follow through might leave an unfavorable impression as to my manhood. And she may not have been as understanding as Michelle was.

"Want to go back to the party?" she asked, as I lay on top of her.

Hell no! That's how I really felt, but instead I helped her up from the bed. I held her hand as we went out the door, then she let it go and told me she would see me in school. I saw Will watching; he nodded me over. We left the party and he was eagerly waiting to hear what happened. I didn't want to lie, so I told him we just kissed. He could tell I didn't want to talk, so he went into how big his house was going to be when he became a famous artist. He did most of the talking that night, while I wondered if I had done the right thing.

I was frustrated and it came out during football practice at the most opportune moment.

Dale was a winner—I could never take that away from him. What I wanted was respect. From the sideline I watched as the varsity prepared for their game. Dale broke the huddle and came over toward the sideline like a proud Clydesdale with his high-stepping trot. He was a wide receiver and Will had no chance of defending him, which was the point of using the junior varsity defense to practice against. The coaches didn't want anyone to get hurt before the game, especially not such a valued commodity as Dale. The season was almost over, several college scouts were courting him, the world was his oyster—and all I could think about was my sister Renee'.

On the next play Will stood next to the sideline waiting for the offense to break their huddle. I motioned to him to let me on the field in his place. He knew what I had in mind, so he looked around to see where the coaches were and stepped off the field as I got on. But when the offense broke their huddle, Dale went to the opposite side of the field. The quarterback called out the signal and the receiver I was defending made a lackluster dash down the field, not wanting to overexert himself before the big game. I began to cheat over toward the middle of the field, figuring the pass was for Dale anyway, and when I saw the ball floating in the air, I fully committed myself to getting there before the ball did. As far as I was concerned, there was no one on the field but Dale and me.

He was doing what all great receivers do, concentrating on the ball. As he focused on the spiraling ball floating towards him, I was focused on the center of his chest. I went for him with the prejudice and malice of a heat-seeking missile. I forced my eyes to remain open until the very last moment. I suspect we left the ground at the same time, and as he went for the ball, I went for his chest. It was going to hurt— hopefully more so him than me.

The impact could be heard clear across the field. I could hear the oohs and aahs through the ringing in my ears. The force of our collision drove us out of bounds and onto the concrete tennis courts. When I finally opened my eyes, I smiled. The crumpled look on his face told me he was in pain.

"Good hit, Lil' Brax," he moaned, hoping to disguise it.

I jumped to my feet and helped him up. As he trotted off, his steps weren't so high and my steps weren't so steady, but I felt vindicated. I knew Dale was going to go on to bigger and better things one day, but I wanted him to remember that moment if he couldn't remember that my nephew was his son.

We had an undefeated season and the championship came down to our cross-town rivals, as it had for the past fifty years. My mother took off early to come see me play. We quickly got behind by twelve points and for most of the first half we passed the ball, trying to catch up. When I did get the ball, I broke a sixty-yard run for a touchdown, then did it twice more. We won the championship. A fantasy of mine had actually manifested, all the way down to my mother being there to see it. I had never seen her more proud of me.

I made the decision to break up with Tess, which was more difficult than I imagined. She was beautiful, smart, loyal, supportive, and morally sound. She would've understood my problem too, if I had told her. So why break up with the perfect girlfriend? At sixteen, what was I supposed to do with a girl like her? When I thought about Toni it was always in the present tense, like going to the movies, kissing, or making love, but when it came to Tess I felt like I was being fitted for a tux whenever I was there. She couldn't understand why I wanted to break up and believed it was because we weren't having sex. Tess was too perfect too soon.

It was a weird and confusing time. I wonder if the word adolescence was invented to actually mean adult with less sense—or is that just a coincidence?

My friend Bigfoot seemed quite confused also.

Besides the gambling, my first memory of Bigfoot back in the seventh grade was of him beating his head against the wall. Trying to impress friends is one thing, but slamming your own head against a wall is another. He was dealing with his own demons and I found out what they were when he came over one weekend to play ball and all the guys were there.

Winners stayed on the court, and he and I were ruling for a

while, then lost to Dale and Barry. While we were sitting out until the next game, Bigfoot went into my house to get some water. When it was about time for us to play, I went inside to get him. My bedroom door was closed and I figured Adrian had slipped one of his girlfriends through the back door. I pushed the door slightly open for a quick peek— and saw Bigfoot and Madison in a tight embrace, kissing.

I hurried back to the game, refusing to believe what I saw.

A lot of girls liked Bigfoot, but he poked fun at them as if we were still in grade school. The banging his head against the wall, starting fights, and the goofiness around the girls all of a sudden made sense to me.

When he came out to play, I studied him for a moment, looking for something weaker in him, but there wasn't—at least, not on the basketball court. We played and didn't leave the court until sundown. I never told him or anyone what I saw, including my brother Madison.

CHAPTER TEN
LIKE VELVET

That summer, frightened that one of us would get into the crossfire of a gun battle across the street, my mother moved us a couple of blocks away. The house had three bedrooms, a large den, and a breakfast area. I took the small bedroom upstairs next to the girl's room, my mother took the den, and Adrian, who was out of school and working, closed off the breakfast area with a sheet and slept there.

Will and I went to Texas Southern University for the summer as part of an outreach program called Upward Bound. It was for students in high-risk neighborhoods. Paulette was entering high school, so she was eligible to participate as well. Along with other students from different high schools we took college courses, lived in the dorm, and worked on the campus for a small stipend every two weeks. It was better than flipping burgers and cleaning toilets.

I was going into my junior year sexually handicapped. I pestered my mother until she finally set the appointment—more than a year after my first attempt at sex. The urologist's confirmed that at sixteen, I needed to be circumcised. None of my brothers were, but for me the doctor said there was no option. When was the humiliation going to end, I wondered? All I wanted was to be a normal male. Was that too much to ask?

After the surgery, I woke up in my room very groggy from the sedation. I remember different nurses coming in, lifting up the sheet, and checking on me. Not that many nurses were assigned to me, which my mother found amusing. The doctor sent me home with strict instruction to change my bandage every day and not to have sex until the stitching healed. He assured me that I shouldn't have any problems after that, for which I was grateful.

On the way home, my mother reminded me of the strict instructions, as if I had been given bullets to a gun. Adrian chuckled at the cautiousness with which I walked, or maybe it was the whole situation he found funny. A week later, I packed my things and met Will and Paulette at Texas Southern.

Coincidentally, my sister Jo, a junior at Texas Southern, was hired as a counselor for the Upward Bound Program. We took courses like English and Math and had a choice of electives. Most of the guys chose weight-lifting or tennis, which was what Jo taught, but I wanted to do something different, so I chose modern dance.

During school Mr. Howard had talked to me about being a dancer in his modern dance troupe, but I kept putting him off. He cornered me and insisted that I see them practice. I went, and discovered that it didn't look as sissified in person as it did on television. One of his female dancers was exceptional. Her gracefulness was captivating—in fact, she was featured in just about every number. It looked fun, but with football and track practice, I really didn't have time for any more extracurricular activity so I never went back.

Now, by taking it in Upward Bound, I could test the water without anyone's knowing how bad I sucked at it—except for Will, who signed up too. The instructor was Ms. Carmelita Laws, a pretty caramel-colored twenty-two-year-old senior, who spoke Spanish fluently. Her job was to choreograph three numbers for the ceremony at the end of the seven-week program. Being typical sixteen-year-olds, at night before falling to sleep, Will and I would talk about how sexy we thought

Carmelita was. There were a couple of girls in the program with whom I shared an attraction, but I wasn't ready to commit to anyone. Girls took the dating thing very seriously; I didn't want to make the same mistake I'd made with Tess.

My job in the afternoon was working at KTSU, the college radio station, and the manager asked me what I wanted to do there. I had never been asked that; I figured they'd show me where the mop and bucket were and tell me what corner to start in.

"I know you like music. Why don't you go upstairs and see if Mr. Sinclair can find something for you?"

It was a black college, and Mr. Sinclair was the only white person who worked there. He was beyond fifty and did the news. He asked me if I wanted to take a shot at it, then handed me a sheet of paper and asked me to read it. My palms became sweaty and I became very nervous. My apprehension must have been obvious because he said, "Don't worry, the mike won't be on."

This time I couldn't change the words around to make them easier to say, as I did in everyday conversation. It had to be exactly what was written. When I finished, he called me a P-popper, which meant I accented the Ps when I spoke. He asked me to keep trying, but it was too late Hotshot had returned, and I was embarrassed and feeling ignorant. He must have thought I was an idiot.

I made up some excuse and went back downstairs, and for the rest of the summer I pulled albums from the library for the disc jockeys. This was the first time I'd elected not to pursue something I wanted because of my speech. I realized that it could affect me for the rest of my life, if I let it. My occupational skills would be limited if I could not express myself verbally, so I began seeing athletics as more than just a game. I could have been mute and it wouldn't matter as long as I scored. I tried not dwelling on it and focused on just having fun that summer.

* * *

Standing outside the girl's dorm, Will and I talked to Tina and a couple of other girls on the second level. It was forbidden for males to be in the female dorm, so we shouted back and forth. It was dusk and my neck was starting to hurt. I told them to come downstairs if they wanted to continue the conversation, but they dared us to come up. We proceeded to go around back and climb up the drainage pipe to the second level. It was dark by then and Paulette opened her window to let us in. Will remained in her room while Tina led me to hers. She wanted to play a joke on her roommate, who was down the hall, and asked me to hide on the floor between her bed and the wall. I had no idea what she had in mind, but just the thought of it was forcing her to burst out in brief fits of laughter.

Tina called out to her roommate and I had a pretty good idea of my role in all this, so when I heard her coming through the door, I jumped out at her. To my amazement, she was butt-naked. I was as shocked as she was. I closed my eyes and threw my hands over them for her benefit, while she went for the towel that she had just thrown across the bed. Unlike the handful of girls in the hallway laughing, she found no humor in it and cursed them as she ran back to the showers.

By then the word was out that a man was in the girl's dormitory, so Tina hurried me back to Paulette's room, where she and Will were talking.

"Come on, man!" I yelled.

We climbed out of the window and onto the ledge. He got to the drainage pipe first and started to climb down, but just then a campus cop climbed out of one of the windows and onto the ledge. "Go! Go! Go!" I shouted at Will, who was only concerned about falling.

I looked down over the ledge and into the courtyard. The drop was about fifteen feet. Will was only halfway down and the cop was well within eight feet of me, so I made the decision to jump. Without another thought I leaped from the second level and hit the ground rolling. By the time Will had his feet planted on the ground, I shot around the corner, leaving him wondering how I had gotten down. Without a siren, a patrol car slid to a halt with the lights flashing and gave chase as we headed toward our dorm. It had rained and there was a puddle of mud in front of one of the side entrances. Remembering that, I jumped over it, but Will wasn't as lucky. He slipped in the puddle of mud and I burst into laughter.

"Come on!" I yelled, holding the door open.

He got up and we ran upstairs to our dorm room and locked ourselves inside, adrenaline soaring through our veins. Drunk with fear and laughter, we heard the police knocking on doors. When they came to ours, the pounding of our hearts should have given us away. I tried not thinking of my shocked and naked friend or the fact that I jumped off a fifteen-foot ledge or Will's being covered in mud. Any one of these threatened to send me into uncontrollable laughter.

The cops left and we laughed about it all that night and into the next morning—although Tina's roommate still wasn't finding any humor in it. She was self-conscious of her weight. I tried reassuring her that everything happened so quickly that I hadn't seen anything, but was just as shocked and bewildered as she was. Most of that was the truth. I hardly noticed her flabby middle or her cocoa brown nipples.

The adolescent antics carried over into dance class and annoyed Carmelita. She ended class early because of our lack of concentration and blamed me for it. She held me over and told me she had expected me to be more mature and disciplined, which embarrassed me, then said that everyone was going to have brief solos during the last number and that I could start working on mine right away.

During class I would sneak peeks at her through the mirror while she stretched. She was so graceful and limber, and watching her bend in ways that I never thought possible was almost hypnotic. I'm not sure if it was my hormones or the harmony in which she could move her body. Either way, I was falling for her, but I was careful with my ogling, stealing no more than a couple of seconds at a time. She would have considered that childish.

One afternoon as I stayed behind to work on my routine, she came over a few times to correct my form and went back to what she was doing. She then called me over. "Come help me warm up," she invited.

She wore old warm-ups, as most of us did, and we sat on the floor facing each other. She effortlessly opened her legs into a Chinese split, pointing each toe toward opposite walls.

"Scoot up closer and put your feet on the inside of my thighs, but don't push," she instructed.

I opened my legs and placed my bare feet gently against her inner thighs. She put her hands on my shoulders and told me to lean back slowly. I did, and her hands slid down my arms until we were holding hands.

"Lean back farther," she told me. I did, until her head was near my groin. I was grateful to be wearing tight underwear. Her hands began crawling back up my arms toward my shoulder as she rose back to an upright position. She looked at me, expressionless; I returned the same lack of expression. I didn't want her to know how thoroughly I was enjoying being that close to her, but I needed to be mature about it. This was just a workout and I was just helping her stretch, right? She repeated that sequence three or four times and thanked me. That meant I was free to leave.

I was noticing how chummy Will and Paulette were getting, but didn't mention anything to them. Honestly, I was glad he was there to watch over her while I spent time with Carmelita. I was no longer staying late to work on my solo. I was there strictly because I liked her.

During the weeks that passed, after class she taught me advanced routines and the basics of tap, which I have since forgotten. I helped her stretch and the excitement of it finally wore off. Her dream was to be a ballet dancer, but her Nubian hips wouldn't allow it. She had a bachelor's degree in dance and decided to take the summer job to think about her future.

Helping her warm up, again we interlocked arms and she leaned forward and I leaned back until her chest was a couple of inches from the floor. She then asked, "So which one of these girls are you dating?"

"None of them," I replied.

"Why not? I know a couple of them are pretty obvious."

I just shrugged my shoulders, not knowing exactly how to respond. She raised and let my arms go. Pushing bangs from her eyes she asked, "What are we doing here, Gary?"

I didn't know what she meant. I was just grateful to be in her presence, so I replied, "What are we doing?" trying to make it sound more like a challenge than an inquiry.

"I'm attracted to you and I think you're attracted to me, too."

"I am," I responded eagerly to dispel any doubt.

"Is the age difference going to be a problem for you?"

"No," I said, trying to hide my excitement, "How about you?"

"I guess I'll find out, won't I?"

After curfew she picked me up and we would sit in her car on the outskirts of the campus and make out. We never discussed how we were going to carry out this relationship. Her job would be in jeopardy if anyone found out. After a week or two she was no longer content with the making out in the car; in class the attraction between us was becoming more obvious. Some of the girls were giving me the cold shoulder and some of the guys started to ask, but I didn't want her to get into trouble by bragging, so I denied it.

The rumor reached the directors of the program. When they asked me about it, I denied it again. I even lied to my sister Jo, who was only a year older than Carmelita. Jo and I had grown closer as I was growing older. With Leon and Ambus gone and Adrian's attentiveness to his girlfriends, Jo defaulted to being my older brother at times. She taught me how to drive, taught me how to play tennis, and gave me girlfriend advice.

Jo knew something was going on and vowed not to tell, so I confessed. She thought it humorous at first, but suddenly fell into the big sister role and began telling me how inappropriate it was. She insisted that if we had to date, we should at least wait until the summer was over.

I agreed all along, but Carmelita did not. She no longer wanted to hide our relationship. It was the principle of it, she would say. I didn't see any principle, but when they asked her if she and I were having a relationship, she owned up to it. She was sent packing that very day.

It didn't make sense to me. We were already dating; why not keep the job too?

She was fired on a Friday. I walked to the girl's dorm and as I helped her load her things, she asked if I would like to spend the weekend with her. How my mother might have felt about that did not enter my mind when I eagerly accepted the invitation—nor did the doctor's instructions of abstinence.

After class I went back to my room and packed my things. Everyone went home for the weekend, so I asked Paulette to tell Mom that I was staying, even though I was not. Will told me to have a good time and they got on the bus and went home, while I waited for Carmelita. She picked me up and said she wanted to introduce me to her father first.

It was then that I found out that her father disapproved of our relationship, and my age was not his greatest concern. They lived in Acres Homes, a well-to-do neighborhood with hard-working black folk hoping to escape the violence in the Wards. Now his daughter was dating some thug she met in a government program and living in the Fifth Ward. She was bringing home exactly what he was running away from, though I don't think I actually qualified as a thug.

Before we got there we stopped off at a department store and she bought me a pair of shoes, a shirt, and some slacks. I always wore jeans and tennis shoes, even to church. I never wore dress shoes or slacks unless it was Easter Sunday, and I had one leisure suit for that. When Carmelita was done I looked like a yuppie, complete with the sweater tied around my shoulders, but I wanted to make a good impression for her and that was all that mattered.

When we drove up, her father was out in the yard raking leaves. He stopped when he saw us pull in the driveway. I was nervous, but Carmelita seemed to be fine. She went over and kissed him on the cheek, though he wasn't as happy to see her and was even less happy to see me.

"This is Gary, Father."

He looked me over and shook my hand limply to make sure none of the ghetto slime rubbed off. I smiled passively, hoping to put him at ease. We followed him into the house, where he went into the master bedroom. Her mother went with him and so did Carmelita, leaving me alone in the room with her fifteen-year-old sister. We smiled at one another and she asked me what school I went to. We talked and tried to pay no attention to the arguing that was taking place in the other room. I think her sister found the whole situation funny.

After about ten minutes Carmelita stormed out of the room. "Let's go!" she told me.

"Bye," her younger sister said.

"Bye," I replied. She was only a year younger, and I wonder whether her father would have objected if I had dated her instead.

We went to a Travels Inn right off the freeway—at least, that's what I think it was. She parked her car and went inside the office while I waited, and a few minutes later she returned with a key that had an orange oval plate hanging from it bearing our room number. That's when I began to feel butterflies in my stomach. It was actually about to happen. After today I was no longer going to be a virgin.

I was nervous and excited at the same time. All I knew about sex came from one or two porn flicks, in which the men did most of the work, so I was feeling a little under pressure. She grabbed her purse and I got out of the car and followed her to the second floor. We entered and she dropped the key on the wood-grain desk and went to the window and closed the heavy drapes. Beneath the window was the air conditioner and she turned that on.

I had never been in a motel, so my eyes wandered. The television was hoisted up in the air and bolted to the wall and it had cable. We didn't have cable at home. There were two huge mirrors, one over the sink that was next to the bathroom and one behind the dresser where the key lay. The second mirror reflected the nicely made queen-size bed.

Carmelita stood in front of me and unbuttoned the only buttons on my brand new Izod shirt and pulled it up over my head. Her eyes examined my chest as she took her fingernails and gently played in the curly black hair that populated the upper portion of her well-developed sixteen-year-old. Standing in the same spot, she undressed me piece by piece. I lifted my leg so she could pull off my socks and pull down my pants. She then pulled down my Fruit of the Looms.

I undressed her as she had done me, piece by piece. Then, lying on the bed naked, she raised her leg and told me to kiss the inside of her ankle. I was ready to explode with anticipation, but I did as I was instructed. I made my way up to her stomach, circled her navel with the moistened tip of my tongue, and before I could move up any farther she placed her hand on my head as if I had forgotten a spot. She rubbed her fingers through my hair, then pressed down on my head and pushed her hips into my face. When she let go of my head, she grabbed the sheet, arched her back, and let out a shrill that had come from somewhere deep inside her. Somewhere I wanted to go. Then she fell limp and brought her knees together.

After a minute or so she opened her legs again and her arms I put myself inside of her. When I started to go too fast or she thought I was enjoying it too much, she would wrap her legs inside of mine to slow me down. "You like being inside of me?" she asked and I nodded. The smell of her aroused me and while the contours of our sweating bodies melded into one, I was in awe of how soft, warm, and accommodating she was. Being inside of her was the most beautiful sensation I had ever felt. "There is no rush," she said to settle me down, "reaching an orgasm is only part of lovemaking."

I'm not sure how long I had to wait, but it felt like an eternity, and when she finally gave me the okay, I did, and it was worth every drop of sweat that she wiped from my face. Afterward, we talked a little before we began again.

We eventually made our way into the shower. She washed me and gave me the towel to do the same to her. That was how we dried one another, too.

That night she fell asleep quickly, but I remained awake, thinking about what had happened. I was elated and looked forward to daylight so we could do it again. Maybe I wouldn't even have to wait till then.

Having shaved two weeks off the doctor's advice never entered my mind until the middle of the night, when I awoke in pain. I closed the door to the bathroom before I turned on the light. When I looked down, I tried not to panic. I had swollen up to twice the size of a normal erection and when I touched him it was painfully tender.

The next morning it was no better, but I was determined not to let this setback affect our weekend. I don't think she ever noticed the difference or my wincing in pain, because she never made mention of it. It only hurt when I entered her, but as we got into it, I hardly noticed the pain at all.

She took me home that Sunday evening to get some clothes for the week at Texas Southern and to be introduced to my mother. Mom was cordial but sour; Carmelita knew immediately that she did not approve of our relationship. My mother found something else to do while we packed, and when everyone was ready to leave, she pulled me aside.

"I guess you think you're a man now?"

No more man than my father, I thought, but dared not say. "I know having sex doesn't make you a man."

Mom and I had always been very close. She was the strongest woman I had ever known, but she wasn't a man, and she had no idea what I was dealing with. The first thread in our relationship had begun to unravel.

Her little boy was now having sex and that was difficult for her to get accustomed to. It was a natural parental instinct, I presume, because Carmelita wasn't having it any better. Her father went so far as to give her an ultimatum; break up with that kid or get kicked out of the house.

Once again I was willing to see her secretively. I was about to be seventeen, and in the eyes of the court that was practically legal, but again she refused. Her father must have had some considerable influence, too, because she couldn't find a single relative who would take her in.

I went to my mother and pleaded for her to be able to stay with us, just until she saved enough money to get her own apartment. My mother could never turn away anyone in need, so she reluctantly consented, with strict instructions that there would be no sex under her roof. I would give up my small room and sleep downstairs on the sofa. With genuine sincerity, I agreed. Mom added, "She's only dating you to get back at her father." I didn't believe it at the time, but maybe that did have something to do with it.

It was fun in the beginning, because she would take me to football practice and the guys would stare at my twenty-two-year-old girlfriend sitting on the hood of her car. The season was a great disappointment after such an amazing sophomore year. I was moved up to varsity, but rode the pine behind seniors the coach was hoping to get scholarships for. When I did play, I did well, but most of the time I left the stadium holding back tears. When I got home, Carmelita knew just how to make me forget all about it. I put the season behind me and looked forward to my senior year when the scouts were going to be looking at me.

As the weeks passed, I started to feel the walls closing in around me. I was still sixteen and practically married. We argued all the time, loud enough to be heard throughout the house. Then she'd want to have make-up sex. The novelty of it was wearing off. I had been sneaking upstairs in the middle of the night, but she seemed to enjoy it more when everyone was up and roaming about downstairs, and no matter how much she promised to be quiet, she wasn't. Afterward I would rush downstairs to pretend that the beading sweat on my forehead, my disorderliness, and the sounds they heard had nothing whatsoever to do with sex.

Our relationship was not looked upon favorably by anyone and rightly so, but the most vocal opponent was Resa. I was breaking rules even Leon didn't dare to break, but there was more to her hostility than Carmelita's living with us. Resa had given up half her life raising us, and began to comprehend the opportunities that went by while she watched her younger siblings grow. Paulette and I were the youngest and the most outgoing of all my mother's children. We were competitive and Resa hated that. We asked why instead of just accepting fate.

Simply put, we bucked the system and I was going too far.

I should have exercised more self-control, but Adrian, who was twenty, was dating a fifteen-year-old girl. And then there was Mom. She was forty-six and dating an eighteen-year-old man. I was sixteen and my girlfriend older than my mother's boyfriend.

He was a nice guy, but it was hard for me to call him Mr. Herbert, so we all just called him by his nickname, Sugar Bear. As corny as it sounds, it seemed appropriate. He was honey brown, about six feet tall, and weighed over three hundred and fifty pounds. He and Mom met at a zydeco club that she and my aunts frequented. Flattered that such a younger man was attracted to her, she invited him to live with us soon after they met. There was not a gathering such as she had with Daddy Jerome, and as desperate as I might have been for a father figure, he could never fill those shoes.

At school the word got out, most likely by my best friend Will, that my girlfriend was living with me. I willingly admitted to it at first, but the novelty of that soon wore off. She had this thing about correcting my speech, and it had nothing to do with my stuttering. As a matter of fact, she never mentioned stuttering; it was my pronunciation that bothered her. I didn't mind at first, because I felt that she was looking out for my best interest, but it started to become a control issue. Our arguments became so violent my mother started to intervene.

Stifled and suffocating at home, I went with Will after practice to help cook and feed his grandparents. A long walk spent talking about our dreams would follow.

After a couple of months, Carmelita had saved up enough to move out, but that wasn't enough to save the relationship. I got the guts to break it off two days before she was to move out. She became very upset, more so that I was breaking up with her instead of her with me. We had thrown the word love around a few times, but if asked today, I think we both would downgrade that to an infatuation on both our parts.

Tess had heard about my living arrangements and also that we had broken up. We remained friends despite her misconception that I had broken up with her because she wouldn't have sex with me. That bugged me, so when she called and invited me over I was delighted. I wanted her to know the truth, so as soon as I got there I went into a complicated explanation about how our breaking up had more to do with me than her. By the time I was done, we were sitting on the sofa, and by the look in her eyes, either she hadn't heard a thing I was saying or didn't care.

Her grandmother had passed away, so there was no more chaperoning. We started to do some intense kissing before she got up and led me down the hall to her bedroom. They lived in a small apartment and I had been there hundreds of times, but never once had I ventured down that hall or into her bedroom. Her two sisters were

126

conveniently watching television in their mother's room across the hall while she was away. Tess was dating another guy, but she was as curious about me as I was about her. When we dated, only circumstance and her grandmother kept it from happening. Now there was neither.

It was a wonderful encounter and didn't feel the same as it had with Carmelita. Emotionally, Carmelita and I never seemed to be on the same level, and that affected our intimacy, but Tess and I were both adolescents, equally unacquainted with the perplexities of sex. Though neither of us was a virgin anymore, together making love was still venturesome and new. She was soft and spoke in moans. Instead of giving me instructions, she would shower my face with kisses and tell me how great it felt, my being inside of her.

CHAPTER ELEVEN

HELMETS AND TIGHTS

Because of *Saturday Night Fever,* across the country disco clubs were full and from the looks of it, I wasn't the only one sowing my oats. It seemed as if the whole world was partying; the only problem was no one was minding the store. There was a blackout in New York City, Three Mile Island had a nuclear meltdown, and finding important people to assassinate must have become difficult because they settled for the publisher of one of the porn magazines Adrian pulled his pinups from. And nearly a thousand people, many of them black, followed Jim Jones to Guyana, where most of them ended up committing suicide.

A few years later disco was out and rap was in and because of the Iran hostage crisis, President Carter was out and President Reagan was in. For sure bellbottoms were out and straight leg jeans were in, and although I still had one, Afros were out and the shag and bald fades were in. Shooting important people did make a comeback, though. John Lennon was assassinated and attempts were made to assassinate the Pope and President Reagan too. They all made headlines for weeks, but none held the same significance as the shooting of J.R. Ewing. He was the only one my English teacher forced the class to write a paper on.

I liked my English class, but even though the teacher pulled me aside several times to compliment me on my essays, I never thought I had a chance at getting into college with it. I had a better shot at a football scholarship because the coach worked hard at getting scholarships for his players, even if it was just a junior college. At practice he cursed, slapped, and jerked us around, leaving the nurturing up to his assistants.

Playing for him was torture because his demeanor reminded me so much of Daddy Jerome. I froze every time he yelled at me for missing a block or not hitting the line hard enough, and God forbid I should fumble the ball.

That football coach knew there was potential in me, though he saw my talent as unsalvageable. It was too deep to get to, and in the short three years he had to work with us, there were other players that he could get more out of.

However, Mr. Howard was willing to invest as much time as it took. He stopped me in the hallway every chance he got, to try to persuade me into joining his dance troupe. With the popularity of movies like *Fame, Footloose,* and *Flashdance,* modern dance was becoming popular. To get him off my back I agreed to attend a practice.

From the rear of the auditorium, I watched him put a tape into the boom box that sat at the edge of the stage. Then he came back and sat next to me. While the students danced, he told me that they performed primarily at school functions. Most of Mr. Howard's choreography was more like unspoken dramas, usually about love and betrayal, performed to current music. I remember thinking there was nothing that was going to get me on that stage in a pair of tights, especially in front of the student body.

When the music ended, all the dancers left the stage except for that one girl. I couldn't take my eyes off her. She moved like a ballerina; the others paled in comparison.

The dance theatre was Mr. Howard's baby; however, it was not recognized as one of the school's official extracurricular activities. All of the dancers were students, so most of the financial responsibility, such as costumes and gas to travel to and from performances, fell on his shoulders.

Public schools that offered modern dance were schools in smaller school districts. The only other school was the High School of Performing and Visual Arts, which we had to audition for; without any formal training we had virtually no chance of getting in. He wanted to offer inner city kids the same kind of cultural exposure, but the district didn't believe the interest was there, so Mr. Howard did it himself. He got support from the school's principal, who allowed him to use the school's facilities to practice. In return we performed at school functions and ceremonies.

He drove a brown 65' four-door Chevy that puttered along, if it decided to start at all, but it managed to get us back and forth to our performances. To bring in more members and donations, Mr. Howard used his own money to rent an old office building in the worst part of the Fifth Ward, on Lyons Avenue. It took weeks to clean. Once it was painted and the mirrors were glued to the walls it began to look like a real studio. He named it the Inner City Dance Studio.

In some ways it was more grueling than playing football. The backlash, which I expected, came in the form of being called a queer, a punk, and a faggot by guys and girls I had considered friends. Madison's homosexuality and our mother's insistence that he not be treated any differently because of it cured me of any homophobia that I might've had. I wasn't blind to the contradiction of dance and football, but some saw it as some sort of betrayal. I laughed along, as I did when the kids picked at me about my stuttering, then I dared *them* to try it. I dared them to get to rehearsal at six in the morning, get banged up at football practice, then go back to rehearsal at eight o'clock that night.

It wasn't dancing so much as it was Mr. Howard that made them question me. I hadn't really thought about his sexuality until he had to fit me for a costume he was making. He measured me around my arms, my neck, and my waist, then he knelt down and took a measurement of my thighs. He slid his arm between my legs to grab the other end of the measuring tape and brushed up against my groin. Immediately I got knots in my stomach. I was too afraid to look down and so petrified that he was going to touch me, it took over every thought in my mind. Should I punch him in the face if he tried anything? He was a teacher and I wasn't sure what to do, so I just stood there stiff as a board. I was relieved when he brought himself upright, wrote down my measurements, and let me leave the dressing room.

I tried to forget the whole incident, though I never understood why I needed to be totally naked.

He was engaged to Maggie, a tall, attractive woman, who right away I thought could do better. She pestered him about getting married, and he was as resistant to the idea as a ten-year-old boy to bath water. I couldn't understand why, but that would become crystal clear in a couple of months.

Paulette and Will joined not long after I did, and with about a dozen students, Mr. Howard had enough to expand the company's repertoire. An awards ceremony was coming up and officials from the school district were going to be there. In the hopes of getting school funding, he choreographed new routines and we spent an obsessive amount of time perfecting them. We left for school at five-thirty in the morning and didn't return until ten-thirty or eleven that night. We saw each other first thing in the morning and before going to bed. We spent more time with one another than we did with our own families. Our parents never complained about the hours because they knew of our whereabouts and liked that we found that sort of thing interesting.

Metra was his primary female dancer and Mr. Howard's showpiece. When he brought in trained college dancers for a master class, they would praise her natural ability. He paired us together for a new number, which meant we would be in very close proximity of one another over the next few weeks. It never took her long to get a routine down and waited patiently stretching in front of the mirror, while Mr. Howard whipped the rest of us into shape. She was pleasant and friendly but stayed to herself.

After school we rehearsed at the studio on Lyons Avenue. The studio being in the roughest part of the neighborhood, Mr. Howard had been robbed at gunpoint and assaulted more than once so we made sure we all left at the same time. Paulette, Will, and I walked the mile home and passed right by the Kelly Courts, a housing project where Metra stayed with her grandmother. It was on our way, so to save Mr. Howard a drive, we walked her home.

Will and Paulette began dating, and who could blame them? They spent so much time together it was inevitable.

While we worked on our duets, Metra spent countless hours in my arms. I loved staring into her big brown eyes. Sometimes I saw her staring at me in the reflections of the mirrors, but when our eyes met, she would quickly look away. When I tried giving her the slightest hint that I liked her, she always withdrew.

When we danced together the intimacy we shared was undeniable. It was like making love without intercourse. Holding Metra and feeling the warmth of her body against mine felt natural. It was soothing; almost healing.

The more we rehearsed, the less Mr. Howard had to instruct. At times he backed off the dance floor altogether to watch us. As the performance drew closer, we rehearsed late into the evening. One night almost at the end of rehearsal, a man knocked on the locked door and demanded to come in. He was an older man and nicely dressed, but Mr. Howard refused to open the door. Metra quickly started to make her way to the rear dressing room, and when the man noticed her through the large window, he suddenly became irate. He started banging and pulling on the door and Mr. Howard threatened to call the police. Shouting more profanities, he got into his car and sped off. Mr. Howard made us all wait a while before leaving that evening.

Later, walking Metra home, I asked what all that was about.

"Just a guy I used to date," she explained, "and I don't feel like talking about it."

I respected her desire for privacy and pressed no further.

When we got to Metra's home, I asked Will and Paulette to go on ahead. While she stood on her porch, I expressed how I felt about her. She was only a few months older, but she rejected the idea of our dating, acting as though I was some high school adolescent with a crush on the teacher. Though she diluted her rejection with flattery, I knew it had something to do with the man who had come to the studio that evening.

He didn't return, so the incident was soon forgotten. But now that she knew how I felt, she began opening up to me.

Her mother had been but a child herself when Metra was born, and Metra wound up living with her grandmother, who, at almost seventy years of age, still cleaned homes during the day to add to her social security. Metra's first sexual experience was being raped at knifepoint and being threatened with death if she told anyone. That experience had lowered her self-esteem and she got involved with an older man who taught her how to hustle, as she called it. She'd distract the clerks while he stole things from expensive clothing shops. Gradually he began pressuring her into having sex for money.

At seventeen, Metra's experiences made her coarse. She was a realist who didn't have time for nebulous relationships. To discourage me further, she told me she was abstaining from sex, in case that was what I was interested in. Either way, she decided our puppy-love courtship was over before it ever began.

That was a big pill to swallow, but despite all that I had heard, I still wanted her to be my girlfriend. Her honesty overshadowed everything else, and I believed her love would be pure and unconditional. Eventually, we did begin dating. Spending so much time with me it was inevitable. Mr. Howard wanted her to have a suitable boyfriend, but for some reason he didn't want it to be me.

Early one Saturday morning I got a call from her. She was hysterical. I knew something was terribly wrong, because she always kept her cool, even when she was really hurting.

"Gary! Help! Gary!" I heard. Then the receiver went dead.

I didn't attempt to call her back; I just grabbed the baseball bat next to the door and climbed out of the window in the gym shorts I had gone to bed in. Moving across the decomposing roof was the only thing I thought through thoroughly.

I jumped down into the front yard, hopped the fence, and began the mile run to the Kelly Courts. Her front door opened to the feeder road of Interstate 10, and as I ran under the overpass I could see a car speeding away from her apartment. I prayed she wasn't in it.

When I leaped onto the porch she came out and threw her arms around my neck.

Standing barefooted and shirtless, I asked "What the hell is going on!?"

Crying uncontrollably, she sobbed, "It was him! He tried to force me to go with him and I didn't want to."

She had convinced him that she would go voluntarily if he let her get some clothes, and that's when she tried calling me. He burst into the room and jerked the phone out of the wall and dragged her downstairs, while her grandmother watched. She was a frail old woman who had warned Metra several times about the company she kept, but she was always told to mind her own business. She did exactly that, that day. She was alone and didn't want to have any trouble with the local thugs. Her granddaughter had gotten herself in that predicament and she believed she should be able to get herself out.

That incident drew us closer together. I felt a need to protect Metra and she wanted to be protected. Exactly what I could have done with a Louisville Slugger against a .38 Special I never had a chance to discover, thankfully. My mother genuinely liked Metra, the first and only girlfriend of mine upon whom she bestowed that honor, but she told me no girl was worth getting killed over.

Before the performance, we were all very nervous. Metra went around assuring us we would do fine. When it was time, Mr. Howard told us to take our places and the curtains opened. My heart pounded when I saw the auditorium filled to capacity. Football and track were held inside stadiums; now I could see the whites of their eyes—some were already laughing at us in our tights. Playing football, after the first clash of helmets or the sound of the starter pistol at a track meet, my nervousness would be over and I'd be running off adrenaline. This was different. I had to remember the routine and stay on the count and hope I didn't look too foolish in the process.

The adrenaline didn't start to flow until I heard the crowd applaud with approval. Then I became addicted.

The officials from the district didn't show, and Mr. Howard was angry about that, but he still wanted to celebrate with an after-party at his house. I had never been to a teacher's home, so I thought it would be interesting.

CHAPTER TWELVE

THE TEACHER

It was a three-bedroom home in a middle-class neighborhood. We ate from party trays, drank a little, and talked until midnight. Those who did not have rides, Mr. Howard took home. He pulled up to the curb to drop me and Paulette off. Once Paulette had gotten out he stopped me and asked if Metra and I were interested in going back to his house. Stephanie, another dancer and classmate of ours, was sitting in the front seat.

Paulette stood on the steps waiting for me while I looked at Metra for her opinion. We knew he was offering his home as a place to have sex if we wanted, and by her expression I could see she wanted to. I told Paulette to go inside and I would be back later. Our mother worked at night then, so I didn't have to worry about her inquiring as to my whereabouts.

Returning to his home, he showed us the room we would be using and left us there. The drapes over the windows were actually heavy curtains, like the ones used in a theatre, and when the lights were turned off, the room was pitch black, even in the daytime. Without the lights we could not see our hands in front of our faces.

We got undressed in the darkness, not knowing exactly were the other was. I waited to hear her climb into bed before taking off my underwear and getting under the covers. We kissed and made love to one of the songs we danced to. Afterward I fumbled about in the dark looking for my underwear, and she laughed at the sound of my bumping into things. My bladder forced me to settle for just my blue jeans. When

I opened the door, a dim light suffused the room and Metra hid from it by pulling the covers over her head.

I crept down the hall and closed the door to the bathroom. When I came out, Mr. Howard was standing in front of me . . . naked.

"Enjoying yourself?" he asked.

I shrugged my shoulders and kept my eyes on his. I still saw him as an authority figure. He looked at me as if he wanted to say something, but before he could utter another word, Metra came out of the room with a sheet wrapped around her brown petite body and grabbed my arm and pulled me back into the room.

Throughout the year we performed at different schools and received an invitation to take part in the Sam Houston State Performing Arts competition. We didn't win, but Metra impressed the judges and was singled out as one of the competition's best dancers. Her natural talent was head and shoulders above the rest of us. She stuck out like a violinist in a company of fiddlers.

Mr. Howard hardly turned down an engagement. If there was enough room to perform a number, he accepted. All he asked for was a donation of whatever they could afford. We performed on two local news channels for a brief commentary on the fine arts in the urban neighborhoods.

It all seemed to pay off when we were invited to perform at the district's administrative building for the superintendent and some visitors. Mr. Howard never gave a damn about his superiors and showed them little respect. It could be fairly said that he downright despised them, but this was an important event. He had done what he set out to do, taken boys and girls from the Fifth Ward, with no previous training, and created a dance troupe that was being requested to perform all over the city—at school functions, beauty pageants, and huge gatherings like the Annual Juneteenth Celebration in Herman Park. He never charged but only asked for donations. We washed cars and had fundraisers, but we came up short every time and he always made up the rest. He wanted the dance theatre recognized as an officially sponsored program; performing for the superintendent could do that.

Maggie, his fiancée, appreciated what he was trying to do, but she was in her mid-thirties and ready to give up on the relationship. They had been dating for more than four years and she had broken off the engagement several times because he never had enough time for her. When he wasn't in school, he was rehearsing or sewing costumes for the upcoming performance. When she tried giving him an ultimatum, it only made him more resistant to the idea. He hated being told what to do and ruled over us like a dictator. No one challenged his authority. We rehearsed until one in the morning and even on school nights, if he deemed it necessary. He had almost as much control over us as our parents did—in some cases more.

Only one teacher seemed to take notice of the kind of hours we were putting in. Mr. Stallings, my substitute homeroom teacher, went to all the football games and saw me dance at the school functions also. At first he was impressed that I was able to do all that and keep up my schoolwork. He thought I was a good kid. But he subtly warned me about Mr. Howard.

Mr. Stallings showed up at rehearsal one morning and watched from the shadows. At the first break, I jumped down from the stage and went to say hello. Mr. Howard, infuriated by this, screamed at me to get back on the stage.

"You better run along," Mr. Stallings told me. "I don't want to get you into any trouble."

I thanked him for stopping by, but instead of leaving, as I expected him to, he sat back down. That angered Mr. Howard, who ended practice immediately, pulling me aside to remind me that he held closed practices. His jealousy was disgusting. It angered me.

Mr. Stallings showed up at rehearsal again. This time Mr. Howard decided to handle it himself. He yelled out, "This is a closed practice!" Mr. Stallings didn't say anything; he just continued to sit.

Mr. Howard told us to stay on the stage, then he jumped down and walked up the aisle as we gathered at the edge of the stage to see what was about to happen. Mr. Stallings stood up, they began having words, and Mr. Stallings seemed to have the last one. I don't know what he said, but Mr. Howard was visibly irritated.

The closer we got to performing for the superintendent, the more hard-nosed Mr. Howard got. We repeated routines over and over until we were totally exhausted. He was a tyrant up until the day of the performance, though on that day he was in a good mood, I was a nervous wreck.

There was an intro before the dance where Will and I had to speak. I had so much trouble with it during rehearsal, I actually expected Mr. Howard to either cut that part out or just replace me, but he did neither. He went over the lines with me patiently and after a great deal of repetition, I was able to nail it without stuttering. Never once did he raise his voice when it came to my stuttering. He screamed and cursed me out for losing count, but never when I stuttered.

During football and track practice, I was always being screamed at. It was part of the game, like helmets and cleats, but every time it happened there was an implosion inside of me that resurrected Hotshot. Chills would sprout over my whole body and I would be frozen solid, just as if I were nine years old again.

Going to practice was sometimes masochistic, but game night made it all worth it. The same was true for dancing. After all the grueling hours of rehearsal, the day of the performance made it all worthwhile.

We were all psyched up after the performance and Mr. Howard asked if I wanted to go to his house.

"Metra's got to go to work," I said then Gloria, a dancer who flirting with me from time to time and whom I found attractive too, whispered some encouragement in my ear.

Sex is still novel for most seventeen-year-old males. It was no different for me. While Gloria sat in the front seat with Mr. Howard, in the rear with me was Yvette, a dancer who had just joined the troupe. Once we got to Mr. Howard's house, he put in a video tape of porn and prepared the room, while Gloria and I made out on the sofa. When he told us the room was ready, Gloria took my hand and I took Yvette's as the three of us went into the bedroom.

In the beginning, we moved about the bed awkwardly and laughed at the simplest things, like the size of their areolas and my two-toned penis. Gloria suggested Yvette be first, so while lying on her side, she watched as we kissed and caressed one another. During intercourse, she rubbed my back and giggled at the sight of our pleasure.

There was a short knock at the door and Mr. Howard walked in without permission. We stopped. Gloria pressed her body against mine and Yvette's to hide herself.

"Can I join?" he asked.

"No!" we all said simultaneously, then broke into laughter at the accord in which we said it. Our temperament had been frolicsome, but his presence brought tension. He left the room, annoyed, and we took a moment to chuckle quietly upon his exit.

With the amount of time we spent together, it was not a great leap from holding the female dancers in my arms on stage to holding them in bed. Our hormones were bursting at the seams, and as indifferent as it may seem, we approached it like an experiment in lab class rather than something intimate. Most of the guys in my neighborhood drank liquor or smoked weed. I wasn't into either, but I did find women probably just as pleasurable.

Maybe it was the strength of the local teachers union or Mr. Howard's refusal to let go of the free love and peace he'd experienced when he was our age, but he did just about what he wanted. The principal confronted him only once that I can remember, about his relationship with a student, after her mother came to the school to complain. She said that he had intercourse with her daughter and had allowed another boy to enter the room and have sex with her too. Her daughter didn't know who the other boy was because the room was so dark.

What her mother was saying was true, because one of the guys who had participated was bragging about it. I assumed the cops were already on their way so I didn't expect to see Mr. Howard in typing class, but it was quite the opposite. There he was, sitting behind his desk, irritated but not overly concerned. We held practice that evening and it was business as usual. I didn't know how he managed to get away with the things he did.

It wasn't just girls he waylaid into bed. He also bragged about having sex orally and anally with guys. I had a high tolerance for his deviance, so he felt comfortable talking to me. I think it also confused him. Telling me was a strategic move, to soften my attitude toward it and to make me feel like it was not a detestable thing. I was not surprised at the boys he chose; their sexuality was in question anyway.

My brother Madison was gay and never had sex with a woman, if you hear him tell it. I grew up tolerant of the lifestyle and treated any homosexual as I hoped my brother was being treated. But what Mr. Howard was doing was different and perverted. After so many years of watching students come and go, he knew when we bloomed sexually and used our natural urges to trespass. When the parents saw their children on stage they praised him for the great job he was doing, but he was methodical in how he erased the boundaries of a relationship. I never saw him smoke marijuana, but I know he used it to lure. I didn't do drugs or drink alcohol, so he was still searching for my vice.

As proud as our parents were to see us on stage, they did not know what went on after the curtains closed. We had a loyalty toward him that was difficult to betray. We felt special being a part of the group. He was the one who had given us that; he could also take it away.

I played other sports and had other venues to express myself, but nothing compared to the high I got performing on stage. For some in the dance troupe, that was all they had. Without it, some would have dropped out of school or gotten seriously into the drug scene. It was a self-esteem boost for all of us and offered Metra an opportunity to go to college.

Mr. Howard was giving us something special, but taking it back a little at a time. For most, he took more than he gave. He was an adult, and while we floundered in the deep waters of adolescence, the smell of our inability to express ourselves or think beyond our years lured him like a shark to bloody water.

CHAPTER THIRTEEN
METRA

Mid school year, Mom decided we were going to move into Sugar Bear's mother's house. Remember, he was the eighteen-year-old who was living in our home as my mother's lover. He was no stepfather and none of us accepted him as that, least of all me.

I was opposed to the move for many reasons. The house was farther away from the school, the studio, and Metra. Adrian and I would have to start sharing a room again, which meant smelly feet and reggae music. Primarily I was opposed to the move because I knew their relationship was a joke. However, she seemed happy and that was enough for all my brothers and sisters. I guess it should have been for me too.

I was vocal about how I felt, so they eventually called me into her bedroom to talk about it. When they asked, I told them the truth; that I didn't believe they were going to make it and when they broke up, we would have to move all over again. He was pretty annoyed, while my mother was hurt and angered by my bleak forecast of their relationship. This widened the wedge between us. For the first time, we were truly at odds. We had always had an open and honest relationship—sometimes too open, I think.

Mom knew of my indiscretions with other girls and she would say, "You're just like your father." That offended me, which was her intent. She liked Metra, as everyone did. Metra was naturally trustworthy, generous, and kindhearted, but her early experiences with men had taught her to be cold and hard. When she tried changing her life, the vipers always tried pulling her back.

When Metra and I first started to see each other, everyone encouraged our dating. I was in school, a clean-cut athlete and academically sound. It was sort of a cliché of the rebel biker dating the popular cheerleader, except the roles were reversed—at least, it looked that way. In reality, Metra deserved better.

Maybe only her grandmother knew that. "Doll," she'd say, "He ain't no better than the rest of 'em."

Out of respect, I would never say a harsh word to her, so Metra took up for me. "He's good for me, Ma'Dear, and that's all that matters." Her grandmother would then resort to muttering under her breath.

Regardless, I loved Metra and she knew that.

After the move I caught the bus or walked the three or four miles to the Kelly Courts to see her. Kelly Courts was a housing project tucked in a corner where Interstate 10 and Highway 59 intersected. It was arguably the worst place to live in the Fifth Ward. When I went to see Metra, especially after dark, I had to be very aware of my surroundings.

Once, an old drunk who thought he was about to be mugged pulled a gun on me. Though it seems humorous now, at the time it wasn't. Looking down the barrel of his Saturday Night Special, calmly I explained that I was just going to my girlfriend's house. I could tell that keeping his balance and his aim simultaneously was not an easy task as he swayed back and forth. I thought about taking off running, but I thought he might pull the trigger out of fear and just my luck he'd get me in the back. After a long thirty seconds, he gathered his balance and wits and allowed me to pass.

Another night after being dropped off at the bus stop, I noticed two guys split up when they saw me approaching. Metra's building was still a few yards away and when one of them wound up behind me, I knew that wasn't a good thing. When the guy in front got within ten feet, I made a quick turn and walked up to someone else's door and knocked. The two men stood on the sidewalk for a moment, to see if I was bluffing. I knocked again and shouted as if I were replying to someone on the other side of the door. "It's Gary. Open up. I'm freezing my balls off out here." I opened the screen door and the men started walking away. If they could have heard the pounding of my heart or waited a minute longer they would have known I was bluffing—it was a vacant unit. As soon as they were out of sight, I jumped off the porch and ran over to Metra's door.

Too often I cut a class to sneak over to Metra's before she went to work in the afternoons. It was during one of these visits that she told me she thought she was pregnant. Her delightful expression told me she was okay with it. For me, panic was gradually building. My first thought was in what manner was my mother going to murder me.

Having ten children of her own, Mom was fed up with babies and warned us not to make that mistake or we would surely have to pay for it. I remembered how disgusted she was with my sister Renee' and the animosity she bore because of it. Sitting in Metra's living room, I was quietly going into shock, but she was calm and cool. She asked me what was wrong, whereupon I told her that I hoped we would go to college and have a family later.

I wasn't ready for a child and thought I had taken the necessary precautions to prevent that from happening. I guess not.

I loved Metra as much as any seventeen-year-old could, but I had my doubts about our spending the rest of our lives together. That meant leaving my child to be raised by another man and taking a real step in the direction of being like my father. Also, the memories of Daddy Jerome came to me like an aneurysm. The piss can, his speech therapy, and the Querk; none of them would be a part of my child's upbringing.

It was I who introduced the option of abortion. She wanted to have the baby, but was not totally opposed to what I was saying. She wanted to continue dancing, and Mr. Howard was trying to get her into Sam Houston State University, hopefully on a dance scholarship.

I was going into my final year of high school and hoped to get a scholarship to college any college, but I never counted on Metra getting pregnant. No one knew she was pregnant, for she continued practicing as if she weren't. For days, over and over, I rehearsed telling my mother about the pregnancy. She warned that having children early would ruin our lives and though I knew she wasn't going to beat me or even murder me, it was out of respect that I feared her. No matter how it came out, I knew she would be furious.

In desperate need of advice, I caught the bus to my father's, which I hadn't done before. I never told him my girlfriend was pregnant; I just asked him stuff like, "What did you think when Mom told you she was pregnant?"

"Whatcha mean, what did I think?" he slurred, holding his glass of Hennessy and ice. "She was pregnant, what was I supposed to think?"

"Well, obviously it wasn't planned. You were married. You must have been scared?"

"Scared, scared of what?" he laughed.

He found my question absurd or humorous so I stabbed back, "The responsibility of raising a child, Dad!"

He had a befuddled expression, as if he had missed the punch line and was afraid to ask what it was. His ignorance offered me my first insight into how he thought.

On the shelf behind him was a black and white photograph that appeared to have been taken in the sixties, possibly even the fifties. The old gentleman in the picture was tall, thin, and dark-skinned; he wore a white shirt, a narrow tie, and a dark hat. He reminded me of a traveling salesman.

"Who is that, Dad?" I asked, pointing.

He picked up the picture. "That's my daddy," he boasted with a hint of sadness, which told me my grandfather was no longer alive.

"Were you raised by your dad?" I asked methodically.

He brought his head up from the picture and looked at me as if I had asked another absurd question.

"Yes!" he answered.

He returned the picture to its rightful place on the shelf and talked about how good and hard-working his father was. I remained silent and wasn't as interested as he was eager to tell me. Instead I took the opportunity to watch him—well, evaluate him may be a better way to describe it. By the way he carried himself and dressed, you could not tell he was a custodian. He was a sharp dresser and liked wearing a cowboy hat and boots when he went out on the town. His boots were made of snake or lizard skin and usually he had a belt to match. He had a gold cap on one of his front teeth and kept his long, hard fingernails cleaner than he kept the convention center floor. His prize possession was the new Cadillac he bought after collecting on a settlement for a fender-bender. On the face of the glove compartment, he had his name embroidered.

I also noticed that he spoke fast and occasionally stumbled over his words. I thought it was the effects of the now-empty whiskey glass. I couldn't deny the facial features we shared; some even said we laughed alike. I hated his high-pitched hoot, and if we did indeed laugh alike, then I regarded it as one of life's cruel jokes. I found nothing funny about our being alike, but he took it as a compliment whenever someone acknowledged our likeness. Don't get me wrong, I cared for my father and wanted him to be in my life, but when I introduced myself I used my birth name and politely corrected anyone who made the mistake of calling me by his last name.

When he told me he had been raised by his father, I felt first surprise, then anger, and eventually envy. Of which I felt the most, I couldn't tell you. I had just taken it for granted that his father flew the coop too. He blew the only excuse I had for him, but in spite of that when he drove me back home that evening, I realized the resentment I had been carrying for him was weakening. Worse than some, but better than others, he was my only father and became a measuring stick for me. I wanted to be a better man and father than he was to me, and I believed if I had a child right then, I would not.

I went into the kitchen, where Mom was standing over the counter making a peanut butter and jelly sandwich. She was using a spoon rather than a knife. That eased my trepidation a little. I greeted her and she greeted me back pleasantly with a kiss on the cheek and went back to making her sandwich.

"Mom . . . Metra's pregnant," I said as if announcing a terminal illness.

She put down the spoon, turned around, and leaned against the sink. Her face was cold, undaunted. Looking into her eyes wounded me and I intermittently looked away after that. Her contempt for me at that moment was crushing.

She said as calmly as she could, "So what are ya'll going to do?"

"I don't know." I left that dangling for a moment, hoping she would offer some direction.

She remained silent and folded her arms. She would never tell me to have an abortion but she would not deter me either. She didn't want any of her children to end up like her, broke, struggling, and as she would say, without a pot to piss in. As far as she was concerned, having a child at that age was going to do just that. What better example could she have than herself?

"You both are too young to have a baby, but people do it all the time." That was the only advice she offered—vague, at best. She went back to making the sandwich that I doubt she ate.

As far as I knew, Metra hadn't told anyone. She was having her doubts, too, and knew I had mine. There was a time when she couldn't shut me up about how I was going to make the pros and buy our families big houses in the country. I wasn't talking about that anymore; I was down most of the time. We still spent as much time as we could together, but the puppy-love days were over.

A product of a young mother herself, Metra had her own concerns about raising a child at that moment in her life. She wanted to go to college, take ballet, and major in dance. It was her way out, as football was for me.

It was a school day and I called her early that morning. She had to catch an early bus to get to the Planned Parenthood Clinic downtown. I wanted to go with her, but she refused and told me to go to school. It would look suspicious if we both skipped dance rehearsal.

I could feel she wanted me to stop her, but I couldn't allow myself to. Neither of us knew for sure if what we were doing was for the best.

My mind wasn't on dance rehearsal that morning. When Mr. Howard asked where Metra was, I told him she was sick. That was questionable in itself because she had never missed a rehearsal, not even when she was sick, but he didn't push the issue.

I went to a couple of classes that morning, but couldn't concentrate for the guilt I was harboring. I waited for the bus and five or six must've passed before hers came. When she got off, it looked like she was in pain. The contempt I held for myself at that moment was greater than any I had ever felt for my father. I was utterly useless, but for some reason she was glad to see me there. And there was no other place I wanted to be more.

I helped her up the stairs to her bedroom and she got into bed. In the fetal position, we lay together and prayed not to go to Hell for what we had done, but mostly we cried. She eventually fell asleep. We stayed like that all day until her grandmother came home. I would have stayed there all night if I could have, but I needed to get home before my mother sent Adrian out looking for me.

As the days passed it became easier to cope, but the guilt never went away. It stayed with us like a dark secret that would someday have its day in the light. Ultimately we would have to pay for the moral crime we committed. Nothing could ever justify what we did, but by staying together and having a family, maybe that would nullify it.

CHAPTER FOURTEEN
CONSEQUENCES

We decided to save our money during the summer to buy a car. Metra started working as a medical assistant for Dr. Robey, a neighborhood doctor whose office was a few blocks from the Kelly Courts. After my summer job, I had saved up four hundred dollars and Metra had three hundred. We put it together and my father offered to take me to Louisiana, where I could find a better deal for my money. We looked at several cars; I settled for a 1970 Impala. It looked like a brown boat when I first saw it. I wanted something smaller and a little sportier, like an old Mustang. He said for six hundred dollars the Impala was as sporty as I was going to get. We bought the Impala and I drove it proudly.

I stopped at Metra's home first. She was excited. She hopped in and we drove to my house to show my family. Everyone was pleased. It wasn't just *my* first car, but the families' as well. Mom rode the bus to work and my aunt took her grocery shopping on the weekends. The only other cars we had occasional access to were a boyfriend's of some sort.

Having a car at our disposal helped out in many ways. When my mother got a better paying job in the housekeeping department at the medical center, I was able to take her to work when Sugar Bear didn't feel like it, which was quite often. On Saturdays, instead of waiting on my aunt to go grocery shopping, she commandeered me to take her. Also I was able to take a few people home after late rehearsals and that helped Mr. Howard.

Unlike sports, the dance theatre was not seasonal, for we

rehearsed and performed all year around. The only thing I was more committed to was football, my only foreseeable path out of the Fifth Ward. So when I heard that the coach was transferring to a cross-town rival, the news was bittersweet. When he yelled, most of the guys didn't take his yelling too personally, but for me his overbearing demeanor and the frame of reference I had with it caused me to feel belittled and that stayed with me for days. Yet if I wanted anyone lobbying for me to get a scholarship, especially during my senior year, it was he. He had the respect of college coaches for turning out not just good athletes, but good students as well. He pushed hard for his academically sound players because he knew they had a better chance at getting a college degree than getting into the pros. I wasn't on the honor roll, but I was on course to graduate in the top fifteen percent of my class.

I drummed up enough courage to approach him and ask why he wanted a transfer. In a roundabout way he told me the talent pool at Wheatley was getting scarce. I took that personally. I ran the forty-yard dash in 4.5 seconds—respectable, but not exceptional. I averaged over four yards a carry and I guess it did look better in the Saturday paper than it did on the 8mm game films. That was his specialty, though. He told scouts the things they couldn't see on film and pumped up players he thought were hard workers and good students while down-playing the talented troublemakers.

But none of that made any difference anymore, because he was out and the new coach didn't have the clout he had.

As the season grew to a close, the scouts were few and far between and by season's end there were no scholarships forthcoming. It was a rude awakening I hadn't prepared for, but it was fitting that one of my best games of the year was against him. I always played better angry—and I was pretty angry that day. I rushed for more than a hundred yards. Afterward I went over to him and shook his hand, hoping to see a little regret, but he barely noticed me.

Out of our clique, Dale was the only one who got a scholarship. I don't think any of us understood why he gave it up to come back home and work a nine-to-five. However, the way things turned out it was for the best. He accepted my nephew and he and Renee' got engaged.

Their relationship was something we never talked about. It had been almost two years since my nephew was born, but I still held a grudge. I hid it except when we played basketball. We still competed as fiercely as we always had. An elbow to the chest was just incidental contact. I enjoyed the rivalry between us because it pushed me to be better. I would never admit that to him, but I would have savored the games more if I had known they would be our last ones.

I came home from rehearsal one evening to an empty house, except for Adrian who was in our bedroom, with his earphones wrapped around his head. He saw me walk in and shout something at him. He pulled off the headphones to hear what I was saying, but I was only moving my lips. I thought that was funny and liked doing that to him when he was trying to listen to his headphones. He usually played along with my childish pranks, but that day he did not.

"Hey, where's everybody?" I asked.

"Mom and Resa are down the street at Renee's." I didn't think to ask why and before I turned away he added, "Dale has cancer."

Stunned, I gasped, "What?! Not Dale!" But he didn't have to say it again.

He was only twenty-two years old and never took a puff from a cigarette or drank an ounce of liquor. Dale wore his self-confidence like armor and I could not conceptualize anything penetrating that. Not even cancer.

I went to visit him after months of chemotherapy and the physical presence in front of me no longer looked like Dale. His massive physique had withered down to skin and bone. He was bald. The only remnants of my friend were his laugh and his resilient spirit. There was a time when I'd thought he was Superman in the flesh, and if that was so, then cancer was surely Kryptonite. He joked about being a good hurdler but now not being able to get over the curb when he went for his chemo treatments. Renee' hated his dark humor and cried often.

During those visits with Dale, we talked about sports and school. Sitting across from him, I felt guilty for being a healthy eighteen-year-old, while he looked more like a victim of the Holocaust. He made it easy for me during those uncomfortable moments of silence by laughing at something on television that wasn't all that funny or telling a crude joke about his condition.

I wanted to tell him how much I valued our friendship, as volatile as it had been. I'd set goals for myself based on his accomplishments and saw him as a measuring stick during a time when I needed something to measure up to. I liked the adulation he got from others for being a good student and athlete; I wanted that for myself, and though I didn't get the scholarship as he did, going to college was still obtainable. Without knowing it, he showed me how adversity could help you grow quicker than prosperity. He helped develop a drive within me that would kick in when the odds were stacked against me. That would be crucial as I got older.

The following summer Dale died. His mother created a shrine in the living room with candles, pictures, and awards he'd won. My sister went through a state of depression, for my nephew Christian hadn't reached his second birthday and would never know his father. Regardless of how I felt about my own father, I still had the option of seeing him if I wanted. Chris would never have that privilege.

Besides Dale, the only other person close to me who had died was my Uncle Charlie, a couple of years earlier. I made a point not to ever forget his death, either.

He had probably saved my mother's life when he pulled the shotgun on A.J. to stop the pistol-whipping years ago, but there was nothing we could do for him. His existence had decayed to being bedridden and my Aunt Edna had to feed and clean him. He was sickly, frail, and clung to each breath as if it were his last. He struggled to hold on more out of spite for my Aunt Edna than for survival. He needed daily care, and that was all he had left to punish her with.

I had come over to see my cousin Patrick, and my aunt pushed and prodded me to go in the bedroom and speak to my ailing uncle.

Poking my head in, I said, "Hey, Unc," if he were in there watching a ball game or something. He lifted his head from the pillow, which I think took too much of his strength, and raised his right arm as if he wanted me to come over. The presence of death loomed over his bed like a canopy. My Aunt Edna, standing behind me, went over to his outstretched arm. She brushed back the few white strands left on his shiny bald head, while he watched me at the door.

"Hey, Unc," I repeated. He tried raising his arm again, but my aunt placed her hand on his forearm to keep it down. We were never close; the only conversation I remember us having was when he accused me of stealing candy, when it was actually my cousin. I took a few steps closer and imitated a smile, hoping to hide the tremendous despair that weighed me down.

Dabbling a moist face towel in the corners of his eyes, my aunt said, "Don't cry. Your nephew Gary has come over to see you. You shouldn't be crying."

My aunt had no idea why he was crying, but I believe it was regret. He had worked for the railroad for over thirty years and had owned several properties. When he got too old to conduct his business, my aunt spent most of the money on other men and didn't pay the mortgage. The house was foreclosed on and they were living on his pension and social security. Now he was poor and about to live out his last days in a small room of a rented house. Defeated, he was dying owning nothing but the small lot on Cleveland Street where I had lived with Daddy Jerome. I did not know which was crueler, Dale's youth or my uncle's despair.

After graduation, I didn't know what to do with my future. Opening the doors on the last day of school was like looking out into a barren desert. I had no real direction to go, but I didn't see many obstacles, either. I never bought into the common vices of the ghetto, like drugs or crime, as some of my friends did—Bigfoot, in particular. He kept getting into trouble and eventually ended up in jail for murder.

I was not ready for college and so I sought out my first real job. My mother had a firm rule that if we weren't in school we had to get a job and contribute to the household. Within the first two weeks of graduating I got an interview with a security company. I could tell that the chubby man behind the steel desk was taken aback by my youth.

"How can I help you?" he asked, turning down the Motorola radio on his desk.

"I heard you were hiring for security officers."

"I'm sorry, but we don't have any openings at this time," he replied quickly.

"I'll work hard and I'm dependable sir. I even have my own car."

"We don't —"

"I'll work any shift anywhere," I persisted. He took a moment to think and I added, "I can work today—right now if you need me to." Determined, I wasn't going to take no for an answer.

I think he liked my tenacity. He called in another guy and said, "Show him where to get his uniform." He wrote down an address and gave it to me. It was a bank downtown and he told me to be there at four-thirty.

Just like that I had my first real paying job.

Proudly I went straight home to try on my uniform and tell Mom. She was proud for me, but we were still estranged. The Sugar Bear fiasco was over and we had moved out as soon as the school year ended. He never kept a steady job and complained when he had to take her to work. It was painfully obvious that he was not as mature as she hoped, for she recalled the relationship as having to raise another child. Duh...!

Will's grandparents had passed away; he also got a security job and moved into his own apartment. For two eighteen-year-olds, we were making good money, but it was a means to an end. I was staying in shape hoping to make it as a walk-on for some college whenever I decided to go. His aspiration was still to become a famous artist and was taking classes at Texas Southern.

Will had always been my closest friend since we were thirteen. We shared many of the same classes, played ball, ran track, and danced. We saw one another more than we saw those in our own family. He was more than a friend, he was like a brother to me and I loved him like one. We spoke honestly with each other—except when it came to his dating my sister. She was already being offered academic scholarships and would be heading off to college soon.

With the aid of Mr. Howard, Metra had enough grants to get her through her first year at Sam Houston State. Her mother and stepfather drove us the seventy-five miles up to Huntsville. After helping her unpack, they left the room for us to be alone. I hated leaving her there, but it was for the best, plus I planned to be with her the following fall.

The adjustment was difficult for her, so I wired her money every payday and picked her up on the weekends if she didn't have to study. Mr. Howard called quite a bit to get an update on how she was doing, and when she was in town we went to dinner with him and Maggie.

For whatever it's worth, I loved Metra as much I could at that time and had no problem putting myself in harm's way, if that's what it took. I missed her and since the abortion I had been faithful to her.

It was Friday night and I was watching *Miami Vice* with my mother when Mr. Howard and Maggie invited me over for dinner. After dinner we sat in the living room and drank wine—well, I drank red Kool-Aid, because I hadn't acquired a taste for alcohol yet.

They kept disappearing throughout the evening and going into the bedroom to talk. I thought that was suspicious, but didn't really give it much thought until the last time, when Maggie returned without Mr. Howard. She gave me a long stare, scrutinizing me, and when she was done she said, "So Herman says you have a little crush on me." By my smile she knew I did, and before I could get past my embarrassment she said, "Come on."

Entering the bedroom, I thought I knew exactly what was about to take place. Mr. Howard wasn't in the room; I figured he slipped out the back door to give us privacy. She must have known about the girls—maybe this was her turn. I didn't know why she was doing it, and to be honest, I didn't really care. Maggie was stunning. She was in her thirties, almost six feet tall, and had a well-endowed chest. Like most eighteen-year-old boys, I was flattered that she even noticed I was alive.

After promising her that I wouldn't go bragging about it all over town, she went to the bathroom and turned on the shower, while I sat at the edge of the bed. To keep out the light, he had the same heavy drapes over his windows as he always did.

In the bathroom, I suspected she was probably smoking a joint or doing a line of coke, but there was no evidence of that. It was just the longest shower I had ever heard of. When she finally came out, by then I had to go, and when I came out the lights were off and it was pitch black, as it usually was in one of his rooms. I could hear her moving about in the bed so I climbed in.

"Where are you?" she said with a giggle. Then she grabbed hold of my arm and pulled me down on top of her. I could feel her huge breast against my chest and we began having sex, but I felt this presence as if we were not in the bed alone. When I felt Mr. Howard's hand on the back of my thigh it startled me so much that I rolled off Maggie and onto the floor. They laughed, and I began searching for my clothes in the dark. As I stumbled toward the door with what I hoped was my underwear, I could hear them continuing with what they began.

Getting dressed in their living room, of all people I thought of Toni. Being a virgin seemed so long ago when it had only been about three years.

Feeling defiled, I went home and headed straight for the bathtub. My mother and Resa were watching television as I zoomed past them, and my mother stopped me with, "You're not going to speak?"

"Hi, Mom. Hi, Resa," I said quickly, then excused myself. A few minutes later there was a knock on the bathroom door. "Who is it?" I shouted, hoping to intimidate them into going away.

"It's Mom."

The lock didn't work anyway, so I collected all the suds and placed them in the appropriate position and pulled down a drying towel for a backup and invited her in.

"What's wrong?" she asked nicely, hoping to get more flies with honey.

"Nothing," I said.

"Well, I was just checking on my baby boy. He never just run into the house and jump into the tub."

"No, I'm fine. Me and Will were hanging out."

I hoped she believed me because if she didn't, I would have just kept right on lying.

I was repulsed by what had happened, but took most of the responsibility for it because I knew something like that was bound to happen. That night I learned that my actions had consequences that couldn't be so easily washed away.

"Papa"
Will H. Montgomery

Grandmother
Olivia Montgomery

"Mom"
Mary J. Braxton at 12

"A.J." and Mom
Newlyweds

"Hotshot" 1967

Mom and Ambus, Uncle Charlie, Resa and Leon in 1956

Sports and Dance

Gary   **Will**

Will   **Gary**

Metra, Gary, Leah, Will, Paulette

The Marines

PFC Braxton

Persian Gulf

Saudi Desert

Mogadishu, Somalia

News Clippings

December 14, 1944

The Liberty Vindicator—Combined with Liberty County News

Negro Victim of Hit, Run Driver

Investigations are being made by the Liberty County sheriff's department concerning accidental death of Will Montgomery, negro, who was the victim of a hit and run driver Saturday night. Fatal injuries were received by Montgomery at 8 p. m., and he was found a little later and brought to a Liberty hospital.

The accident occurred, said Chief Deputy Sheriff V. R. Shauberger, a quarter mile west of the ABC Club on Highway 90, just out of Liberty. Frank Farmer of Liberty called an ambulance for the injured negro, whose right arm was broken in a number of places and a gash cut in his right side.

Montgomery died at 2:02 a. m. Sunday.

Occupational hazard

Teacher, shot in front of team, plans to

A teacher who was shot while instructing a drill team at Wheatley High School said today he plans to return to teaching despite his constant fears about the "violent area" where the school is located.

Man stabs sister to death, then is shot by brother

A 42-year-old man with a history of mental problems stabbed his sister to death early Sunday before being shot in the neck by his brother, police said.

THE TEN

Top Row: Gary, Paulette. Second Row: Ambus, Jo, Madison.
Third Row: Riley, Renee'. Bottom Row: Resa, Adrian, Leon
and Mom (Bottom Corner).

CHAPTER FIFTEEN

THE FRESHMAN

Metra and I didn't hang out with Mr. Howard and Maggie that summer as we would have normally, and she thought that was odd but never inquired as to why. We worked and prepared for the fall semester, and I looked forward to being away from home. I quit my security job, packed my belongings, and Metra and I drove up to Sam Houston State.

When I picked up my schedule from the counselor's office, I noticed that most of my classes were remedial. I asked the elderly lady, who was probably born and raised right there in the small town of Huntsville, why I had to take those courses. She explained that I was reading on an eighth-grade level and my math skills, outside of addition and subtraction, were nonexistent. There had to be some mistake. I graduated at the top fifteen percent of my class. I wanted to tell her that, but I was too embarrassed. She waited for a reply or for me to take the schedule. I took the schedule.

For football tryouts, I was in tiptop condition, and while we executed different exercises a coach took notes. On the bench press I can't remember how much weight I lifted, but I pumped the required amount and a couple more for good measure. At the horizontal jump, I knew I put up impressive numbers because the coach nodded his head with approval. I did well at the agility test also, and finally it was down to the forty-yard dash. I matched my best time with a 4.5 and when the list came out the following day, I was on it. I had made it on a college team.

After a few weeks of practice, the bills for tuition, housing, and food began coming in. My government grant didn't cover all of my expenses, so I went to the head coach and explained my situation. He told me that I had to play a full year in order to be eligible for a scholarship. He went on to tell me that I would make a good addition to the team, then he patted me on the helmet and wished me luck.

I did more growing up after that conversation than I did in the three years I was in high school. I knew right then that I seriously needed to think of something else to do with my life—but what else could I do where stuttering wouldn't be a hindrance? I didn't know and that placed more emphasis on obtaining a degree of some kind. The only question was how I was going to make up four or five years of reading and arithmetic in one semester.

I was given a job stuffing envelopes for some department and running errands back and forth across the campus. By four o'clock I was done with class and work. Ever since I was thirteen I had been involved in some form of extracurricular, so just returning to my dorm didn't seem natural. I was used to the camaraderie of being a part of a team and longed for that familiar sense of belonging.

I considered the dance program, but when I wandered into their practice session there were no black guys. It was the abilities of the few guys they did have that intimidated me most. They had formal training; the instructor could feed them a whole routine from her chair. Compared to them I had no dance training. Back home, Mr. Howard demonstrated what he wanted and we just copied—and he wasn't formally trained either.

I could have pledged a fraternity, but running around campus in ladies' underwear or having a senior member ride my back while leading me around on a leash, wasn't challenging. Carrying around Daddy Jerome's can for five years was all the degradation I needed for a lifetime. I was looking for something that had a purpose.

The Rangers were something totally different. It was an R.O.T.C. organization whose initiation was running new members through a mini boot camp at the end of the semester. If you were still there, you became worthy of wearing the black Ranger beret. It was exactly what I was looking for; a challenge football didn't give me. As if that wasn't enough, I also joined the school's rifle team. I wasn't very good at it, but they were badly in need of members.

Metra took dance classes, and though she had an abundance of natural talent, she was lacking formal training also. She took ballet to overcome that, but Biology was not so easy to overcome. Her major was nursing and it was a critical course, so she spent most of her money on tutoring lessons. She resided in a cooking dorm and couldn't eat in the cafeteria unless she paid, so I snuck food out.

The small town of Huntsville couldn't exist if it weren't for the state prison and the university. We felt out of place. We studied together at the Student Center, where the students hung out to play video games and watch television. With the little extra money we had on payday, we got a couple of burgers and sat in the grass and studied.

On the weekends we drove home if we had gas money, but I spent most of my weekends playing war games in the national park with the Rangers. We checked out M16 from the National Guard Armory and wore fatigues. We started off with about twenty-five guys but quickly dwindled to about twelve. Our acne-faced, red-headed lieutenant liked yelling, but he stopped far short of making me angry. I could tell he didn't have much experience with black guys and was wary of me, but I was quiet and did well at following orders.

I hated the boot camp initiation tactics, but I had never voluntarily quit anything either. That would be challenged one night standing in the middle of a dark forest.

We all stood in formation and the commanding officer left us to go find a good place to make an ambush. One of our sergeants was carrying a loaded .357 Magnum. The red-headed lieutenant gathered his other two sergeants in a huddle and there was some debate before they broke. The lieutenant gave us the long speech about what size balls it took to go charging up a hill to your death. When he was done he held up the gun for us to visually inspect, then he loaded a single round in the cylinder. He spun the cylinder, then slapped it closed and put it to his head. He shut his eyes and pulled the trigger—to an empty chamber.

We were all stunned.

Then he gave the weapon to one of the sergeants, who also spun the cylinder once, placed it to his temple, and closed his eyes. I tightened my body, hoping this crazy guy wasn't going to kill himself right in front of my eyes. When the hammer fell I could see the relief in his eyes.

Now it was the last guy's turn, and he was not as gung-ho. He stepped out of the formation, having second thoughts, and the red-headed lieutenant took the gun and went to him. The other sergeant followed and they were both on him like a pack of dogs.

I was ready to start walking toward the highway if they thought I was going to put a gun to my head.

After a few minutes of being verbally beaten down, the sergeant gave in. The lieutenant spun the cylinder around for him, closed it, and offered it to him. He hesitantly took the weapon and brought it to his temple as if it weighed a hundred pounds. He left it there while the other two sergeants laughed at his cowardice. This was stupider than any fraternity hazing I had ever heard of.

It took several attempts before he finally pulled the trigger. I held my breath. When the hammer fell to another empty chamber he almost collapsed from exuberance.

They never offered the gun to any one of us. I was relieved, because that would have been a long walk back to the campus.

Nothing that exciting happened on the rifle team. We lost most of the matches we entered, and my marksmanship left much to be desired. My mother wrote me often, though I was only an hour and a half away. I made sure not to mention the Russian Roulette incident.

I also got letters from Leslie, a petite sixteen-year-old hazel-eyed girl on Mr. Howard's drill team. We'd exchanged numbers a year earlier and all we ever did was talk on the phone occasionally. She was an only child, and our conversations consisted of her complaining about her mother and her grandmother. We would stay on the phone for hours until she fell asleep. She had a boyfriend and I was dating Metra, so we wrote letters to one another.

Being the only child, Leslie knew how to get her way when she really wanted to, as she did when she came by the house with her grandmother a few minutes before I was to drive up to Sam Houston. She was very reserved when it came to showing her feelings, having been reared in the old-school way where women never let on if they liked a fellow. Her grandmother, Mrs. Moore, rarely let Leslie out of her sight. She took her to school and picked her up. Allowing her to come to see me off was significant. We had merely been talking over the phone, so Leslie must have whined for days to get that privilege.

It was an innocent relationship, but as the semester wore on, our infatuation grew.

By the time the semester was ending, so was the Ranger initiation. I made it through a grueling weekend of calisthenics, obstacle courses, and yelling to be able to wear a black beret that I bought with my own money. After the ceremony, I threw it in my closet and closed the door on the Rangers and any thoughts of joining the military. My grades were low; if I wanted to remain in school I needed to do better in the spring. I resigned from the rifle team as well, determined to concentrate on nothing but academics for the next semester.

Metra was not as lucky. She was failing. Even acing all her finals wouldn't bring her grades up enough to pass, so she decided to catch the Greyhound bus home before the Christmas break. Though she talked about coming back to school, I knew she wasn't going to. Her heart wasn't in it and it had nothing do with academics. She wasn't going to be a dancer, so the next best thing for her was having a family. Our relationship had also run its course and we both knew it.

Helping her pack was solemn, for obvious reasons. She didn't say very much and then she asked, "It's that virgin, isn't it?"

I had no idea she even knew about Leslie. My roommate had gone to class one afternoon and left her in the room to wait for me, and she found my stash of letters from Leslie. They were explicit in how we had grown to feel about one another.

For all that she had experienced in her life, quitting Metra for Leslie was as bad as quitting her for a white girl. My sister Jo was

totally in love with her first, though they had broken up. So was Renee'
with Dale. Even my mother was still in love with A.J., and he beat the
hell out of her. As hypocritical as it was, I have to admit that Leslie's
inexperience did play a part.

Metra said nothing for a long time, then the tears began
glistening in her huge brown eyes, but none fell. *I take it back, I take it
back,* is what I wanted to say, fighting desperately to keep from caving
in. Hurting her was the hardest thing I ever had to do. She was a good
woman—even at that age I could see that. She would always be by my
side, through sickness, health, and even poverty. Metra was, in many
ways, like my mother. She didn't ask for much from a man but was
happy as long as he was compassionate, loving, and respectful. She
didn't care how much money he made as long as he brought it home.

As a boy listening to my mother cry, I couldn't understand why
any man would not want her. I promised myself that I would never hurt
my woman the way she had been hurt. That was a promise I wasn't
going to be able to keep. I loved Metra, but for me there was something
ominous about our relationship. When I thought of our future all I could
see was our having three or four children, living in the same
neighborhood I grew up in, and barely getting by. Or even worse, I
would not be there to raise my children. I saw myself making the same
mistakes—not only those of my mother, but those of my father as well. I
can't explain why I felt that way, but I did and sometimes you have to go
with that.

PART III

CHAPTER SIXTEEN
YOUNG HEARTS

The family was living across town in a three-bedroom apartment in a better neighborhood. Resa, Jo, and Adrian all worked and stayed at home. We could stay with our mother indefinitely as long as we went to school or contributed to the house by working, but it had to be an honest living. There was enough money that the refrigerator was always full, and not only could we afford boxed cereal, but we had cable television too.

It was MTV's first year on the air and computers were just being introduced to the world with a commercial during the 1984 Super Bowl. Geraldine Ferraro became the first female running mate of a presidential candidate; Desmond Tutu won the Nobel Prize. When I was able to get home on the weekends I watched as much MTV as Resa and Mom could stand; Huey Lewis, Tina Turner, Michael Jackson, Madonna, Prince, Men At Work, Cindi Lauper. The first time my mother saw Boy George, she slapped the arm of the sofa, shook her head, and said, "The world is going to hell in a hand-basket!" I'm sure a lot of people thought so too.

The sultry voice of Marvin Gaye had been silenced at the hands of his father that year. Vanessa Williams became the first black female to become Miss America. Martin Luther King's birthday was on the verge of becoming a nationally recognized holiday. Also, some of the guys I danced with were getting sick and no one really knew what it was until the news broke about Rock Hudson dying of AIDS. And my eldest brother Leon was somewhere taking his first hit of crack.

The weekends I was home from college, I stocked up on food because I could no longer afford eating in the cafeteria. I had an unpaid balance from the previous semester and each payday that cost was taken out of my measly check. So was tuition and books, which left me with a ten-dollar bill to eat with for the next fifteen days.

With ten bucks, I bought a pack of wieners, a loaf of bread, and sandwich spread. I was not partial to sandwich spread, but I got it for practical reasons. It had more crap in it than regular mayonnaise and with only a wiener a day, I needed the extra nutrients. I'd boil the wiener in an old percolating coffee pot around two o'clock in the afternoon and wrap it in a slice of bread. Without a refrigerator, those wieners lasted just long enough.

Metra and I could lean on one another when times got rough, but we were no longer dating and I was there alone. Paulette had academic scholarships and was doing well at TCU. She started studying drama and also broke it off with Will. He took it hard but finally moved on and eventually began dating others. So did Metra. She didn't write me or call; that was just how she was. She was giving me what I wanted even if she believed it wasn't the best thing for me.

Leslie and I were dating exclusively. I looked forward to her letters, but they were not enough. I wrote her almost every day and was glad to see the semester coming to a close. By the end of the year I was taking all college level courses and could have filed for a federal grant as well as a federal loan, which I didn't do the first time.

I would like to say that not returning to Sam Houston had everything to do with the one-wiener-a-day diet, but in reality that had nothing to do with it. My main reason for going home was because I wanted to be close to Leslie.

When the semester was over I left and got a job reading meters for the local utility company. I enrolled in night school, but the most important thing to me was being with Leslie. Mrs. Moorehouse liked me and she knew that my interest in Leslie was more than physical.

As a family we hardly spoke of Daddy Jerome. However, I did begin to tell Leslie bits and pieces about him, but never about the can. I hadn't seen him since the night he stayed over and gave me the bit of advice about running through the line with my eyes open. The only one who even mentioned his name occasionally was Leon—and hardly in the presence of our mother. He hated him with a passion and told us repeatedly that he was insane.

Being raised by my Aunt Edna, Riley never felt the rope or the Querk and laughed at the absurdity of Leon's statement. Actually, we all laughed at Leon, because he looked so serious when he said it. Yes, Daddy Jerome was overzealous when it came to disciplining us, but I didn't believe his sanity was in question.

He was my only reference when it came to a live-in father; I still held a deep respect for that. He provided for seven children who were not his own and protected us from those who would otherwise break in and rape my mother or one of my sisters. He was the only man vying for the job, and the boys just had to take one for the team. That's just the way it was.

It might have been a Sunday when my mother got the phone call. I don't remember her saying a single word, just putting down the receiver. She was so visibly disturbed that what little color she had, seemed to drain right out of her. She began feeling around for the arm of the sofa as if she were blind.

Resa asked, "What's wrong, Mom?"

After taking a minute to calm herself, she answered. "Jerome's been shot." Before we could wrap our minds around that she added, "He killed his sister Clara and his brother Albert had to shoot him."

What!? Why would Daddy Jerome ever want to hurt his sister Clara? What could possibly go so wrong that the soft-spoken Uncle Albert would shoot his brother?

I read the article in the paper the next morning and couldn't believe what it said about him.

I needed to see Uncle Albert, but was not sure if he even remembered me. Regardless of how I felt about his brother, I was no real blood relation. We referred to him as our uncle, though, and I hoped he would remember that.

As soon as I walked into the restaurant he began to smile. He recognized me, but didn't remember my name. He called me Adrian, but I took no offense because he hadn't seen me in about twelve years. We made small talk about my family, but he knew why I had come. It was difficult for him to talk about it, but he voluntarily told me what happened in those early morning hours.

He began by saying that Daddy Jerome had fallen on hard times and he and his wife were separated. He was living with his sister Clara and still worked at the barbecue restaurant, off and on. On the Fourth of July about 2:00 A.M. Uncle Albert was awakened by a hysterical call from his sister. She and her boyfriend had been awakened by the huge silhouette of Daddy Jerome standing in the doorway of their bedroom, naked, in one hand holding the bible and in the other a butcher's knife.

It was difficult for Uncle Albert to keep eye contact with me. He looked down at the counter or over my shoulder as he spoke. That was easier for me too. He went on saying he could hear his sister screaming for Daddy Jerome to stop before the phone went dead. He grabbed a gun and sped over as fast as he could, running red lights, hoping a police officer would chase him, but none did.

When he got to within a block of her house, he heard loud music coming from someone's home. The closer he got, the more he realized it was gospel music and it was coming from his own sister's house. When he drove up, he saw her boyfriend in his underwear, sitting in his taxicab. He hadn't called the cops because he was a married man and didn't want to be implicated.

Albert entered the house cautiously. The music was so loud it was distracting, so he went over and turned it off. As he proceeded to the bedroom, calling for Clara, the silence bothered him more than the music had. When he entered her bedroom he could see that the walls were splattered with blood. His sister was crouched over between the bed and the wall. He knew immediately she was dead. She had several stab wounds about her shoulder, chest, and head. He turned and saw Daddy Jerome standing next to the dresser and on top of the dresser, a bloody knife.

In his pocket, he had his hand on his gun. "What's wrong, Jerome?" he asked gently, hoping to soothe the giant.

Knowing what was in his pocket, Daddy Jerome responded by telling him to kill him. Albert's eyes were wide and I could tell he was trying to make sense of it as he demonstrated how Daddy Jerome slapped his palm down on the knife and picked it up. He pleaded for him to put the knife down. Not until he began to come toward him, did he pull out his gun. He gave him several more warnings before finally firing one shot. The bullet entered Daddy Jerome's neck and paralyzed him from

187

the neck down.

He had been having mental problems a few years prior to the incident; his wife had warned Albert that his brother was dangerous. One evening he sat outside in the cold, wearing nothing but his underwear. She couldn't get him to come back inside so she called Albert, as she always did when she couldn't control him. Albert came over, sat down next to his brother, and put his arm around him. Daddy Jerome laid his head on Albert's shoulder, and after a few minutes Albert convinced him to go back into the house.

After the shooting, when Albert was allowed to see him at the hospital, outside of being paralyzed, he said he seemed fine. In good spirits, you might say. He wanted to believe it had all been a bad dream. When he asked where Clara was, Albert replied coldly, "Don't you know?" His demeanor became solemn and he turned his head away.

Mom asked if anyone wanted to go to the hospital with her to visit him. I was the only one who took her up on the offer. We got off the elevator on the floor where the criminals were kept. We walked into his glass room and saw a thousand tubes coming out of his body. His head was facing the door, and when he saw us, I could see a smile gradually forming on his jolly face. My mother was meek as she grabbed his hand and began rubbing it, as if he could feel it. With the back of her other hand she caressed his scratchy cheek. He must have liked that, because he closed his eyes as if her touch was quenching a great thirst. It was as if nothing had changed between them.

It was important for me that he saw that I was not weak or feeble, nor was I ignorant or slow. Most of all, I wanted him to see in my eyes, in my body, and in the way that I carried myself that Hotshot was dead., The person who stood before him was a man; there wasn't an ounce left of the little boy that carried his piss can back and forth to the commode.

He looked at me and I asked him how he was doing. As always, I never noticed it, but apparently he did.

"Hotshot," he laughed. It was uncomfortable being called that, and to hear it come from the same voice that created it, disturbed me. "You still stutter," he said, then managed to move his head slightly, back and forth, as if to say that after all these years I still hadn't learned some lesson that he had invested so much time in teaching me.

My intent was for him to see that I was big, strong, and smart enough to go to college. I needed him to feel ashamed for making me feel less than worthy. That wasn't what was happening. Being in his presence not only brought back those feelings of powerlessness, but the affection I had for him also. I placed my hand on his forearm and felt the caring gentleness he showed us at times. Nothing could ever make me forget that he was there for my mother when our fathers were not.

His visitations were restricted to family only, so we never got the chance to see him again. From complications due to his paralysis, he died of pneumonia a year later. His death left me disillusioned. I was looking for closure and there wasn't any. There was no one else alive, other than myself, who knew the depths of the degradation that I felt during our speech therapy sessions, so if I pretended it didn't happen, it didn't? *Right?* After all, he had been out of my life longer than he had been in it.

But those years from the age of three to almost nine, must have been crucial years in my psychological development, because nothing really changed after his death. When I knew I was on the verge of stuttering, my mind would scrabble over my limited vocabulary for another word that meant the same thing, but flowed easier. It worked most of the time. That was how I was getting through interviews and general conversation. When it didn't work, though, I would begin to hyperventilate, and once that started, my jaws would just lock up.

I tried making it appear as if I had just lost my train of thought, but internally I was still feeling that same terror I felt as a child. I was just better at hiding the upheaval that was going on inside of me. I knew no one was going to pop me on the forehead or whip the Querk from around the bedpost, but the fear of being labeled as stupid or just being held back for it, replaced the fear of abuse.

Daddy Jerome's death was like removing the brain tumor after the damage had already been done. I had to learn to communicate without relapsing into Hotshot every time I stumbled over my words. I knew people who stuttered worse than I did, and they acted as if it was nothing. It was just a speech impediment, but I could never accept that. I was convinced that my stutter was intertwined with Hotshot, leading to a constant struggle of which one of us would have control over my life.

Not a single soul knew what was going on inside me. Each of us got something different from Daddy Jerome, depending on our age, our attitude, and our gender. None of them would have understood, so I kept it to myself. I spoke to Leslie about some things, but she didn't know the depth of it either.

Leslie and I spent most of our time on her green sofa with her mother, Betty, sitting across from us, reluctantly chaperoning. She had taken a bad fall as a baby and her mental capacity was primarily that of a thirteen-year-old girl. Some guy in the neighborhood knocked her up and never took responsibility for it, so Leslie never knew her father. Mrs. Moorehouse catered to Leslie because of that, and that made her mother jealous. Leslie was embarrassed by her mother's mental incapacity, so there was always tension between them. They squabbled like sisters over trivial things, such as whether to watch *Fantasy Island* or *The Dukes of Hazard*, and the ending played out virtually the same way every time: Mrs. Moorehouse would storm in, telling them both to stop the bickering, then turn to Betty and scold her for being childish. Feeling outnumbered, she would leave the house and go to a small bar around the corner to drink a Coke. Mrs. Moorehouse forbade her from going there, but she did it every time. Once Mrs. Moorehouse returned to her bedroom to watch television with her husband, Leslie would dim the lights and look at me with a conniving smile.

Though her tactics may have been questionable, she knew how to get what she wanted. She wanted to be with me and I wanted to be with her. After a few months of dating, her grandmother had begun allowing her to come to the apartment we lived in. We would lie on the floor in the living room and watch MTV. When no one was paying attention, we would slip away into the bedroom I shared with Adrian, and that's where the real serious making out happened.

We went as far as she wanted and I always stopped when she asked. The day finally came when she did not want me to stop. It wasn't long before we were under the covers and down to our underwear. I was experienced sexually, more than I should have been, but this time things were different. Being that she was a virgin, I felt a sense of responsibility to her that I had never felt with anyone else.

My sisters, Jo, Renee', and Paulette, had openly discussed their first times with me, as I had mine with them. For each of them, their first time was less than desirable and even less enjoyable. After listening to their expectations, I remembered how tragic that was and didn't want Leslie to experience that. She had been waiting for this moment for a long time; I wanted it to be as she had imagined it.

Under the covers with our naked bodies pressed up against one another, I could tell she was nervous. I would be gentle and she knew that, but she was not on the pill. This was an important moment in her life and I wanted it to be perfect, so to ease her fear of getting pregnant I told her I would not reach an orgasm. I'm not sure if she believed me or not, but making sure her first experience was special was more gratifying. Plus, I didn't want to gross her out by pulling out.

I laid my weight on top of her and I felt her hands timidly guiding me. We gently made love in my bunk bed, and it was not easy keeping my promise, but I did. There would be time for that I was once told during my first time. I was letting Leslie know early on that I was in this all the way. I wasn't looking at her just as a girlfriend. I wanted her to be my wife.

That night, on the way home, she cuddled beneath my arm and laid her head on my shoulder. She was finally mine and nothing was going to ever break the bond I was forging between us.

Reading meters for a utility company happened to be the perfect job for me, because I didn't have to speak that much and it paid better than security work. All I had to do was jump approximately three hundred fences and fight pit bulls, Rottweilers, and every little piss-ant dog, that had more courage than sense. And there was never a day that it was too cold, too hot, or too rainy to read a route. Promotions were judged on attendance, injury, and errors. My first day, I took notice of the older guys limping around with braces on their legs and workman comp claims being reviewed. I didn't want to be in that department for long, so, hoping to get promoted quickly, I never missed a day, never complained about the route, and was awarded for having fewer errors than anyone else.

Mrs. Moorehouse knew my intentions were to marry her granddaughter, so she put a little more slack in the leash—and we used every bit of it. Leslie talked to me every night until she fell asleep on the phone. On Saturdays, I picked her up about two o'clock and we would spend the whole day going to the movies, then to Sizzler's for the all-you-can-eat steak and shrimp, and ending the evening at our favorite motel. If we missed her curfew by a few minutes, when we drove up, Mrs. Moorehouse would be standing on the porch, arms folded. She always began scolding me first; being that she'd left her granddaughter in my care, but Leslie knew just how to calm her. From her purse, she would pull a napkin full of shrimp, and all would be forgiven.

Neither one of us was ready to have a baby, so we went to the clinic so Leslie could get on the pill. We signed in about eight in the morning. After waiting three hours, Leslie went to the front desk and the lady told her she would be seen after lunch. Watching people come and go, she went to the desk again, where the lady said she had called her name and no one responded. I had been there all day too, and told the woman no one had called Leslie's name, but she wasn't hearing it and told us we had to reschedule our appointment. Leslie was already cutting class to be there; getting another whole day was going to be difficult.

Before we could reschedule the appointment, she got pregnant.

I wasn't as scared this time; in fact, I actually started liking the idea of her having my baby. I wasn't afraid of what my mother would say anymore. I wasn't in high school anymore and had a good job. In a year or so we would be married anyway, so I didn't see it as such a bad thing as I had when Metra had gotten pregnant. You might say that I thought having the baby would only complete the union we had already created. However, Leslie was not as optimistic as I was. Her grandmother had always bragged to the neighbors about what a good girl she was, while their daughters were coming up pregnant. Now she was going to have to eat crow.

I kept very few secrets from Will. He knew how deep my complex with Hotshot went. He also knew about Leslie's pregnancy. He told me if I really wanted to have the baby, have it accidentally slip out in front of her grandmother—she would never agree to an abortion. He was right, but I couldn't have done that to Leslie. If she sought approval from anyone, it was her grandmother. If Mrs. Moorehouse had disapproved of me, I would have been long gone, so I understood the importance of not disappointing the one person she sought approval from.

When Leslie told me she thought an abortion would be the best thing, it wasn't what I wanted; my first impulse was to do as Will had suggested. Although I was as equally responsible for the child as she was, I had less than an equal right in the decision to have an abortion, so we scheduled it. We went to the same Planned Parenthood Metra and I had gone to. After it was done, I took her back home and we hardly talked about it again. If it troubled her, she never showed it.

It took me a little longer.

Jo and I moved out of the family apartment and shared one of our own. Will began reading meters with me. We liked telling everyone we were brothers. We may as well have been. We doubled-dated, and while I was steady with Leslie he went through a couple of girlfriends. We were making good money and bought ourselves better cars. I replaced the Impala with a candy-apple red Trans Am with chrome wheels. He bought a Mustang. Together we were young, black, and twenty-one, as they say. We didn't feel like the proverbial man was holding us down. If we worked hard for it, we knew it was obtainable, regardless of how much we had to make up just to be on an even playing field.

Reading meters, we were susceptible to the elements. Under the blistering southern summer sky, we fried like eggs, while in the winter; our hands would be frozen into hooks from grabbing the tops of fences and hoisting ourselves over them. Not until we got in the van and thawed out did we know if we'd caught a splinter.

Someone was always sick, so when Will missed a couple days, I didn't think anything of it. On the third day, I went to his apartment with Leslie and he was in bed with the flu. I prepared that honey, lemon, and whiskey concoction that my mother gave me when I got sick and gave it to him with two aspirin. He sipped on it, while I sat at the edge of the bed telling him if he didn't get back soon, it would start to affect his ability to transfer out. Upset at my insensitivity, he snapped back with, "You think I want to be sick!"

I made sure he didn't need anything else and told his younger brother, who was living there with him, that I would come by the next day after work to check on him. After dropping Leslie off, I went home.

Very early the next morning I got a frightening call from his brother. "Gary, William's not breathing! William's not breathing!" he shouted.

I told him to call 911, and by the time I got there Will had already been taken to the hospital. I ran through the emergency room hallways, looking for him, and when I found him, the paramedics were trying to hold him down while the doctor administered something to stop the eruptive convulsions he was having. Everything was moving too fast for my mind to comprehend. A few hours ago he had a common cold; now his body jerked and quaked violently with seizures. I thought he was dying before my eyes. A nurse pulled me away and escorted me to the waiting room.

I was told a few hours later that Will had slipped into a coma and the doctors had no idea what caused it. He was comatose for two weeks before coming out of it and when I entered his room, he looked at me strangely, as if he didn't expect to see me there. He asked what had happened, and as we talked I realized he had lost some of his memory. He thought we were still sixteen years old and didn't remember anything after that.

At sixteen, Will and I had just begun to be friends, so I spent hours in his hospital room telling him all the things we had done. I reminded him of the time we crept into the girl's dorm at Texas Southern and how I had to jump down from the ledge when the cops began chasing us and how he slipped in the mud as we made our getaway. He didn't remember that, which saddened me.

With Leslie's help, I brought Will up to the present by bringing pictures, ribbons, and trophies he received during high school. He was amazed that he had no recollection of it, and his eyes lit up like a child listening to a fairy tale when I talked. After a while, our conversation tended to go round and round because he could not retain something I had said ten minutes earlier. Many times, he would ask me to tell him a story I had already told him. He liked hearing about our antics and we were beginning to connect again, but that was because of my being there every day, rather than a rediscovery of any genuine emotion. It was disheartening that all the long walks, all the talks about our past and our future, were no longer memories we shared. I'd expected our futures to change, but the wiping out of our past caught me off guard.

I asked the doctor if the hot toddy could have caused his high temperature, and immediately the doctor dismissed it, but I never got a straight answer as to what brought on his sickness. After several months the doctors settled for epilepsy as the cause though he had never shown any symptoms of it before.

Will seizures and loss of memory were so severe that he would never fully recover and when he was discharged from the hospital, he had to remain under a doctor's care. He was admitted into a sort of halfway-house for those who were mentally disadvantaged. He hated it and didn't believe he belonged there. When the doctors allowed me, I picked him up on Saturdays and dragged him around with Leslie and me. We would drop him off in the late afternoon and that still gave us time to do what we wanted.

When I did think he was regaining some of his memory, a seizure would usually wipe it out. I didn't really understand what happened to Will, nor did I understand why it had to happen. It just didn't seem fair, but I was beginning to accept the fact that our friendship would never be as it was.

CHAPTER SEVENTEEN

MAN OR MOUSE

I hadn't seen or spoken to Mr. Howard until he showed up at the hospital to visit Will. He went to see Will as often as I did, and that rekindled our friendship. I put the thing with Maggie behind me. He never brought it up and neither did I. When Will was released Mr. Howard was the only other person that picked him up from the halfway house and took him to the movies or for a bite to eat. He let Will watch videotapes of us dancing and it fascinated him that he could not remember any of it.

Will, being a little superstitious, used to say that bad things came in threes. I wonder if he was right. Daddy Jerome died, Will got sick, and one afternoon, Metra called—the first time since our breakup—and told me to turn on the news. It was a report that a teacher at Wheatley High had just been shot in front of his drill team. Of course, that teacher happened to be Mr. Howard.

I hated to admit it, but my first thought was that the "chickens had come home to roost." I figured a father of one of the young girls or some guilt-stricken boy had come to get even. Mr. Howard had lots of friends but he also made some serious enemies. Some were thugs who had an experience or two with him when they were in school.

When I went to visit him at the hospital, Maggie was there. There was an outpouring of affection for him. He had a room full of flowers from well-wishers and Maggie really stayed glued to him. I thought that was wonderful. Maybe this was what he needed to realize what he had in her. I believe whatever she had done with me had been prompted by him, and that made it difficult to look her in the eye. There were a few times I could feel her eyes examining me; other than that, she never gave a hint that it ever crossed her mind.

It wasn't chickens coming home to roost, as I had expected—it was just the opposite. Mr. Howard was shot protecting the girls of his drill team. Three young punks came in and began harassing the girls. Mr. Howard was throwing them out when one pulled a gun and shot him. He was lucky to be alive.

When he returned home, we started to hang out again. I put him in the category of an older brother. I was never invited to hang with my elder brothers, so I responded by ostracizing them as well. My mother said to stay away from drugs, so I used that to justify not including my elder brothers in my life—which may have been their reason too.

I heard Mr. Howard indulged, which would explain a lot, like why the girls were so available and why they kept their mouths shut. That's all speculation because if he did, he kept it from me. I was ignorant to it and wouldn't have known unless he was smoking right in front of my face.

Leslie's birthday was coming up and she was dying to get married. It was going to be difficult raising a family on a meter reader's salary, so I asked her to wait until I got promoted. As fate would have it, I got promoted during the month of her eighteenth birthday and we set the date for a month later. When I told my mother, she said we were too young and if we really loved each other there was no rush. I knew the speech. She had given it to Leon and Resa before. If Mom warned us of something it was usually for good reason, but this time I was going to show her that she didn't know everything.

When Leslie and I met for the first time, she was fourteen and I was eighteen. She was an only child and before any talk of sex or love, I was more like a big brother to her. Over four years our relationship evolved into something greater. Paulette was doing well at TCU and through conversations with her I could tell she was maturing. Getting away from the family had been a positive thing in her growth. In her own way, Leslie would have to spread her wings too, and I didn't want to prevent that. The kind of growth I wanted for my own sister I wanted for my wife, but I didn't want her to outgrow me as Paulette had done Will.

Speaking of Will, the doctors would not release him for the wedding, so I had to choose another best man. With five brothers, that should have been an easy decision, but I held some resentment for almost all of them, Leon for running away and leaving, and Riley and Ambus for just forgetting I existed. Madison I held no resentment for, but we weren't that close. For Adrian, I probably held the most resentment. He was my last chance to have the older brother every little brother dreams of. It started off great with us wrestling on Sunday mornings after church, but he started the drug thing and we drifted apart. I wanted him to be more like Dale. Blinded by that resentment, I chose Mr. Howard to be my best man. Adrian would have understood my choosing Will, but not Mr. Howard. He never said anything to me and I didn't think he cared, so I never tried explaining. Only through my mother did I later know that he was disappointed.

Leslie didn't mind my bringing my English Bulldog to the ceremony, as long as he was wearing a tuxedo. The accomplished tailor he was, Mr. Howard made a tux for the dog to match mine and his. My only excuse, we were young, dumb, and having fun.

Leslie and I exchanged vows in the rose garden of Hermann

Park. The whole family embraced her like a sister. My mother didn't have much faith in the marriage, but she treated Leslie as if she were one of her own. Leslie returned that affection by having great respect for my mother. We knew we were very young, but I thought I could compensate for that. College was never for Leslie; instead she wanted to participate in beauty pageants. That led to modeling bathing suits for a girlfriend who owned her own store. I could tell that was a serious boost to her self-esteem. I gave her as much support as she needed. I never tried controlling her in those ways, but I had others.

We moved into an apartment on the southwest side of town. It was in a nice neighborhood and only a couple of miles from my new job in my new department. Unlike meter reading, I could retire in that department, but I took evening college courses anyway. Leslie was a secretary at an insurance company downtown and we enjoyed our independence. We wanted to put off having children until I got my degree. What I was doing wasn't considered skilled labor and there was also the phobia about my speech. Daddy Jerome would have called getting my degree, "improving my hand."

One of my co-workers stuttered worse than I did. Meeting him would be significant in how I viewed Hotshot. I had never before worked with anyone who stuttered, but James was the most respected person in our group of eight. He didn't eat red meat or pork and didn't profess to be of any religion. He was his own man and never caved under pressure, even when management was around. He spoke up every time he disagreed, stuttering all the way through it, but no one dared finish one of his thoughts or even snicker. Everyone, black and white, respected him because he stood up for what was ethical, and that had nothing to do with the color of his skin. He was wise and turned me on to Malcolm X and Medgar Evers. If we had been in a prison, he would have been the cell block philosopher.

He was almost ten years older than I was, but he was in excellent shape. Our competitiveness had more ferocity than Dale's and mine had. One day we played racquetball, played basketball, and bowled—all within a six-hour span. Being around James made me realize that it was what I said, not how I said it, that gained respect. James was the sharpest brother I knew.

He had a bachelor's degree in business and served in the Army, but our job only required a high school diploma. We took meters in and out; that's what we did all day. It was the most likely step up from meter reading. When I asked him why he wasn't moving up and utilizing his degree, he fed me some bull about not wanting to be a house-Negro. The true answer was because he could retire there and his impediment wouldn't get in the way.

Psychologically, we were in the same place when it came to our speech, but there was a difference. His speech impediment had been diagnosed as neurological; I thought mine was mostly psychological. As formidable a foe as Hotshot was, I felt fortunate. That was something I could possibly control, if not overcome. I don't think that was true for James.

Another difference between us was that I sought out opportunity to fail, instead of avoiding it. At the community college I had taken a few public speaking classes as part of my curriculum, so when our supervisor asked for one of us to give a brief presentation about an upcoming charity event, I volunteered. Standing at the front of the conference room while everyone piled in made my knees weak. I cursed myself for being so masochistic.

I began addressing the audience of twenty or so, and when I felt an episode coming on, I did the word replacement game to avoid stammering. About ten minutes into the presentation I started to feel my throat tighten. I tried dismissing it as the natural fear of speaking in front of crowds, but my little word substitution game started to fail and I was sounding more like Porky Pig. I wanted to run out of the room and find a corner to vomit in, but I stood there and continued.

When it was done I was relieved, but by not being able to say exactly what was in my head, I felt inadequate, insecure, and self-conscious. My mother had always told me that a real man held down a job, paid bills, took care of his children, and was a loving husband. I was doing most of that, but the conversion from mouse to man hadn't happened yet, so I sought that validation from the only person who I thought could bestow that honor; Leslie.

After two beauty pageants she decided it was too expensive and too much work. She stayed with modeling bathing suits and I didn't mind it so much, it was just that most of the gigs were in nightclubs. When I went with her I was shocked at the meat-market atmosphere. Forbidding her to do it was justifiable in my mind, but I would never invoke that kind of authority, for I knew the negative effects it would bring. It was something she loved doing, and as long as she was faithful and loving me, I swallowed my pride.

The manner in which I tried controlling her was pushing my point until she conceded, whatever that point may have been. Before going to bed, sometimes she expressed sorrow for not knowing her father. Her mother and grandmother never pressed the issue with the boy that got her pregnant—probably because they weren't exactly sure if he was the one. I didn't see what the big deal was. After Daddy Jerome and getting to know my own father, I'd learned that having one wasn't all it was cracked up to be, and I told her that. Then she reminded me that at least I had that choice. She was right.

I wasn't able to help her with her father, but I was very attentive to most of her other needs. With our pristine credit, I surprised her with a new car. For birthdays she got diamonds and fur—which wasn't that difficult, since we didn't have children. I paid the bills and we shared the cooking duties. I wanted her to know beyond a shadow of a doubt that she could depend on me.

Leslie, on the other hand, had always been reserved with her emotions. She got my car pinstriped and bought me another dog when Hammer died. That meant a lot to me, but her greatest outpouring of affection came when we made love. Other than that, she wasn't very affectionate. We laughed, talked, and joked around, but her well didn't run as deep for me as mine did for her. However, getting her to love me more was just a matter of letting her know how deep my well actually ran. I'd move mountains to let her know just how deep that was.

One night after a conversation about her father, I figured he had to pay a utility bill so I got one of the ladies at the front desk to pull his name, and it came up. His address wasn't even a mile away from our apartment. I really wasn't sure what to do with the information. How was he going to respond to the invitation of getting to know his daughter? For a couple of days, I made a few drive-bys through his affluent neighborhood before deciding to stop.

When I knocked on the door, a fair-skinned, good-looking gentleman in his mid-forties answered. I asked if he was Michael and he told me yes. I could hear his wife and children roaming about in the house and I motioned for him to come out. He never questioned who I was or why I was there. He just stepped out and closed the door behind him.

I asked if he remembered Betty from the Fifth Ward. After a moment of pondering, he cautiously admitted to knowing her. To put him at ease, I explained that I was his daughter's husband and all her needs were being met; I just wanted to know if he was interested in talking or hopefully meeting her. He agreed without a moment of thought, as if it was something on his to-do list and he just hadn't gotten around to it.

I got home first and could hardly contain my emotions when she walked in. Her eyes glazed over when I told her what had happened and that he would call her around eight.

She didn't take a shower, as she usually did when she came home, or even think about dinner. On the sofa she lay against me, chewing her lip and wringing her hands for more than an hour, waiting for his call. When the phone rang she was as frightened as she was relieved. She answered it and this huge smile formed on her face, as one did on mine. To give her complete privacy I went to walk the dog. I felt as if I had finally done it. This was the thing I needed to show her how much I loved her, and now the floodgates would open and the void between us would be filled.

When I returned, she was sitting on the sofa. By the tracks of her tears, I could see it had been a pretty emotional reunion; then I realized her tears weren't from joy. He'd told her that he was happy to know that she was doing fine, but he was unable to have a relationship with her because his wife would never allow it. *That punk ass mutherfucker.* I couldn't believe it.

She cried herself to bed that night, and I felt I had done her more harm than good.

Outraged and disgusted, I went to his home the next day. His wife answered the door. She acted as if she knew who I was. Then he came out and begged me to go away and not to return. He had other children, who knew nothing about Leslie. I told him again that she needed nothing from him but a call once in a while, even if it was just on her birthday, but he insisted that I leave his property and forget about the two of them having any contact. With that, he went back into his nice home and closed the door.

I could feel Leslie gradually slipping away from me; the first sign was when we stopped talking. I had explored and experienced a lot in my twenty-four years. I was extremely independent and did pretty much what I wanted. For Leslie, I was her only reference, and in more areas than sex. She needed to know how much of her thoughts were her own and how much were implanted. She was also curious about other men. It was never spoken, but it was a natural reaction for her to have. Also, our worlds at work were very different. She worked in an office environment and the men around her wore nice suits and cologne. After a day in the field I came home sweaty and when I jumped out of the shower, I was off to school. She stopped talking about her day and didn't really listen to mine when I told her.

It wasn't so much about me; it was simply her need to know her self-worth. She couldn't tell me she wanted to experience life without me, or that I was such an overwhelming presence that she could hardly have a thought that wasn't associated with me. And now I had even invaded into her thoughts of her father.

Making love dwindled to once a week, if that, and for her, even that was becoming a chore. Our relationship started to change into something unrecognizable. We argued about my obsession to control her thinking and her buying things we couldn't afford. Checks started to bounce, and the minimum payments on our credit cards were becoming difficult to make. The tension between us would last for days, but not being desired is what tore at me the worst.

This made her modeling more difficult to handle. I saw how the men responded to her and I was as desperate to have her as they were. When I told her how I felt, she was usually unresponsive, which only served to make me angrier. I started getting into her face, hoping that my rage would trigger something to let her know that our relationship was breaking down and that if we didn't begin to communicate soon; we were going to regret it. She would sit quietly and tune me out. Nothing I said could get through.

Our arguments started to become more violent, mostly because of my screaming and cursing. She responded the way she always did, which only added fuel to the fire. To keep it from escalating I went to Jo's apartment to stay there for the night. Jo listened, but offered little advice. I didn't want to go to my mother, because she had never wanted me to marry Leslie in the first place. I could have talked to one of my brothers, but none of them had ever really taught me anything. Adrian was four years older, Ambus was at least six years older, and Leon was almost ten years older; none of them had taught me how to drive, play ball, or what my first time would be like. What I didn't learn by trial and error I learned from my mother or my sisters.

Jo and Paulette were the most open-minded, but neither had ever been married. Resa did meet a good-looking man and was so smitten she married him after a few weeks. Mom told her that he was no good and begged her not to marry him, but she did just as Leon and I had done and got married anyway. Twelve weeks later he called her at work and said that the police were after him and he was moving to Dallas. He never told her why the police were chasing him just that she should walk off her job and go with him. She told him no, and when she got home all his belongings were gone. The marriage was annulled and the experience deeply wounded her. She moved back home and never forgot that our mother had been right about him.

Resa would never leave the safety of that nest again. She never remarried, and the few relationships she had were never serious. Like our mother, she had given up on men—and these were the two people I was seeking marital advice from.

Resa believed that a woman's body was her own and if she said no, then that's exactly what it meant. It was that simple. When she was done, I felt as if my knuckles should have been dragging the ground to expect sex when my wife didn't feel like it. I had no say-so in the matter.

My mother was a little gentler when she said, "I know how you feel, baby, but A.J. forced me into sex and I didn't like that." I understood what they were saying and it sounded right, but I felt like there was more to it than that, so I sought out a man's opinion. When I spoke to Adrian he said that was what porn was for.

One day on my route I saw my old girlfriend Tess in an

apartment complex I was working in. We were surprised and happy to see one another. She was living there with her son and her mother. She invited me in and we sat on the sofa and looked at our high school yearbook. We laughed at the afro I was sporting and I joked that I must have had the very last one. She got around to asking me why we broke up. That was a good question, because I couldn't remember anymore. She was a great girlfriend and was never stingy when it came to showing me affection.

By her smile and the way she made an effort to be close, nothing had changed, either. She was still holding something for me, and I was holding more than a week's worth of testosterone. I asked about her mother and we continued to make small talk. My loins told me to grab her and grab her quickly, before she changed her mind, but maybe this was just another test of faith. She scooted closer to me and the smell of her freshly bathed body aroused me. The tie on her turquoise silk robe was barely clasped. If I were to slip my hand inside of her robe, what would she do? Honestly, I did want to be with her and she wanted me to. It had been a long time since someone lusted for me and it felt good, like I was being validated again.

That stamp of validation needed to come from Leslie, though, so I told her I had to go back to work and walked over to the door. She knew I was married and with a soft peck on the lips, she let me know she didn't mind—at least, I hoped that's what she meant. I kissed her in the corner of her mouth to insinuate that I was just taking a rain check and not turning her down.

After her modeling gigs, Leslie would take a shower and climb into bed. Usually by the time I got out of the shower she was pretending to be asleep. I would remain awake for hours, staring at the ceiling, wondering where her rights began and where mine ended. It started taking me longer to get to sleep, and listening to her snore only served to annoy me further.

I started to have stomach pains that only half a bottle of antacid could stop. I found out it was an ulcer. That evening after dinner, I told her I was at the end of my rope and we couldn't go on as we were. She responded as she always did, saying she didn't know what to do or how to fix it, then having nothing else to say. I acted no differently, screaming and shouting, trying to get her to understand the severity of it. When the verbal abuse began, she went into the living room to get away from me.

"Whatha fuck is your problem," I said, following her. "I'm tired of dealing with this shit, Leslie!"

She turned and responded, "I'm tired of this shit too! And maybe the problem is I'm just not happy with you, Gary!"

I was stunned by her confession, and as she crumbled toward the floor, I could see in her wild eyes that she hadn't grasped it yet either, that I had slapped her. Inside of me there was this overwhelming sense of empowerment. It was like holding a gun for the first time. At that moment she was poised to hang on my every word. Now I had her undivided attention, something I hadn't had from her in a very long time, but it came at a heavy price.

My mother was afraid of A.J. and I didn't want that fear for Leslie, so I went to her. She allowed me to help her to her feet. I kissed her wet face and promised not to ever lay another hand on her.

By morning there was no physical evidence that it had ever happened, but I doted on her, hand and foot, trying to make up for it. That was impossible. With a single strike, I had wiped out every good thing I had ever done.

Sometimes just to get away, I visited Will. He had recovered enough to get his own place and enroll in art school. He tried carrying on with his life as if nothing had changed, but he would have seizures during class, on the bus, and quite often right in the middle of one of our conversations. After it passed, whatever had been said prior to that was pretty much lost.

One evening when I went to see him he had a bandage on his arm. When I asked what happened, he proudly unwrapped it like a war wound and exposed a third-degree burn so severe it left a deep crevice.

Looking at the pinkish cleft, I asked squeamishly, "How did that happen?"

The question appeared humorous to him; he wasn't all that sure himself. Putting events together as if it were the first time he'd thought about it, he said he'd been cooking and must've had a seizure. When he came to, eggs were on the floor and grease was splattered across his arm. I'd thought living alone agreed with him until I saw that burn; now I wasn't so sure.

Will wasn't listening to that. Going back to the nursing home was no option for him, and I wasn't in any position to argue. Leslie and I were having problems, and Will moving in with us would only make things worse.

He liked showing off his artwork and gave me a self-portrait he painted in class. He showed me sketches, and I pretended to be impressed when I was really choking on a heavy dose of reality. He wasn't going to be a famous artist and I wasn't going to be a ball player.

We were only twenty-five and I wanted to ask him how things had gotten so bad for us. He was on disability and suffering with seizures; I was dealing with an ulcer and barely able to hold my marriage together. Nothing was turning out as we'd expected. Like one of his paintings, we needed to start over on a fresh, clean canvas.

I had always joked that I might go to the Marines because that always struck a chord with my mother. She thought the military had changed her sons for the worse. Leon was in and out of the brig. Her smart, well-mannered son Ambus came back a dope smoker and hating the world. When Madison came out of the service he also came out of the closet. The Marines were the worst of them all, she would say. They were crazy and that was no place for a black man. It sounded funny her saying that, with her straight hair and pale face. She was also a woman; how could she have any idea what I was dealing with?

But I still held great respect for her opinion, so when I confessed that I had hit Leslie, her cold stare filled me with shame. She was disappointed because she expected more out of me—probably more than all her sons, now. Over the past year she'd watched me change, and neither of us liked who I was becoming. And I couldn't hide behind the veil of immaturity, either. Leslie and I needed a fresh start and Uncle Sam could foot the bill, plus I could still go to college. Going into the Marines started to sound like a good idea.

I spoke to Leslie about my idea to enlist and she agreed that it might be just what we needed to get back on track. I spoke to a recruiter at the nearby mall. I wasn't interested in being a grunt; he knew my interest was mainly for the college benefits. After taking a few tests, he told me I qualified to sit behind a computer for my four years, as a purchasing clerk. Having been a grunt once himself, he bragged that during wartime, all Marines are expected to be infantrymen, if needed. We hadn't had a war in twenty years so that didn't bother me. I was just inquiring, anyway. It was just an idea.

At home we were going round and round, like one of my conversations with Will. The cycle of screaming and shouting persisted. I spent many nights on my sister's sofa and when it was just too embarrassing, I got a room at a motel. Leslie was not even sexually attracted to me anymore, and that was a hard pill to swallow. I thought we would always have that. From the few attempts at intimacy we did have, I knew by her lifeless touch that she had already thrown in the towel. The responsibility of our making it or not, fell squarely on my shoulders. The pressure wore another hole in the lining of my stomach and I got another ulcer.

This time I admitted myself into the hospital and after probing a camera up my butt, the doctor came into the room. "Gary, your stomach looks like World War Two," was his exact words. I thought he was joking, but he wasn't. Then he added, "You're too young, Gary. Whatever is ailing you, you're going to have to get rid of it."

"I know doc, I know," I said, pacifying him.

"The next step is to have bleeding ulcers, and believe me, you don't want that."

The doctor confirmed what I already knew. The thought of bleeding ulcers frightened me as much as the thought of losing Leslie. It was time to do something, for my marriage and for my health, so I asked Leslie again if the idea of enlisting still appealed to her. She never told me to enlist; she always said, "I think it's a good idea." She answered most of my questions like that. I reminded her that once I enlisted, it couldn't be undone; we were going to have to live with it for the next four years. She responded, "It'll make us or break us, won't it?" And I surely couldn't argue with that.

Leslie had her doubts, but she looked forward to leaving Houston and starting over. We hardly left the state and had never really been away from our families. The thought of it rejuvenated our relationship. I felt hope for us, for we had a future again. She felt it too. She was initiating sex, and it felt wonderful to see her passionate, to feel me again.

I kept my ulcer a secret from the Marines while I waited for my day to leave. It was reason to be rejected and I did not want that. I put my job on notice and told Will my plans. He didn't understand why I had to go. It was too complex to go into, so I explained it as if it was one of those macho things I had to do. He accepted the news as if I had said I was going up to Austin for the weekend.

I longed to know what the Will who knew me since I was thirteen would say. Would he tell me I was crazy and try to talk me out of it? Would he tell me Leslie wasn't worth it and to let her go? It wasn't as if I was enlisting right out of high school. I was twenty-six, with a well paying job with a solid company. The military would be a cut in pay and I would be leaving the support of my family.

For those reasons, I put off telling my mother, because I knew she was going to tell me that I was throwing away a bright future and making a mistake. She feared that the military would change her baby boy, as it had her other sons, but I was changing anyway—and not into something either of us was proud of.

Mom was in the kitchen when I walked into the apartment. I

asked if she would come into the living room because I had something to tell her. I knew my mother wasn't going to be happy with what I had to say, so I left Leslie at home. She took a seat on the sofa in front of me and I just went for the gusto. "Mom, I'm joining the Marines."

"Don't do it, Gary," she responded immediately. "That's not something you want to do. You see what they did to your oldest brother Leon . . . ."

"It's too late, Mom. I've already done it."

She was startled for a second, then became angry that I had made such a huge decision without at least consulting her. With venom she said, "That wife of yours is not going to wait on you. You know that, don't you?"

"We're looking forward to it, Mom," I said with a snicker to show her how ludicrous her remark was. "I'm leaving in about a month."

She ended the conversation by getting up and saying, "Well, that's that. You've already done it so I guess there's nothing else to talk about."

It was my life that was falling apart. This was no scrape or cut she could make feel better with a kiss or a bottle of sugar water. It was one of those man-or-mouse decisions, and my mother could offer me nothing in the way of advice.

When I got back home, Leslie opened the door before I could take out my keys. I went straight into telling her how it had gone, but left out the part about Mom saying that my wife wasn't going to be there for me. Leslie didn't make a remark and that's when I noticed the somber look on her face, as if she had something horrible to tell me.

"What's wrong?"

"Will. His sister called. He died."

Will had suffered a seizure during his sleep. The neighbors complained about the smell coming from his apartment and the maintenance man went in to investigate and found him dead in his bedroom. It was a hot Houston summer; he had been dead for about a week.

I drove to his apartment and the door was locked, but the windows were open to air out the apartment. I climbed in and the pungent odor of a decaying corpse forced me to clasp my hand over my nose and mouth. I then removed it. It was Will, my best friend.

In the bedroom, there was a dark brown stain on the wall, where his head would have been if he had fallen out of bed. In the bathroom, his toothbrush was still sitting on the sink next to his razor and a bar of soap. I returned to the living room and sat in the same seat I'd sat in a couple of weeks ago. I wanted to cry, but couldn't. A major part of our relationship had died a while back; I'd just been trying to nurture what was left of it.

I thought of us as teens and how he was the first to befriend me when I moved to the Fifth Ward. How he always took a knee with me, to pray after I scored a touchdown, and how he did a great imitation of the Eddie Murphy laugh. Also letting Leslie and me borrow his apartment before I had my own; that was where I proposed to her, too. And of course the time he slipped in the mud while we made our escape from the campus police at Texas Southern.

I had mixed emotions about being the sole caretaker of all those memories.

CHAPTER EIGHTEEN

MARINE

In San Diego the Marine Corps Recruit Depot sat in the valley, and the beautiful homes that were wedged in the green sloping hillside looked down on the base. It was such a contrast to the flatlands in East Texas. The air was cool in the morning, like a cold drink after a mint. It seemed like heaven compared to the Wards, but I rarely got the chance to enjoy it.

We had chow at four-thirty in the morning, had physical training until eleven, then took showers and had lunch. The next two or three hours were spent in class, then to the drill field for two more hours before going to dinner. At night we had mail call and though they fed us, my real source of nourishment was Leslie's letters. She wrote about how much she looked forward to our future and how much she starved for me. That was nice to hear because she hadn't in a long, long time and I was starving for her also. She sounded as if she really missed me, but the letters were short—sometimes a page, maybe—though I was grateful for that. We seldom had the privilege of a phone call so I was depending on those letters to keep me going. I read them over and over. Once my training was over we were going to have children and see the world together.

At night, lying in my rack, I could hear the whimpering. Most of the guys, including myself, questioned if we had made the right decision to enlist. I chose the Marines specifically because it was like killing two birds with one stone. It was going to fix my marriage and help me rid myself of Hotshot. Everything the Marines represented was the opposite of how I felt about myself, but the irony of it was that I was subjecting myself to the same level of abuse and ridicule that created Hotshot in the first place. And now that I think about it, my reason wasn't that different than my brother Madison's to join the Navy. We were both looking for some kind of exorcism from ourselves.

I was surprised at my performance in boot camp. I far exceeded my expectation and my speech didn't hinder me at all. The military was more results oriented and not as image conscious as the real world. I was a squad leader and after thirteen weeks of boot camp, I was promoted to private first class and awarded for being the highest marksman in my unit. I don't know where that skill came from, because if you remember, in college I was the worst shooter on the team. Becoming a Marine far exceeded anything I had ever done and was a major milestone in my life. With my mother and Leslie at my graduation, it was by far my proudest moment.

I had a ten-day leave before going to North Carolina for more training and Leslie seemed excited about our future. We walked through the rose garden where we had gotten married and even took a weekend trip to Ft. Lauderdale. Being with her hadn't felt that wonderful since the very first time we made love, except this time I didn't have to hold back. It was wonderful, but it would not last.

Halfway through my leave she started to become withdrawn again. When I wanted to meet her for lunch she always had something pressing to do, and when we were together she seemed preoccupied with her thoughts rather than our future. One afternoon when she did have time to meet me, we took a walk in the nearby park. That's when she told me she wanted a divorce.

I was stunned. The whole purpose of joining the military had been to keep that from happening. I reminded her that I'd quit my job and totally turned my life upside down. I said that our first week back together proved we still had a chance. She didn't look convinced. I thought all I needed was time and surely she would see that being apart would be a mistake.

My perception of the military at that moment began to change. Instead of helping my marriage and bringing us together, it was now keeping us apart.

When I pleaded for some explanation, she could only tell me that it just wasn't working between us. She wasn't even willing to give our new future a chance. By her stern conviction I knew there had to be someone else. She finally conceded that she had met someone, a businessman eleven years her senior. As if I were stupid, she said they were just friends and our divorce really had nothing to do with it. Ignoring that, I told her she could come to North Carolina with me; she didn't have to wait for my permanent duty station. I hadn't cleared that with the Marines yet, but I was going to worry about that later. She then told me casually, "I just don't think I love you anymore."

I had never put up any pretenses and I wasn't doing it that day either. As clear and as precise as any words I had ever spoken to her, I looked into those hazel eyes and supplicated, "Leslie, I love you. Please don't do this."

She responded with silence, her eyes frozen with contempt.

I turned around and walked away, hoping she wouldn't see the apathy I felt. I wondered how long she had known she wasn't coming with me. If I had detected the slightest hint of doubt, I would not have enlisted—she must have known that.

She tagged along behind me, trying to convince me that it was over between us. She spoke with a stinging certainty that cut deeper than her words. The more I heard it the tighter my fists clenched, hoping to expel the tension that was building inside them. She said more than she had ever said in any of our arguments. She was confident; as if there was no doubt that she was making the right decision. By the tone of her voice, she felt safe and secure, not only with her decision, but also with me.

There was nothing I could do. She knew I always followed through on my obligations, no matter what they were.

Standing behind me, she spat, "Besides, why do you want someone who don't want you?"

No matter how much I loved her, I was still holding the pride, jealousy, and anger of a man scorned. I swung around and slapped her across the left side of her face. The force ripped her from her pumps, leaving one of them stuck in the dirt, as she stumbled backward and down to the ground.

Watching her sprawled in the mud, I didn't feel the same level of regret that I'd felt the first time I hit her. Still burning from the contact, I offered her my hand. Crying, she pushed it away, but I helped her to her feet anyway.

Now she finally had what she needed, justification. I had given it to her on a silver platter.

I had a couple of days left before I had to catch a plane to California, then another to North Carolina for six more months of training. I'm not sure how he found out about what was going on with Leslie and me, but Mr. Howard called and invited me over. He seemed more empathetic, probably because he and Maggie had gotten divorced. Sitting on his sofa, he offered me a drink and I asked for a glass of water. He asked what was going on. A few tears fell as I told him about Leslie and he handed me a tissue. It was so embarrassing, but he listened and seemed to have genuine concern as he scooted a little closer and said, "Gary, I love you." It sounded perfidious, and it wasn't because he was bisexual; it was because he knew I was not. "Gary, I can't make all your problems go away, but I can make you forget them for a little while."

"I'm cool," I told him, hoping he would leave it at that.

He scooted even closer. "I have something that will relax you and I can make you feel better. All you have to do is just sit back and relax."

Slouched on his sofa, with my face toward the ceiling, I didn't have to look at him to see what he meant by that. I knew what he was trying to tell me.

At that moment I really needed a friend to talk to. He was the closet thing I had to Will, and after all, he had been my best man. But all he wanted to do was persuade me into some kind of sexual act. I excused myself to go down to the convenience store for a grape soda, something I knew he didn't have in his refrigerator, and I never came back.

My mother was sick with worry. She thought I was going to do something crazy and I wasn't too sure I wasn't. All kinds of things ran through my mind, from murder to suicide. As far as the military went, it was the last thing on my mind. I wanted to stay home and work on my marriage.

The day before I was to leave, Mom came into the living room where I was sitting in the dark. She turned the light on and sat next to me. The scene looked familiar, but the person was usually one of my sisters. Mom told me that all I needed to do was get up the next morning, and with each day the hurt would go away.

She asked, "You know what you'll be left with once this crisis is over?" I didn't respond. "Your actions. Don't forget that, young man." Who knew that better than she? After dispensing that advice, she asked what time my flight was. She wanted to make sure I was not planning to go AWOL. I must not have responded soon enough because her voice began to tremble. "Baby, don't mess up your life over some stupid little girl. I know you're hurting, but this will pass."

Without making me speak, she left.

Mom was an expert on heartache. No matter how bad she was hurting she got up every morning and did what was needed. Now I knew the kind of strength that took.

I got a flight the next day to North Carolina, where I was to undergo more training. I made sure not to stand out, as I had in boot camp, but just fade into the background as much as I could. During the week I spent most of my day in training classes, and on the weekends I took the five-mile walk to the mall in town, just to turn around and walk back. A time or two I contemplated "accidentally" jumping in front of a passing car. The idea was to get injured just enough to get sent home, but I couldn't get past the possibility that I could get maimed in the process. If Leslie didn't want me the way I was, how was she going to love me if I was any less? This idea lasted as long as it took for the car to pass.

The walks took chunks out of the day; the rest I filled with an obsession for running and lifting weights. Food was plentiful, but I resorted to only eating one meal a day and getting up at five in the morning for a five-mile run, whether it was with my unit or not. It was just something to do to occupy my mind.

One night the duty officer called me to the phone and it was Leslie. She had been so cold towards me I didn't understand why she was calling, so I asked.

"I'm just calling to see how you are doing," she said with attitude, indicating that she didn't want to get into a discussion about our break-up. We spoke about twenty minutes, and before hanging up she said, "I still love you, Gary." And I still wanted to believe that.

She called me two or three times a week, for months, and had not yet mailed me the divorce papers. She shied away from conversation about reconciling, so I still didn't understand why she was calling. I clung to the hope that if she was still calling then there was still something left between us.

As graduation grew closer, so did our anniversary. I called her that morning. Houston was an hour behind, so when she answered it was seven o'clock in the morning.

"I just called to say happy anniversary. I know it's not very happy, but I wanted to tell you that anyway."

There was silence for a moment, then in a surrendering breath she said, "I had sex with Kevin."

Hearing that from her mouth on our wedding anniversary was incomprehensible. I was stunned by her heartless confession. She said it as if she had relieved herself of a heavy weight. That was the final insult and she knew me well enough to know that, but she never considered the longevity of her words.

I hung up the phone without saying another word, my mind racing, my heart pounding, and my stomach on fire. It was a natural impulse to reject what I'd heard, so I did physically what I couldn't do mentally, I began vomiting. Once my stomach emptied, I dry-heaved until my throat was raw.

Shackled to my commitment, I wiped my tears and dragged myself into the training class thirty minutes late. The usual punishment was three pushups for every minute you're late, but the instructor didn't say a thing.

The divorce rate for the Marines is the highest of any branch of the service, so they knew who was married and who wasn't. We also lived together and worked together, so it wasn't difficult to figure out that I was having marital problems. One of the sergeants had taken me to the enlisted men's club to try and cheer me up. I didn't drink at the time, so after four or five beers, instead of cheering me up, he ended up depressed from being away from his own girl. By the end of the night I was helping him back to his barracks.

I moseyed through each day until the final day of training, when we learned where we would be stationed for the next couple of years. I was assigned to an infantry unit that was normally stationed in California, but was in Saudi Arabia at the time, patrolling the borders of Kuwait. The likelihood of my joining them there was very good.

I was home on leave for a few days when Leslie called and asked if I would sign the divorce papers. I had no objections and met her at the notary to do so. I was not trying to talk her out of it anymore, but asked her only one question. "Are you sure you want to do this?" She took a deep breath as if she wasn't sure, then nodded yes. I signed them with only one stipulation that she was not to be allowed to use my name anymore. She was surprised that I would ask for that; it seemed trivial to her. We parted with barely a hug.

I figured I was not going to hear from her again, but she called once more. She said there were things of mine at her apartment and she wanted me to come and get them. She answered the door in a big shirt, no bra, and some shorts.

"There's a box in the closet," she said, locking the front door. I followed her to the bedroom and she climbed back into bed and continued watching television. I grabbed the box and carried it to the center of the living room, when I heard her say from the bedroom, "Let's talk."

She turned the television off with the remote and asked how my training was coming. We talked about that, then she said, "I still love you, Gary. You probably don't believe that, but I do."

I wanted to believe that. I leaned over to kiss her, hoping she wouldn't reject me, and she met me halfway. In a matter of seconds our clothes were off and she was receptive to my slightest touch. I was going to be shipped to the Persian Gulf and neither one of us knew what that meant. Never seeing each other again was a real possibility. We surrendered to the kind of thirst we had for one another when we were dating. It was easy getting lost in the moment.

"Did you miss me?" she asked.

Before I could answer, the telephone rang, severing our last intimate moment like fingernails on a chalkboard. We both froze at the sound of it, and she knew exactly what I was thinking. By the second ring we both went for the phone; I got there first.

"Hello!" I said, hoping whoever it was would notice that there couldn't have been a more inopportune time to call.

There was a long silence, then a hesitant man's voice asked, "Is Leslie there?"

"Yeah, she's here, but we're making love—"

"No, we're not, Kevin!" she screamed. "No, we're not!"

I slammed the phone down in total dismay. I couldn't believe she was disclaiming our intimacy. With my mental and emotional state, her callousness surprised me. Looking at her, she resembled the person that I thought I knew once, but her actions were so different—even her words were not words she had used before. I put on my clothes to leave, but even if it was just for a fleeting moment, I wanted her to know the pain I was feeling. Squeezing the last breath out of her became the only thing worth living for.

I didn't want her to be confused about my intentions, so I snatched her from the bed and threw her against the wall, with my hands tightly clasped around her neck. I could feel her bare feet kicking my shins. She tried screaming for help, so I tightened my grip around her neck until her primary concern was breathing. She squirmed like a helpless child, and the harder she fought the tighter I squeezed. I squeezed as long as it took for her to stop fighting, and I still held on a few seconds longer to ensure that she knew that her final minutes on this earth had arrived.

When I let go, she crumbled to the floor and grabbed her throat. My anger was still there—so was the desire to kill her—but I loved her too much to destroy her life. All I had left were feeble threats. She must have known that, because she didn't take off running. She stayed there and just begged for me to let her go.

"I'm not holding you, Leslie," I replied, and as I went to grab the box of my belongings there was a knock at the door. It was the police. It was quite obvious that she had been roughed up. Immediately the policeman closest to me pulled out his cuffs; the other asked her if I had hit her. Before she could answer, I admitted to it.

I turned around and he started to cuff me. I had never been cuffed before in my life—that was something I took pride in—but I figured it was worth it.

She intervened. "No! I don't want him to go to jail."

I was grateful but refused to let her see that. In only a few months my life had drastically changed. I wondered if she grasped the gravity of that.

Biting on her red nails, she stared at me with uncertainty when I stooped down to pick up my belongings. I went to hug her goodbye, but one of the officers stopped me and she intervened once again. We had spent almost nine years growing up together. We held each other tight for about twenty seconds while she cried and I promised myself that the tear coming down my face would be the last. With my belongings, the police escorted me to my car and waited until I drove away.

Leslie was still in my system and I longed for her like an addict. I saw the Gulf War as an inconvenience, like court-ordered rehabilitation, and I was about to go cold turkey. There would be no weekend visits, no phone calls, no chance encounters, no updates from acquaintances, and no way of knowing if she was happy or sad. She was being amputated from my life, and that scared me more than going to war.

The only reference I had of war was Vietnam and the black and white clips of wounded soldiers being carted off on stretchers to helicopters. Vietnam had been so disgraceful to the country's image that I thought we would never enter another conflict like it. I was mistaken.

Though I was totally unaware of it at the time, all this was taking a toll on my mother as well. At the airport, before I boarded the plane we hugged tightly. Watching Leon self-destruct was hard enough, but he had been on that course since he was about thirteen. I had always played it safe by finishing high school, keeping a steady job, and going to college. The only real risk I ever took was going to see Metra when she lived in the projects. Going through a divorce and going to war was more than my mother thought I could handle, so she spoke softly, as if I might crack.

"Be careful, baby. Don't try to be no hero."

When we hugged it became apparent that she was not going to let go anytime soon, so I did. Her trembling lips tried saying goodbye, but her tears would not allow it, so she settled for just staring at me. Her eyes told me that she wished that chasing my demons away was just a matter of showing me there was nothing underneath my bed. I flashed a smile that was supposed to comfort her, but I don't think it did.

We both thought that becoming a man just happens, like growing facial hair and turning eighteen, but it had nothing to do with either. Being a man is a state of mind and without either of us realizing it, somewhere, somehow the conversion from mouse to man had occurred.

PART IV

CHAPTER NINETEEN
SUPPLY GUY

In the dark of night, we were flown into a Saudi Arabian airport. We were loaded on buses and taken to a military base. It was about two in the morning when we got there; most of the camp was asleep except the armed guards patrolling the gates. We were taken to an office, where I was asked several questions about my next of kin, marital status, and dependents. After being processed we were separated into groups. That night, ten or fifteen of us were taken to a small barracks to get some sleep. The sun was going to rise in a couple of hours so I didn't try to sleep, but I must have, because some happy Marine woke me by tugging on my boot.

"PFC Braxton?"

"Yeah," I said, rising from the top bunk.

"I'm Lance Corporal Miller. I'm with the Third Light Armed Infantry Battalion. Come with me."

My host immediately dispensed with the formalities and told me to just call him Kenny. You were supposed to always address another Marine by his rank or last name. Still brainwashed from boot camp, I chose to call him Miller. He was from Riverside, California and liked to talk. He told me not to expect to see any women—they were all on the other side of the camp and most of them were already hooked up with some other jarhead. He pointed at the tents where I would go to get hot food and the basic aid station where I could get medical attention. After the tour, he brought me to a tent full of guys sitting behind laptops. Miller left me there and I stood in line until one of the Marines called me over.

He typed while I answered the same personal questions I'd answered earlier that morning. I was also asked if I had made out a living will and if I hadn't he would have done one right there for me. He asked who my beneficiary was in case I died; even when I was not thinking about Leslie, things like that brought her to mind.

My smiling host returned just as I finished signing and initialing what they told me to. He must've had it timed right down to the minute. He took me to a group of tents that he called home. They were positioned so there would only be one way in or out of the compound. He warned me we were standing outside the officer's tent then yelled out, "Sir, Lance Corporal Miller reporting with PFC Braxton!"

"Come in," a voice yelled.

He pushed back the flap and we stepped in and stood at attention. "Captain, this is our new supply guy, PFC Braxton."

The skinny captain closed his book, got up from his cot, and came over. He told us to stand at ease and asked how long I had been in.

"About nine months. I just got out of supply training, sir."

"You know where the chow hall is?"

"Yes, sir."

"Get some breakfast and report back to me in half an hour." He looked at Miller as if I didn't understand English and said, "Take PFC Braxton to the chow hall for breakfast and bring him back here."

Miller was entertaining; he ran his mouth nonstop. All I had to do was say "ah hah" and he kept right on talking. Usually it was about his on-again, off-again relationship with his girlfriend. He was missing her bad and cherished every letter she wrote him. He was about twenty-

234

one and still had a year left in the Corps. I envied him for that. He asked if I had a girlfriend. I told him no and we left it at that.

The tent was filled with rows of picnic tables and Marines eating breakfast. We sat down with our trays and he ate like a madman, leaving food in the corners of his mouth. By the time we got back to our makeshift home of tents there were about forty Marines in a single-file line, blocking the entrance. Their clothes were dusty and their faces were layered in dirt. It appeared to have been weeks since they had bathed or had hot food.

"That's Bravo Company. They've come back from the front. They'll be here for a week to get some R&R, then they'll go back out to the front."

We squeezed through and the captain was waiting for me behind a desk that looked more like a card table. While looking over my personal file and drinking a hot cup of coffee, he made mention of my high rifle score and my age.

"You're twenty-six, PFC." Sergeants and corporals were twenty-six, and that was two or three ranks above me. A private first class my age had been busted down a few times or enlisted late. He didn't see any court-martials so he concluded, "I guess it took you a while to make up your mind, huh PFC?"

Whether that was a question or a joke, I wasn't sure, and I wasn't exactly in the mood anyway, so I remained silent. There was a commotion behind me like horseplay—he looked over my shoulder to see what it was. The grunts of Bravo Company were hassling a smaller guy as he tried entering our compound. He was covered in dust like they were and when they finally allowed him in; he pulled off his helmet and goggles, exposing his blond hair and pale face. He was a chubby, frail, white guy who stood about five foot four. By the expression on the captain's face, he didn't like how the grunts were disrespecting one of his men, but I think he thought it was more dignified to let him fight his own battles.

"That's Corporal Sampy," he said, getting my attention again. "He's the supply guy for Bravo Company. He's attached to them to make sure they get everything they need. They're back for a little rest and relaxation. You'll be taking Sampy's place when they return to the front."

He stared at me as if he expected some reaction, so I just said, "Yes, sir."

"Go help Sampy and introduce yourself to Gunny Hawk."

Before Corporal Sampy could get a badly needed bath, he had to replace torn long johns, lost canteens, worn-out boots, and anything else they needed.

As I helped replace gear for over forty men that day only two names stayed with me, Gunny Hawk and Sergeant Connors. Connnors was a white guy, kind of soft-spoken, but his men listened intently when he gave an order. Everyone tried to get something extra, maybe two canteens instead of one, an extra pack to carry contraband, or an extra pair of boots. Everyone except Connors, all he asked for was a crewman's overalls, large. His were tattered and torn, but he waited until all his men had gotten theirs before getting his own. By then we were out of his size.

Gunny Hawk reminded me of my eldest brother, Leon. They were about the same age, the same size, the same skin tone, and the same sense of humor. He asked me for a case of heat tabs. Unknown to me, these were a luxury because they were used to heat water for coffee and warm the MREs (Meals-Ready-To-Eat). The prepackaged meals the guys carried around in the cargo pockets of their fatigues. I lifted the case of heat tabs and set it on the counter, when the captain came over and stopped me.

"You know better than that, Gunny Hawk. You get the same amount of heat tabs as Alpha, Charlie, and Delta Companies."

The Gunny looked at me and said, "No hard feelings, PFC," and laughed it off as if the attempt to get more had been worth the try.

The captain pulled me aside and told me that everyone was going to try to be my friend; the officers might even try intimidation to get whatever they wanted. It was my job to make sure every Marine had what they needed, nothing more and nothing less—including officers. Then he sent me back to the counter.

Gunny asked if I was married or had a girlfriend back home. *Damn!* That was the second time I was asked that, and it wasn't even ten in the morning yet. I was going to have to get used to being asked that question. It must have been a measuring stick of some kind that had more insight into my character than race or religion. The second-most-asked question was how long I had left in the Corps. When they found out I was fresh out of training, they chuckled. No Marine was more envied than a short-timer with a woman waiting for him. I had neither.

I told him I was divorced, as if it were of no consequence. He didn't make an immediate comment, which made me feel that he saw straight through me. The Gunny enlisted when he was a teen and still had that mischievous nature about him. What he knew about being a man, he learned from the Corps. He lived hard and played just as hard and never took anything too serious—except his family. He knew that a divorce without consequence did not exist. Having a woman meant everything to him and second to her was God.

The week waiting for Bravo Company to leave, I worked like a slave. But that kept my mind occupied and I didn't have time to think too much about Leslie. When it was time for Bravo Company to return to the field, I stuffed almost everything I owned into a backpack and climbed into the bed of a five-ton truck with other Marines. We traveled two or three hours over a barren desert before we came to our destination.

The truck finally stopped and one of the guys said, "Home sweet home."

I jumped from the bed of the truck and into an ocean of sand. There were no trees, rocks, or grass as far as the eye could see. There was nothing standing but the makeshift outhouse and a few military vehicles parked in a huge circle, which I was standing in the center of. There were no landmarks of any kind; the location could only be found by its longitude and latitude. The unit, called the Combat Train, was made up of drivers from Motor Transportation, medics from a Navy medical unit, and supply guys. It was a roving truck stop that supplied food, gas, and medical attention when needed. There were a few Hummers, but mostly the circle was made up of diesel tankers and five-ton pickups like the one I had come in. The tankers had only ten wheels and were half the size of an eighteen-wheeler. They were all parked in a large circle about two city blocks in area. Other than us, the only living thing that moved about was the black beetles that came from holes in the sand.

Thirty or so Marines crowded around the truck to ask if we had brought mail. I had noticed the orange bag earlier and wondered why it wasn't drab olive green like everything else was. It was given to a sergeant and while he went through it, their eyes gleamed as if it were Christmas morning. I didn't know it, but I would soon salivate at the sight of the orange bag myself.

Since mine was a new face, someone with higher rank asked me who I was. "PFC Braxton. I'm the new supply guy for Bravo Company."

He pointed at a truck about two hundred yards away and told me to go see Corporal Gable. I slung my rifle over one shoulder and my backpack over the other and began walking. The soft, cream-colored sand swallowed my heels, making each step heavier than the last. Three young white guys stood in the distance and began to take notice of me as I got closer. One of them pulled a cigarette out of his mouth and flicked it away while they gathered together.

When I finally got there, I announced, "I'm PFC Braxton, the new supply guy; I'm looking for Corporal Gable?"

He seemed disappointed not to see Corporal Sampy. They all were. "Hey, I'm Corporal Gable," he said, sticking out his hand. I shook it and he introduced the others. "This is Corporal Hayden and Lance Corporal Telly."

"That's not my name," the big bald one interrupted. He had shaved his head—it was easier to keep clean that way—and Gable made a joke out of it and began calling him Telly, as in Telly Savalas. He told me his real name, but unfortunately it didn't stick like Telly did.

Gable told me I would be sharing the tanker truck with Hayden, as Sampy did. For months we had to share a living space the size of a car's front seat. Hayden tried hiding his bad luck behind the same lame smile I was wearing. They were all younger than I was, by three or four years. I knew it was going to be awhile before we warmed up to each other, if we ever would. Regardless, we were going to have to live, sleep, and eat together like brothers.

In our backpacks we stored all our belongings, clothes, boots, socks, toothbrush, underwear, food, letters, and items from our care packages we didn't want to share. Hayden stored his backpack behind the seat in the cab. We already had limited space and didn't have room for another, so I had to strap mine to the side of the tanker. It was Motor T's truck and with three motor transport guys and one supply guy, that was just the way it was. The only thing I really wanted was solitude. I let that be known right away by putting on my headphones and walking out a few hundred feet away from the camp to sit down in the sand.

Just before sunset I started a letter to a second-grade student in my sister Jo's classroom. She'd sent me a huge envelope with letters from her students wishing me well. Instead of writing the class as a whole, I wrote each child a personal letter; if a letter had a child's home address, I sent it there. I enclosed Iraqi money so they could have something to remind them of this wonderful time in their lives. I remembered how special I felt when Tonka responded to my letter when I was about their age and what kind of impact it made on me. I hoped my letters would bring that same kind of joy into their lives.

An hour or so later, Gable called out to me. The sun was going down; it was time to go to work. Bravo Company patrolled the border in case the Iraqis tried a surprise attack. Our job was to meet them wherever they were that night and supply them with fuel and food. It was a long drive—maybe two hours, sometimes more. We could go as fast as we wanted in the open desert, but the sand and lumpy terrain hindered us from going much faster than fifty or sixty miles an hour.

Hayden and I followed in the tanker behind Gable and Telly. Using headlights would run the risk of giving away our position, so the moon was our only source of light. We drove around for a couple of hours, stopping from time to time for Corporal Gable to look at the compass. Hayden and I talked a little and I gathered that they thought I had been busted down, which would explain the huge chip on my shoulder. I told him I hadn't gotten busted down and he also learned that I was from Texas. I've forgotten where he was from, but he had only a year left in the Corps and wasn't reenlisting. That was about the extent of our conversation before I put my headphones back on.

We finally met up with Gunny Hawk in the dark of night and he led us to another spot not far away and began calling in one vehicle at a time. The vehicles were called LAVs (Light Armored Vehicles), and even with the large gun mounted on top, they didn't look all that menacing. With the pointy nose in the front and a flat rear, they looked more like tipped-over milk cartons on wheels. They were really small tanks that rolled on tires instead of on a track. The diesel engine whined, sounding nothing like the diesels I'd heard before. One by one the LAVs came in to refuel and get MREs for about two days. It was a pit stop, except we came to them instead of them coming to us.

We also brought mail; if we had any, Gable would give it to the Gunny. He supervised as each vehicle came through and introduced me to the senior men on each vehicle. I didn't remember any of them except for Sergeant Connors. He was about my age and happened to notice I was wearing a Malcolm X pin on my flack jacket.

"You know Billy Joel mentions him in his song, 'We Didn't Start The Fire'?"

Looking at his tattered and torn overalls, I responded, "Overalls, large. Right?"

He smiled and nodded his head yes. I pulled out my pad and jotted that down, putting his name next to it. The next vehicle was Captain Ray's. He was the highest ranking officer—the big cheese, you might say. If there was a hill to be charged, he would have been the one giving the order. The failure or success of a mission lay solely on his shoulders. When he spoke, everyone stopped what they were doing and listened, even if it was just to say good morning. While his vehicle was being refueled, the Gunny introduced me.

The steel double doors at the rear of the vehicle fell open and Captain Ray stepped out. He was a huge man with a deep voice to match his menacing presence. He reminded me of Daddy Jerome. *Damn! It seemed that I just couldn't escape that man.*

"This is PFC Braxton, Captain. The new supply guy I told you about."

"Nice to meet you, PFC Braxton," he said wrapping his huge hand around mine and shaking it. Gunny Hawk moved around him almost like a house Negro, even though both of them were black. He was an ex-football player—Michigan, I think—and everyone was in awe of him. His aura was one of extreme self-confidence and his men seemed to believe in him because of it. He smiled and spoke heartily, as if he owned the air and was allowing the rest of us to breathe it. He reminded me too much of someone else. I spoke to him only when I had to—but surprisingly, never stuttered.

The anger and resentment I was harboring for having my life turned upside down, gave way to nothing. Not even my stuttering. Regardless of where my feet were planted, emotionally I was somewhere else and just didn't care about what anyone thought of me. It was sort of liberating.

When we returned that night, most of the other trucks had returned also. They performed the same function as we did with the other three companies. I untied my cot from the side of the tank and unfolded it. Hayden slept on the opposite side of the truck. The desert night air was cool and the stars were so bright, it seemed that I could reach right up and pluck one. It wasn't long before I could hear Hayden snoring while I lay awake waiting to fall asleep myself.

The divorce had kicked my ass. It was difficult finding something worth caring about. Most of my emotions were drained except for the angry thoughts of Leslie floating in and out of my mind. I wondered what she was doing and what she was thinking. Was she thinking of me, and if so, how often? Was she concerned? Did she lust for me as I did for her? Was there anything about me she longed to feel again? Was she regretting her decision to leave? Or was she happy? I wanted to know and I hoped that in a letter she would tell me. And when I did fall asleep, my mind played cruel jokes on me, letting me feel her, smell her, and even hear her voice again. The disappointment was so overwhelming when I woke, that it took hours for me to shake the depression.

The days were not much better than the nights. They were always the same, mundane and endless. Most of it was spent doing nothing but reading letters for the fourth or fifth time, listening to my headphones, or reading a book. I kept my distance from Hayden, Telly, and Gable and never gave them an opportunity to get to know me. The only thing I looked forward to was mail call, which only happened two or three times a week. I got letters from Mom, my siblings, and more letters from students at my sister's elementary school. I was extremely appreciative of any mail I received, especially when it came with a care package.

Hayden and I had little in common, but we made the best of the situation and shared our care packages when we got them. The cab of the tanker was our only means of shelter. It protected us from the sandstorms, but offered little when it rained. Water poured in from holes in the ragtop roof, and when a puddle would form in the center of it, we took turns pushing it out. It was actually better sleeping outside in the rain, at least that way we could stretch our legs. He liked listening to Andrew Dice Clay on his Walkman, chewing tobacco and farting while we ate. Though the rooms I'd shared with my older brothers were small, nothing prepared me for the cab of a truck.

A raid across the border was planned, so we left the safety of the combat train and traveled with Bravo Company. They escorted us once or twice a week to a refueling point twenty or thirty miles back. The Gunny did most of the escorting. He and I were developing a good friendship, although he had about five stripes and ten years on me, but in private he treated me as if I were equal. He missed his wife and children and talked about them constantly. She was Asian, the proprietor of a brothel he'd patronized when he was in Korea or Japan. When he wasn't talking about her, he was reading her letters.

His persistence over several weeks forced me to open up about the divorce and he listened objectively. I told him how long we had been together and how we broke up. I even told him about the abortion.

After he was sure that I had given up as much I was going to, he asked, "Do you still love her?"

"I don't know."

He took that as a yes and said, "So what are you going to do about it?"

"Nothing. I don't want to ever see her fuckin ass again!"

"Do you think she still loves you?"

After a long pause I replied, "I don't know." Regardless of what had happened, I believed she did, but what did it matter? Somewhere I heard that love sometimes is not enough and I believe that is true. I was still living in the desert, sleeping in the rain, and living out of the cab of a truck with a total stranger. The Gunny smiled as if he knew how to solve all my problems with one swooping blow. "What?" I asked to get him to say what he was thinking.

"Brax, ya'll just need to have sex."

"What!"

"When you get back home, ya'll just need to hook up once more just to screw." What the hell kind of philosophy was that? I thought he was joking until I realized he was really serious. "After ya'll make love, you'll be the best of friends. Watch and see."

He said it as if he knew from experience, but I disagreed and he laughed it off as if I had no choice in the matter.

Over the days leading up to the raid, we bonded in many ways I wish Leon and I had. My list of supplies was filling up my pad, so I suggested that we take a run back to the rear. The request wasn't like asking to go down to the convenience store on the corner. The trip would take us about a day, and could not be decided upon by either of us. Gunny brought me to Captain Ray's tent, and when the captain called me over, I showed the list I had accumulated. The raid was coming up and he wanted his men to have everything they needed, so he gave his permission. The Gunny and I left that very night.

In a Hummer, we arrived about two in the morning. The camp was huge and called Tent City for obvious reasons. It had hot showers, hot food, and telephones, even a makeshift store where we could buy junk food. That early in the morning, the only thing open was the tent with the phones, but the line ran out of the tent and down the main dirt road. The supply tent was closed for business too, but not to the supply guy.

I tried to jam as many supplies as I could into two or three sea bags without waking anyone. Miller must have heard me, for he came into the tent, wearing long underwear and untied boots. He asked if I needed help loading; when I refused, he seemed thankful and went back to his cot.

I got most of what was on my list and a little extra. The extra stuff was not for me, but for trade. On the way, the Gunny enlightened me on the value of being the supply guy. After loading down the Hummer, he introduced me to other supply guys from other units. All of them were sleeping, but none took offense to being awakened that early in the morning. They all seemed to know the Gunny, or at least knew of him. With our unit's interest in mind, we bartered like sports agents, trying to get the most for our clients. By the time the sun rose I had everything on my list.

On our way out, we again passed the tents with the phones and I thought about Leslie. I wanted to speak to her, but it scared me, too, because I wasn't sure if it was going to do me more harm than good. I slept a little easier each night and took that as a sign of progress and didn't want to backslide. I wanted to call my mother, though, but the

Gunny kept right on driving.

Once we had gotten several hundred feet away he said, "I'd love to call home, but that line's about two hours long."

"No problem, Gunny." It was clear we both wanted to call home, but duty called.

The day before the raid, I distributed all the gear. When Connors stepped up I went into another box that was set to the side and pulled out a uniform that was the size he'd requested.

"Thanks, PFC Braxton."

He then dug into his pocket and gave me the Billy Joel tape he'd spoken of weeks earlier. I assumed he was more into Country Western. As a token of my appreciation I gave him an extra box of heat tabs.

The following night we lined up and headed for the border where the Iraqi soldiers patrolled. Once there, the LAVs got into position. Captain Ray's vehicles stopped a few hundred yards back; so did Hayden and I in the tanker. He gave the word and they sped off into the night. Through binoculars, I watched from the hood of the truck and listened to the radio as Captain Ray barked out commands. When the enemy was in sight, the vehicle commanders described their position in relation to the hands of a clock; "Enemy vehicle at two o'clock," or "Enemy vehicle at nine o'clock." The 25 millimeter guns rattled off like small cannons and afterward I would hear, "Enemy vehicle destroyed." Apache helicopters swooped down and hit their targets at will. The Iraqi vehicles burned so hot, the thick steel armor glowed like a branding iron. It was difficult for me to imagine that there were brothers, sons, and fathers inside of them.

After ten or fifteen minutes the excitement wore off, so Hayden and I sat on the hood and shared a can of Pringles and a box of Teddy Grahams. The Iraqis eventually got the message and retreated, so the confrontation lasted about half an hour, probably less. As our convoy headed back to camp without suffering a single casualty there was this aura of invincibility, the kind you feel after putting a thirty- or forty-point whipping on another team.

Without headlights, we drove though the darkness of the open desert with only the moon and the night vision goggles to help us see where we were going. Without landmarks, it was easy to get lost so we made frequent stops. While Hayden drove, I snuggled down into the seat for the long drive back to camp, hoping to steal minutes of sleep in between the bumps.

We had driven about half an hour when the truck came to an abrupt stop. We sat idling for a few minutes while Captain Ray got his bearing in the darkness—or so we thought. Two Marines in the vehicle in front of me jumped out and ran toward the front of the convoy, while two guys in the vehicle behind us ran past. There were no explosions or gunfire, so I continued trying to get some sleep and Hayden decided he would do the same.

A good time later a blinding spotlight and the clamor of a helicopter landing on what seemed to be right on top of us forced Hayden and me to unravel ourselves from our respective corners. Whatever was happening superseded any concern about giving away our position, but we thought nothing of it and curled back into our corners.

My curiosity caught up with me and I left the vehicle and began walking toward the front of the convoy. I could see that one of the vehicles had been rear-ended by another. The hatch was smashed in like a beer can, and the thick steel doors dangled from its hinges like a rickety gate. As I made my way through the cluster of Marines, in the center I could see three bodies lying in the sand. Their heads were swollen and blood and other fluids ran from every orifice of their cracked skulls. One of them was Connors. His vehicle had been rear-ended by the sharp nose of another, and he and his men had been virtually crushed by the impact.

Watching them being carted off to the awaiting helicopter was a surreal moment. It was almost identical to the news clips of the war that ran every day during my grade school years. It reminded me of the unrest I felt then and that something had come full circle, but I wasn't sure what it was.

At sunrise, Captain Ray gathered us all together and officially announced that Connors and two of his men were dead. He spoke highly of them, as if he knew them well, and said we should be honored to have known them. He also said death was a part of war and reminded us of our righteous cause. God was on our side, he alluded, and Connors and his men were by His side looking down on us. While he spoke some cried, but the speech didn't move me. As a child I had heard something similar from my mother. She believed in knights in shining armor, though she never met any. She believed that good always prevailed, despite how her life turned out, and that God took those we loved because He needed another angel in Heaven. I guess that meant Daddy Jerome too.

I questioned every basic principle I was ever taught and concluded that what happened to Connors had nothing to do with luck, karma, or even divine intervention, any more than what happened to the Iraqi soldiers who were incinerated in their vehicles. I realized that I had never really believed in most of those principles anyway. After all, I never knew an honorable war, or an honorable man that hadn't been brought down by scandal or a bullet. Growing up, the nightly news served up heavy doses of right going unrewarded and wrong going unpunished. Marriage no longer meant forever, and sex didn't have to be sacred as long as it was safe. Friends weren't to the end, fathers didn't know best, and mothers were hardly virtuous.

CHAPTER TWENTY

TREES OF FIRE

After closing the club with my aunts, Mom would get up a couple of hours later to go to Mass at six in the morning. When she got back, she started Sunday dinner so she could have the rest of the day to relax. Adrian hated getting up at the ungodly hour of four-thirty to walk to church. I was an early riser so it didn't bother me that much, plus it gave me almost the whole day to find something to get into. Everyone else went to the ten o'clock Mass, then around two in the afternoon, we all gathered in the tiny kitchen to eat dinner, everyone except my mother. One of us would take a plate to her bedroom so she could watch television while she ate.

Jo, Paulette, Adrian, Ambus, and I sat at the table, while Leon and Resa stood over the sink. Back then Leon was content picking arguments with Resa; the only crack he was familiar with was the sound of the large wooden spoon when she hit him over the head with it. Underneath their bickering, Ambus and Jo talked about homework while Adrian scavenged off everyone else's plates for chicken bones that might still have meat left on them. And Paulette and I spent our time wisely, throwing green peas on the floor, hoping no one would notice them.

One Sunday afternoon I was looking for someone to play with. Ambus and Leon had gone to visit friends, Jo was studying, Resa was out of the question, and Adrian was in the boys' room sketching in his pad. Usually I could wear him down, so I climbed on his shoulders, punched him, and attempted a headlock to entice him into wrestling. Ignoring my harassment, he flicked me off like a pesky insect. If all else failed, I could always count on Paulette. I'd find her in the girl's room lying on the floor in front of her Easy Bake Oven. She was happy to have me lie there with her and watch as the tiny cake browned.

After eating more than my share, my mother called out for me and I went running. In her bedroom she was lying in bed with her arm over her face, as if she were blocking out the sun, except all the shades were closed.

"Baby, bring me a couple of aspirin?"

I had gotten aspirin for her many times before, because of her migraines. Pulling the bottle down from the medicine cabinet, I tried opening the cap, but couldn't. I tugged, pulled, and jerked. I even used my teeth, but the cap wouldn't budge. I did everything but smash it against the wall.

When I entered Mom's room she sat up, grabbed the glass of water next to the bed, and waited for me to give her the aspirin. Noticing I was having trouble, she softly said, "Let me do it, honey," trying not to bruise my ego. I didn't say anything but just kept trying to open the bottle, so she leaned back against the headboard and waited.

Trying to suppress the urge to go into a temper tantrum, I conceded with, "I can't open it, Mom. It must be stuck."

I gave it to her and she twisted the cap right off. In an attempt to save what little manhood I had developed, she offered, "Look, honey, it's one of those new caps. It's childproof."

She said it as if that should have brought me some kind of redemption, but it only proved the point that I was still a little boy. She showed me how to open it and I was grateful for that, but with Hershey bars doubling to ten cents and now childproof caps, I felt that the world was against me.

252

I was summoned again and though I recognized the voice, I still wasn't sure if it was actually him.

"Gary!" he called again.

It was Ambus; to him it was as if I didn't exist. He was six years older than I, and though we lived in the same house, we seldom interacted; when we did, he was usually yelling at me for messing up his bed or playing with his G.I. Joes. I didn't know what to expect when I heard him calling from the front yard.

I walked out onto the porch and he was in the street leaning against a bike, with one of his white friends from school. They would steal bikes, then swap the seats, handlebars, forks, and tires, and paint them so they couldn't be recognized. Then they'd sell them.

"Here," he said. I didn't know what he meant. "Here!" he said again, grabbing my hand and putting it on the handlebar. Surely he wasn't giving me a bike. He hopped on his friend's handlebars and they rode away. I wasn't sure what delighted me more; the fact that I had my first bike or that Ambus was the one who had given it to me.

At the end of Cleveland Street, the downtown skyscrapers stood waiting for me. Without telling anyone, I rode off toward them. Passing a friend's house without stopping, it felt good to be on my own. I liked the feel of the wind against my face and the sound of the knobby tires rolling over the red bricks that paved Andrews Street. It was the bumpiest street in the neighborhood and also the prettiest. It's said that the first black settlers, almost a hundred years ago, laid each red brick by hand.

At the edge of downtown or the end of my neighborhood, depending on how you looked at it, was our church. It may as well have been the edge of the world for me, because I had never been farther from the house alone. I turned my bike around and peddled back the other way. Wharton Elementary was also about a mile away from the house, except in the opposite direction. Like the church, I never ventured past it alone, either.

I was familiar with only one other place, Buffalo Bayou. The trees were always full no matter what time of year, and the grass on the hills was softer and greener than any grass I ever played in. There were people stretched out on blankets with picnic baskets, dogs chasing Frisbees, and couples taking their Sunday stroll. There was also a bike trail that would allow me to do just what I wanted; escape. Just once I wanted to get away. Ride as far and as fast as my legs could take me. I wanted to be free of the neighborhood and free of the people in it, including my family.

With my t-shirt fluttering behind me, the faster I peddled the farther I felt myself getting away from those confining influences. I rode for hours, taking breaks underneath overpasses. I even took off my shoes and socks, rolled up my pants legs, and waded in the bayou. The fact that no one knew where I was pleased me. Not that I wanted anyone to worry—I just needed to stretch my wings a little, even if it meant a butt whipping. Only the rumbling of my empty stomach could change my mind, and the great thing about the bike trail was that it snaked through and around Buffalo Bayou, so I could ride as long as I wanted and still be home in time for supper.

Hearing the screen door slam, Mom came out of her room, "Where have you been?" she asked.

"Riding around."

"Riding around? On what?"

"My bike."

She cracked the screen door to see if the bike was as imaginary as my friend Johnny Macro. Her eyes were puzzled when she turned back to me, but she must have put it together because she never asked where I got it from. I kept it for a couple of days, then she made Ambus get rid of it. It was the principle of it, she said, and I didn't put up a fuss. I was old enough to understand what she was trying to do. But stolen or not, being liberated from the clan even temporarily was empowering; I felt less like a little boy and more like a budding man. I looked forward to being the master of my own destiny.

* * *

The Saudi Arabian desert was not exactly what I had in mind.

When mail came that afternoon, I got a letter from my father. That rather surprised me, since he couldn't read or write, but it was a dictation by his wife, telling me to be careful and that he was thinking of me. At the bottom he scribbled his name, which brought to mind that it was Mom who taught him how to write it. I cared for my father because it was expected and though we smiled and acted as if we knew each other well, we really didn't. When I got back home I wanted to rectify that.

I'm not sure how many weeks passed before the Gunny and I were allowed to go back to the rear to restock. The Gunny said it was going to be our last trip back before going into Kuwait. I didn't have to ask him what direction that was in. In the distance I could see the sky was black, like a coming storm. It was the burning oil fields. We had a day to get to Tent City and back.

Since most of the infantry units were moving forward, Tent City was a ghost town. The single dirt road that ran through the center took us straight by my supply tent. We got the gear we needed and a little more, then went by a friend of the Gunny's. I stayed with the vehicle and he returned ten or fifteen minutes later, with a guy holding a case of hamburger patties under each arm.

The guy asked, "Whatcha got to trade, PFC?" I would have given him the Hummer for those patties, but he settled on a couple of pairs of desert boots and an AK-47 I took off a POW.

With everything we needed we headed toward the exit gate, when the Gunny slammed on the brakes.

"What's wrong?"

"You didn't see that?"

"What?"

"There's no waiting line for the phones."

Alongside the road he parked in a somewhat parallel position and without saying another word we dashed into the tent. It was filled with small cubicles; inside of each were a folding chair and a regular house phone sitting on a desk. I went to the nearest one and he went to the farthest to have more privacy.

It was a little past midnight there, but at home I think it was in the morning or afternoon. I called my mother and she cried as soon as she recognized my voice. It took a moment to gather her composure before she could ask me if I was being careful. She brought me up to date on my siblings. Paulette, who was living in New York, had landed a gig as a chorus girl in the Will Rogers Follies, a musical that was preparing to travel across the country. Leon had returned to Houston and was living with a lady—that's all she would say about him, though I pretty much knew the rest. The others were working and carrying on with their lives.

Taking advantage of the situation, I called as many people as I could. One of them was LaVerne, a mutual friend of Leslie's and mine. After a brief conversation, she offered to contact Leslie to let her know that I was on the line. I wasn't sure if that was a good idea, but I couldn't say no. I wanted to hear her voice and to know why she hadn't written me. La Verne put me on hold and returned with a number. Leslie wanted me to call her.

We made small talk by asking about each other's families. She was as nervous as I was. She never offered to explain why she had not written and my pride would not let me ask. It was not long before we ran out of things to say and the silence became uncomfortable. The Gunny came up, but turned away to give me another minute.

"I gotta go," I said.

"All right," she said hesitantly. "Be careful, Gary."

"I will."

I'm not sure when it happened, but closure had finally come. When we hung up I wasn't sad or depressed, nor second-guessing anything I said. There was a calm inside me that hadn't been there for a while, and like it or not, our lack of contact had actually helped me. It was a sink-or-swim situation, and though I took in a lot of water, somehow I made it to the other side of the pool.

The Gunny was giddy as a little boy after speaking to his wife. Excited, he began telling me how she'd planned his first night back. She was going to prepare a hot bath for him, then lead him to their king-size bed and rub his body down with lotion to soften up what six months of wind and sand had done. He didn't have to tell me what was coming after that, but he did anyway.

You lucky dog, I thought, but soon I tuned him out and spent the rest of the drive gazing at Orion's Belt in the clear night sky.

At daybreak I stood just beyond the camp sipping hot coffee and examining the morning. There were no trees or buildings to eclipse the orange sun rising from beneath the earth's surface. It appeared closer than normal. I can't remember what I was thinking at the time, but the stiff breeze against my cheeks made me realize I was smiling.

Along with the meat patties, the chow hall gunny hooked us up with charcoal, lighter fluid, and bread. We dug a hole in the sand, used some steel fencing, and threw the patties on our makeshift grill. One of the guys had a football and the captain gave his approval to play as long as no one got hurt—he didn't want anyone to break a leg before they could get shot.

After several raids and hundreds of surrendering prisoners, the burning oil fields were finally the only thing that stood between us and Kuwait City. The black smoke literally began blocking out the sun and the closer we got, the darker it became. Night was falling and the darkness it brought happened so quickly we didn't have time to gaze at the phenomenon before it was totally pitch black. With night-vision goggles we gathered together and decided to wait for daylight before continuing. There was absolutely no visibility with the naked eye; the thickness of it had me fighting back episodes of claustrophobia, something I had never experienced before or since. We all stayed close to our vehicles and if anyone ventured out to relieve himself, he had to have a buddy who would maintain voice contact so he could find his way back. In the distance there was this bellowing, like volcanoes on the urge of erupting. I don't think any of us got any sleep that night.

It was around eight in the morning and the sun barely seemed to rise. We had the visibility of dusk. Across the desert's horizon I could see what had kept us up all night. As we entered the oil field, it was like entering a forest of fire. In all directions these forty-foot infernos roared like angry demons abruptly awakened from years of slumber. I had never seen flames so deep in color. The radiant yellows and intense oranges, braided together and spiraling toward the heavens, had a hypnotic charm. The smoke, liquid thick, mimicked the movement of clouds as it loomed over us. Though the closest flames were yards away, I could feel their warmth against my face. It was a beautifully lethal spectacle the likes of which I knew I would never see again.

Drizzling down upon us was this black, oily mist that coated our clothing and faces, like a second skin. The toxins in the air and the smell of hot tar were finally getting to me, so when we stopped, I took a moment to stretch my legs and see if throwing up would make me feel better. Because of the continuous night bombings the wreckage surrounding us resembled a salvage yard. There were charred and mangled vehicles, some with their bloated occupants still behind the wheel. A few feet from the truck was a corpse that I hadn't noticed when I stepped down. Broken and bent in unimaginable ways, it appeared more like a discarded puppet than a man. I climbed back into the truck and when I looked across the horizon again, it looked as if God had punched holes in the earth and Hell was spewing to the surface. You can say that my wish to escape had come true. I was as far from the old neighborhood and my family as I could have ever imagined.

CHAPTER TWENTY-ONE

MISFITS

I was in the truck writing a letter when Hayden jumped in the cab and began banging on the steering wheel like a madman. Before I could ask, he shouted, "It's over, man! Sadaam surrendered." Ever since the first day I set foot in Saudi Arabia there had been rumors about our leaving, so I didn't get happy just yet. But when I stepped down from the truck, I could see how quickly the mood had changed around camp. I knew then it had to be true. We congregated in small circles and talked about all of the things we would do on our first day back. I wasn't thinking any further than a double-meat Whopper and a long, hot shower.

Until our departure from the Middle East, we stayed at Tent City, which is where the Gunny and I separated. He stayed with Bravo Company and I went back to my supply unit. We would see each other mostly in passing after that.

The flight back to the States was about thirty hours; we spent most of that time sleeping. As the plane descended, the anxiety in the cabin was as thick as the Irish whiskey they served us during the brief layover in Ireland. We disembarked from the plane section by section, and when I finally set foot on U.S. soil it was like exhaling after months of holding my breath.

On the runway, I found my sea bag in a pile and slung it over my shoulder. Blocking the exit gate was a huge cluster of civilians and Marines. I snaked my way through the kissing, crying, and embracing until I came to the charter bus that was waiting to take us back to base. Looking out of the window at my buddies and their wives, I'd be lying if

I said that wasn't the most difficult part of my entire Persian Gulf experience.

We had a few days off and that night I was assigned a room in the barracks with Miller, my host in Saudi. His home was in Riverside, which was only a couple of hours away. His mother invited me to come, but I refused. Apart from sharing the experience of coming home to my own family, the experience of being back was best savored alone. I got to the room, peeled off my uniform, and stepped into a hot shower. I sat down on the tile floor, pulled my knees to my chest, while the water ran.

After more than an hour in the shower, I put on a clean uniform and bought that double meat Whopper.

The next morning I was eager to see what my new home looked like. At seven in the morning I stood on the balcony of the barracks and looked out over the base. It was in a valley of the Mohave Desert and there were hills and mountains as far as the eye could see, with clouds hiding the tops of the highest ones. Enjoying the aroma of women's perfume and hearing the sound of passing cars, it took a moment to absorb the reality that I was actually back. A few months earlier I saw my enlistment as dead weight holding me down; now I was seeing it as a springboard into whatever my future was to be.

After eating a hearty breakfast at the chow hall, I called my mother to let her know that my leave had been approved and I would be home in about a month. In the meantime, I was going to need some of my clothes that Leslie had put in storage.

I called Mom back later that evening and she sounded upset and reluctant to tell me why.

After badgering her into submission, she forced me to promise that I wouldn't get mad. "It's all gone. Everything is gone," she said.

"It's all gone. What's all gone?"

"Your clothes, everything you had."

The manager of the storage facility told her that Leslie had come by and taken some things out of storage but never came back. When they tried contacting her about past due payments, she would not return their calls. They had no choice but to auction off anything that was of value and discard the rest.

I didn't really care so much about the clothes, pictures, awards, letters, or even my poetry, but losing the Mighty Mo Jeep my mother bought me for Christmas when I was eleven, was a heartbreaker. Even then I knew it was expensive, but somehow she had managed to get it.

I didn't understand why Leslie had to be so vindictive when it was she who left, but I wasn't going to waste another minute of my life trying to figure it out.

My mother was rather surprised at my indifference. When I went home on leave I could feel her eyes watching me. She analyzed every expression and gesture, looking for damages, psychological or physical, that the military had done to her baby boy. I think she concluded that it was too soon to tell.

I decided to visit a few friends, the first of whom was Metra. She was living in the Kelly Courts, the same housing development she'd lived in when we were dating. When she answered the door I could tell she was surprised, but not pleased.

"Hey, Metra," I said with a huge smile.

"Do I know you?" she asked through the screen door.

How could she have forgotten me? Then she began throwing her eyes over her right shoulder at the man slumped down on the sofa with his mouth twisted.

Not wanting to cause her any problems, I said, "I'm Gary Braxton. We used to dance together with Mr. Howard."

"Oh, yeah . . . . How have you been, Gary?"

We did that for a few more seconds, then I excused myself.

She called me later that night and explained that he would have given her a hard time if he knew that we had dated. I told her there was no need to apologize. We met for lunch the next day and she told me she had five children, but was not married. When I asked why, she replied, "I'm still waiting on you."

We talked fondly about the old times and I made a point to apologize for how insecure and selfish I was back then. She laughed as if I was being silly. We talked about the abortion, and she said at the time she wasn't ready for a child either, but I knew she was saying that for my benefit.

I visited other friends, like Barry, Dale's younger brother, but the one person I really wanted to see I could not. Will had been cremated and did not have a gravesite. All I had were memories and places that held them. I drove down the streets where we walked and by the house he lived in—even by the old dance studio. It was then that I truly felt his loss. I was curious to know what would have become of him and what he would have thought of my life.

On base I was becoming acquainted with a group of guys I would never forget, either. Being a purchasing clerk, I sat at a desk from seven-thirty to four-thirty and had weekends off. Outside of guard duty or field maneuvers, the hours weren't much different than a banker's. I enrolled in a university and began taking evening courses. Things were looking pretty good. Room and board was free and I couldn't get fired or laid off. And being an hour away from Palm Springs wasn't bad, either.

When Miller didn't reenlist, I became the unofficial platoon sergeant. At the ripe old age of twenty-seven, I was fondly referred to as Grandpa since most of the other guys were barely old enough to drink. Living and working together, day in and day out, we became close and told each other things that some of our closest relatives didn't know. I came to value their confidence and respect.

Samuel was nineteen, a tall white boy with blond hair. When he was ten years old he walked down to the local police station and told the desk sergeant that he was being sexually molested by his father. After his father's arrest, he was shuffled from foster home to foster home until he was old enough to enlist. He never said much about his mother, so I never asked. If it were high school we would have voted him most likely to climb a tower and shoot people.

One of my favorite Marines was Newman. His mother was white and his biological father was Hawaiian, but Newman did not know him well, if he knew him at all. His mother remarried and he was raised on a small cattle ranch in Nebraska. I could tell not having a real relationship with his biological father bothered him, as it does most young men, but he did not dwell on it. He was a handsome guy, well fit, with a permanent tan. The only things he loved more than the Cornhuskers and beach volleyball were partying and drinking. Newman and I chose the Corps for the challenge but had no aspirations of reenlisting. We both saw it as a temporary thing. We cut corners and stayed off the base as much as we could.

Another Marine who would become one of my closest friends during this time was Ericson. He was a lifer from the time he was born, because it was some sort of family tradition. He was a little over a hundred pounds and was no taller than five-foot-three, which made him the smallest Marine on the base. He had to get a waiver to enlist because he did not make the weight requirement, but he lived and breathed the Marine Corps. His uniform was always pressed, his boots were always polished to a glossy shine, and he was tough as nails. If you made him angry, he could berate you so bad that you swore he was ten feet tall.

Outside of his extreme attention to detail, there was no other way of knowing he was homosexual. I had already concluded that by the time he decided to confide in me. Telling him about my brother Madison put him at ease; I could see the relief in his face that I was not one of those passing judgment. He was a better Jarhead than any of us, and if he had been six feet, he would have been the perfect Marine. A chosen few knew about his sexuality, but never dared mention it. If our commanding officer were to have found out, it would have been the end of his military career.

I brought my car back with me and went to Palm Springs almost every weekend, for no other reason than to mingle with anyone who wasn't associated with the military. One afternoon I went down to see a movie and noticed a young, fair-skinned girl sitting with an elderly white couple.

I snuck peeks at her between sips of Coke and apparently I wasn't as subtle as I thought, because she smiled and waved me over. With my bucket of popcorn, I walked across the aisle and sat next to her and introduced myself.

Her name was Stacey and the elderly couple was her parents. She was beautiful, very energetic and just turned twenty-one. After the movie I asked about spending more time with her and she said if that was what I wanted, then just follow her home. So I did. They lived in a small suburb just outside of Palm Springs. Typical of the neighborhood, there was a pool in the back, so we sat out there and talked.

She hardly took a breath as she told me all about herself. Born in Chicago, she had a twin sister named Tracey, who was living with a boyfriend. Her folks had adopted them when they were babies and came to California in the hope of the girls being child stars, like the Olson twins, I guessed. She boasted about having been on an episode of *Different Strokes*.

She then lifted her shirt and pulled down on her pants just far enough to show off the scar that was left after her appendectomy. That was just how she was. She changed subjects quicker than a traffic signal, and had this childish, giddy quality as if she was unaware that she was a full-grown woman. She was spontaneous and spunky, and when I went to see her, her excitement was always just over the top. Her parents were very accommodating, as well. They knew I lived on base and offered me a room for the night if I wanted.

One night we decided to take a drive and she cuddled next to me. We drove about ten miles out of town and parked in the desert. She wanted to sit on the trunk and count shooting stars. I had done that so much in Saudi that it had lost its romance. I didn't tell her that, though. I hadn't been intimate in a long time and our kisses were vigorous. She seemed to like that. Maybe it had been a while for her also. We hopped down from the trunk and partially disrobed in the open air of the desert. It was a warm night so I left the car running to keep it cool—but when we went to open the doors, they were locked.

I tried maintaining my composure with my jeans around my ankles and visions of the Manson family coming out of the hills. We needed to find a way into town before I could even think about how to get the keys out of the car. The only extra key was in my room at the barracks, sixty-two miles away without anyone with a car to bring it to me. She pulled up her pants and tried hiding her amusement. She thought the whole thing was hilarious and suggested that we hitchhike, as if that was the next logical choice. We walked out to the highway and sure enough, a trucker picked us up and dropped us at the first convenience store we came to. There I got a coat hanger from the store's clerk and we hitchhiked back. The whole time she never panicked or even acted concerned. I tried to be as calm as she was, but don't think I pulled it off.

There were very few women on base and even fewer that were single. Companionship was a hard commodity to come by if you didn't have a car. Like me, Newman hated staying on base and went to visit his girlfriend every chance he got. She lived near Los Angeles and it took money to get away for the weekend, so our paychecks went fast. Helping another unit move, he came across a stack of blank ID cards that only needed to be filled in. He made himself an ID that made him old enough to drink, and being the entrepreneur he was, he took the others and began selling them. When he showed other Marines what they could be used for, he began selling them like hotcakes. It was illegal, but I figured if they were old enough to die for their country, they should be able to drink, so I thought nothing else about it.

Samuels got in on it with Newman and they both began selling them. I was bringing home about seventy dollars twice a month, after bills, and Newman knew I could use the money so he offered me a couple to sell. I turned him down at first, but as the weekend grew closer I reconsidered.

I got to Zelda's early that Friday night, about nine, and hung out around the club looking for some young Marines to get turned away at the door. It didn't take long. We were off base and in our civilian clothes so the only way we could tell we were all Marines were by our haircuts. I approached them like a ticket scalper and explained how the cards worked. After a moment all four of them began pulling out their wallets. I told them I only had two, and just like that I had a hundred bucks. That was enough for gas to take Stacey to a movie and to the all-night diner.

I don't know how many of the fake IDs Newman and Samuels sold or gave away, but about a month later someone got busted with one of the phony cards. When asked where he got it, he sang like a bird, pointing out Samuels and Newman. I returned that Sunday night and Ericson told me what was going on. He also said that my name had been implicated by Newman's roommate. Fresh out of boot camp, Newman's roommate was an ex-drug dealer who was a born-again bible-thumper; he swore we were all going to Hell for our transgressions. It may not have been Hell, but we were facing a court-martial and if found guilty, we would have gotten time in the brig, as well as a bad-conduct discharge.

That Monday morning the commanding officer called us in one by one. Samuel went first, then Newman. When he came out, he yanked me toward the wall and said, "Deny that you got any cards from me."

"What!"

On the other side of the door I could hear the CO shouting for me to come in. Newman continued, "I didn't give you any."

He walked away quickly and the CO opened his door and ordered me to take a seat. He looked visibly disappointed and it was difficult to look him in the eye, but I had to.

"Were you aware that Newman and Samuels had possession of these ID cards?"

"Yes sir, I did."

He began taking notes on a pad and while his head was still down he asked, "Did you report this to anyone, Corporal?"

"No sir."

He stopped writing and looked at me. "Why not?"

"I didn't see the harm, sir."

After giving me a scathing stare he went back to his writing, then asked, "Did you have any of these cards?"

It was the question he had been leading up to the whole time. The answer had tremendous consequences; he was asking the prisoner if he was innocent. I thought about what Newman had just said to me and how despite living in the toughest parts of Houston I had managed to avoid criminal activity and going to jail. I had never been placed in handcuffs, which was an achievement for most black guys my age. Words like integrity and honesty came to mind also, but by far what ran through my mind the most was what was I going to tell my mother?

I looked in my commanding officer's green eyes and calmly responded, "No sir, I did not accept any of the cards."

I said it with a straight monotone voice that he could not read anything into. He stared at me for a moment and wrote something down again. He gave me a long speech about how I should have taken the contraband and reported Newman and Samuel. I gladly took my lumps and walked out.

When the investigation was over, Newman and Samuels were court-martialed, busted down to the lowest rank possible, and restricted to the base until they could be sent to the brig in Camp Pendleton. I went to Newman's room and did not know exactly what to say. I thanked him for what he did and he acted as if it was nothing, or more as if it was expected of him. We hung out occasionally and when he got a nipple ring, which was against regulation, I didn't tell, but when he was late to formation or physical training I put him on weekend guard duty as I did everyone else. He said he didn't see how squealing on me was going to help the situation, and he was sure I would have done the same for him. We didn't talk about it anymore, but what I owed Newman could never be repaid.

We all looked out for him as much as we could, not allowing some gung-ho Marine fresh out of boot camp to disrespect him for being busted down. There was no retaliation toward his roommate, other than the men no longer trusted him. They worked with him when they had to, but no one volunteered for the job. He stuck to his bible and I could never blame a man for that. He eventually got orders to transfer to another unit, which we all would sooner or later, unless we were discharged first.

CHAPTER TWENTY-TWO
SHE TALKS TO ANGELS

Stacey's parents went away for the weekend and she answered the door wearing a white camisole and a G-string. She lured me outside to the pool with her sweet scent, though she wasn't wearing any perfume. She dodged my attempts to kiss her on the mouth as she began unbuckling my belt.

Stacey seemed to know exactly what she wanted and was relentless at getting it. With my pants down she straddled me on the lawn chair and with her palms resting in my chest hair, her hips began thrusting back and forth. It had been awhile, but it was our first time and I couldn't go out like that. I tried sports, politics, anything that would take my mind off the feel of her thighs sliding against my hips or the softness of her breast in the palm of my hands. Pumping and panting, she smiled as if she knew the outcome before I did and reveled in the sight of her control over me.

We eventually made our way to the bedroom and she locked her arms around me, as if I was going somewhere. Just below her ear I drug my tongue across the peach fuzz on her neck, and watched the chills spread across her shoulder.

I heard her whisper, "It's been such a long time . . . ." as if it wasn't meant to actually be heard.

I'm not sure how many times we made love that day.

Her parents returned on Sunday evening and I greeted them at the door. Her father was indifferent as always, never getting involved. It was as if the adoption had not been his idea and he refused to take any responsibility for its outcome. He was an engineer on an Air Force base and only came home on the weekends. And I don't think he really wanted to come home then. Her mother's mood puzzled me. Helping her with one of the bags, if I hadn't known any better, I would have sworn she wanted to ask me how the sex was.

Stacey kissed them both and I went to the car with her father to help get the other luggage. Unloading the car, we said nothing to each other.

I started getting this feeling that they knew something I did not.

We saw each other every weekend except for when my unit was restricted to base. The racial tension in Los Angeles was high because of a beating some white policemen put on a black suspect which happened to be caught on tape. When they were acquitted of the charges, a riot ensued and my unit was put on standby in case the local authorities needed help.

To be totally honest, the whole thing caught me off guard. As far as my military experience went, race was hardly an issue. We were all considered one color, and that was green. We only had different shades of it, as they say. I trusted Newman and Ericson with my life and neither was black. Rank was the most important factor over race, religion, and sometimes sexual preference.

A unit from Camp Pendleton was called into Los Angeles, and we never left the base that weekend. It wasn't a total waste, though, I finished a couple of term papers that were due and got whipped by Newman in a couple of games of pool. That week I got a call and I figured it was Stacey wondering when I was coming back down.

"Hi, Gary," the voice said timidly, "it's Leslie."

"Leslie!" I said, shocked. "How did you know where to find me?"

"Remember," she said brashly, "I used to be your wife." But there was still an uncertainty in her voice, as if she expected me to hang up at any moment.

She began making small talk as we had done the last time, but I didn't like the pretentiousness of it. The only thing I needed from Leslie was answers, so I interrupted her with, "Why didn't you write me?"

"I didn't know what to say," she responded quickly, as if she had rehearsed it. "I didn't even know if you wanted to hear from me."

Trying to hide the outrage that was beginning to surface, I had only one other question. "Why did you allow my things to be auctioned off?"

Her response to that question came just as quickly. "I had no idea they would do that. I figured they would call your mother first."

Her excuses gave me no satisfaction and I'd known they wouldn't before I asked. She went straight into hoping we could be friends and knew that would be asking a lot. There was this long period of silence before she began telling me that her grandmother had Alzheimer's and had to be put into a nursing home. I remember thinking how lucky she was to have known her grandmother. For all that I knew my lineage began with my mother.

She also said that her mother, Betty, wasn't doing all that well either. Even when we were dating she could be quite belligerent, and with the mind of a child and the body of a middle-aged woman she was difficult to control, so she was being shuffled around from relative to relative.

Without addressing whether or not we could be friends, I asked if she had spoken to her father, hoping he had a change of heart. She said that he still had doubts that he actually was her father. After another long period of silence she said that she was marrying Kevin. I gave her a half-hearted congratulations and after that neither one of us had much more to say. I realized that her fondest memories were growing up on Christie Street, and I happened to be a part of that. Memories were all we had between us now, but I didn't hate her enough to take that away.

Stacey and I had been seeing each other for about three months and I'm not sure if we ever officially began dating. She did joke about going back to Houston with me, and I played along. There was something about Stacey I liked. She had no idea how badly I wanted her to be who she seemed.

When two or three days went by and I had not heard from her, I called her home. She wasn't there. A day or so later I called again, but she still wasn't there. That weekend I went by her parent's home and they hadn't heard from her either. How could she just vanish like that? I asked if they had contacted the police. Her mother explained that Stacey was unpredictable like that, and she would most likely be back soon. We had never discussed the boundaries of our relationship, so I tried not to worry.

That Sunday I returned to her parent's home and they still hadn't heard any news. Just as I walked down the drive, an older model car pulled up to the curb, with three or four black guys in it. They were real thugs, not to be confused with what Carmelita's father thought I was. He would have treated me like royalty if he had known the difference. The door opened and Stacey climbed out of the back. She saw me and stormed past, as the car sped away. I called out to her but she ignored me.

"Here we go again," her mother said when she entered the house. Following Stacey, she told me, "Don't waste your time, Gary."

I knocked on her bedroom door and she shouted for me to go away, but I went in anyway. She had taken off her shirt and was lying across the bed in a pink bra and a pair of soiled jeans that had once been white. Her hair was knotted. She looked and smelled like a vagrant.

"What the hell happened to you?" I asked, unsure if I wanted to know the truth.

"Go away, Gary. Please!"

Her mother stormed in and began shouting at her, calling her a tramp. "Go to Hell!" Stacey shouted.

"Why don't you tell Gary where you were?" There was a moment of silence, then she said, "Stacey is a drug addict. She's addicted to crack."

I didn't know what to say, but everything started to make sense. She assumed sex was her most important asset and offered it freely. Her mother was hoping her association with me would help her, and she must've held out as long as she could.

When her mother left the room, she rolled over and looked at me. We both just waited to see what the other would say, but I had nothing, so she popped off the bed and said, "Hey, I'm going to take a shower. Let's go for a ride."

I drove and she talked for a long time with the kind of ignorant honesty a child would have. She said that all she really knew of her real mother was that she was an addict and she and her twin were adopted soon after birth. As the girls got into adolescence, their parents, who were approaching retirement age, found them more difficult to control. At the age of thirteen, her sister Tracey moved in with her boyfriend's family, leaving Stacey alone. She got into drugs and the rest was history. She went to Los Angeles on crack binges, selling her body and hooking up with a crack dealer who helped her score with older men for money. Sometimes I think she was bragging about her promiscuity, but who could I judge, after all the things I had done?

"The only reason I was at the theatre when we met is because a judge put me in my parent's custody until my court date." When I didn't respond, she added, "My attorney thinks the judge will send me to a rehab."

We went to the all-night diner and ate breakfast, and when I took her home she didn't want to get out, so we sat there and I listened to her talk some more. She got excited when her favorite song came on the radio, She Talks To Angels by The Black Crowes. The song is about a female drug addict. How appropriate I thought. At daybreak, her mother came out to get the morning paper.

"I guess I better go." She got out and turned back to me. "So when am I going to see you again?"

"I'm not sure," I said hesitantly. "Maybe next weekend." And by the look on her face she didn't believe me.

I drove away upset, and when I got to the base I went straight to the shower. I scrubbed myself to a reddish tint and brushed my teeth until my gums bled. It was embarrassing and I felt duped, but I was not as angry at her as I was at myself. My only experience with drugs had been my brother Leon and that gave me some idea of the magnitude of her addiction.

Ambus, like me, stayed away from drugs—until he joined the Army in the early seventies, when it was rampant. Adrian was smoking dope by the age of sixteen, but neither of them allowed it to destroy their lives. Leon, on the other hand, had been an addict for two-thirds of his life.

In the early eighties he moved to Los Angeles, where he hooked up with women or whoever could fund his addiction and give him a place to stay. He made an attempt at straightening out his life by marrying and having twins, but even that could not keep him from going back to the pipe. Fed up with the pressures of raising a family, he disappeared one day. He returned to Houston and moved in with Mom and Resa. My mother had a ring with ten birthstones representing all ten of her children. After a long argument he ended up admitting to pawning it for twenty dollars.

Unable to live with them anymore, he moved into a dope house and helped them run it. They were squatters; the building had no electricity or running water and was on the city's list to demolish. Those who wanted to come in and smoke paid in dope or cash. Fueled on crack, a fifth of Sysco, and Thunderbird, he provided security while another guy was the lookout; there was usually a woman who supplied the sex. I guess that was Stacey's role during her hiatus.

They lived on corn chips and Ramen noodles that they boiled over an open flame. For money he mugged people or burglarized homes. Leon was tagged the bike man because he stole two or three bikes a day and sold them for a crack rock. He admits to being addicted to the lifestyle as much as the drug, but he could only handle the filth for so long.

Very handsome, he would eventually find someone willing to take him in. After they got fed up, he'd steal from them too, wreck their cars, or just disappear. He would eventually show up at Mom's doorstep for a hot bath, a hot meal, and to get his clothes washed. Maybe that's all Stacey had come back for.

Keeping my word, I drove down that following weekend. When I showed up, she ran outside and jumped in my arms, as a child would do. She tried kissing me, but this time it was me dodging her lips.

I set her back down on the ground with a confused expression on her face as I told her, "We can hang out, but we won't be intimate."

"Yeah, right," she said, laughing as if I were joking.

That weekend we went to see *Malcolm X*, which was a strategic move on my part. She'd never heard of him and I wanted her to see what an addict could do once they straightened out their lives.

We spent our time taking long drives and sometimes I brought her to the base for a change of atmosphere. Since I had no roommate, she slept in my extra bed. During the day we'd go up to the top of the hill and look down on the base. She'd wrap her arm inside mine, as if we were in an adolescent courtship, and tell me some grand story about wanting to live in a mansion with a husband she called Lord. Even when she wasn't on crack, her ability to detach from reality disturbed me.

When her court date came up, she was sentenced to a rehabilitation center in Orange County as her attorney had said. It surprised me to roll up on a three or four-bedroom house in a residential neighborhood with nothing but a chain-link fence to keep out everything she was trying to get away from. There were about five other women living in the home and two or three were pregnant. Men visited as I did, but were not allowed to call, so Stacey called the barracks often. She grabbed hold of the idea of going back to Houston with me, as if it were a goal of hers. I didn't encourage or discourage her, but when I did give it thought, it usually played out the same way every time; I would be driving through my old neighborhood at two in the morning looking to find her in a crack house.

We sat on the bench in the backyard and I listened to her worry about her sister Tracy, who was dealing with her own drug problem. Her mouth moved constantly and rarely did she say anything of great interest. While her gums flapped I examined her, searching for the reason that kept me there. If it wasn't sex or friendship, what was it?

The answer lay not behind her crystal brown eyes, but in the reflection of them. It was me, trying to be the knight in shining armor that never came for my mother.

Looking back, I had always done that. It was I who put more emphasis on locating Leslie's father than she did. And Metra, my need for her to feel protected sent me running to a gunfight armed with only a baseball bat. Now it was Stacey, the hooker with the heart of gold. This necessity to be everything they needed in a man overrode my common sense long before I ever kissed a girl.

My mother confessed to being in love with only three men in her life, A.J., Daddy Jerome, and a man we called Mr. Train. Realizing none was my father, she quickly explained how charming and funny he was hoping not to offend me. She didn't. My father was more the court jester than a knight in shining armor.

However, Train was not his real name, but all his friends called him Train. When he was a small boy he was hit by a car and instead of lying there injured, he jumped up and ran home. As fast as a freight train someone would later joke and the nickname stuck. I liked Mr. Train. A veteran of the Korean and Vietnam Wars, he lived in Alabama with his wife and daughter. Because the job market was better, he spent months at a time working in Houston before returning home. Once he and Mom started seeing each other, they wouldn't stop for ten years.

He was jet black, tall and strong like Daddy Jerome, but gentle and humorous like my father. On the surface he appeared to be a quiet man, almost passive, but those who knew him didn't make that mistake. When he was in town Mom would be in such a joyous mood that it once resulted in a ten-cent increase in our allowance. In the summer they sat out on the porch, and after about an hour, I would come out to sit with them. Sometimes she would shoo me off, but mostly she let me stay and sometimes even left us alone to talk. He asked about school and tried getting me to think about what I wanted to be before I knew I had to be something. When everyone was speaking down to me, he seemed to choose his words more carefully, as if he knew I was absorbing everything around me.

Secretly, she wanted him for her own, but never pressured him until she found out that one mistress wasn't enough for him. The other-other woman happened to live around the corner; one day she noticed his car parked in front of her apartment. Unlike Daddy Jerome, he didn't belong to her so she couldn't confront him. Instead she went back home, collected his Otis Redding and Sam Cooke albums, and called me into her bedroom.

Crying, she said, "These are Mr. Train's records. I want you to take them around the corner and give them to him." Before I could ask, she said, "You'll see his car." She fell into her pillow and when I didn't move she muttered, "Go ahead. I'll be all right."

I moped to the door with his records underneath my arm. When I looked back, her red hair was sticking from underneath the pillow she had placed over her head to muffle her cry. I did as she told me, and when I got to his car he came out. I couldn't help but smile; I was glad to see him.

"Here you go, Mr. Train. Mom told me to give them to you." It looked like all the wind had been knocked out of him to see me there, and he probably wished for once I wasn't absorbing everything around me. He bent down to accept the albums and asked how she was doing. "She's crying," I said.

He looked at me as if he owed me an apology, then said, "Tell her I'll call her later."

"Yes sir."

When I got back home, her door was closed, but I could hear her sobbing. It was after six o'clock and our favorite show, *Sixty Minutes,* was on, but I was apprehensive about entering. I could hear Resa consoling her and with only a squint, she could make me feel guilty for just being a part of the gender.

I went to my bedroom, where Adrian was listening to reggae while trying to find an empty space on the wall to pin up his new *Penthouse* centerfold. I sat in bed trying to comprehend why men hurt Mom the way they did. She was beautiful, loyal, a wonderful cook, and a great housekeeper. She was nurturing and kindhearted. She put money in the basket during Mass, went to confession, and lied only to bill collectors. Couldn't they see how perfect she was?

I'm not sure if Stacey saw me as her knight in shining armor, but I was there when she was released from the rehab. Her eyes were clear; she looked fantastic and still had that bubbly personality that made her unique. Her mother was pleased; they got along great for the first few weeks. Stacey had chores and a curfew and she was fine with that. Even when she was hounded about trivial things, like eating the last of the chocolate chip ice cream, she held her tongue. I thought that was a good sign.

A large amount of my weekends were spent studying for exams or researching a paper in the Palm Springs library. I dropped by one Saturday to see if Stacey wanted to go to the library with me and afterward take in a movie. For weeks she had been helping around the house and taking her mother's crap, so she was eager to get out. She asked permission and without a second of consideration she was told no. Stacey didn't respond right away, but by the look on her face, I could tell she was about to go off. She insisted on going with me, and this time it was clear that she was hardly asking. Her mother, after thinking for a moment, seized the opportunity to come out of this without an incident and, more importantly, maintain the illusion that she had control. She gave Stacey her hollow permission and a few dollars, I guess to make sure we didn't run out of gas again.

At the library, Stacey helped me look for books. Along the way she picked up a romance novel and sat down to read it. She read faster than I did and was quickly caught up in it. I left several times but she never noticed my absence.

Watching her, I wondered how long it would be before she was back on the street. Each weekend I expected her mother to come to the door and tell me she wasn't there. I'm not exactly sure what motivated her to stay—maybe she was sick and tired of being a junky, or maybe she really expected to go back to Houston with me. Either way, what I had to tell her next would eventually flush out the truth.

With my banker's hours, college courses, and hanging in Palm Springs, it was easy to forget I was in the Marines. I was not a lifer like Ericson and anyone who spent just a few minutes with me knew that. But if I made a commitment, regardless of what it was I followed through.

I was unclear of the purpose of our mission in Kuwait, but a few weeks after returning from the Persian Gulf, I saw a PBS special about Somalia and how so many people there were starving. Although I wouldn't call it praying, that night before going to bed I asked God if I ever had to be sent anywhere again, let it be there. As luck would have it, just more than a year after that conversation with Him, my unit was being called to go to Somalia for Operation Restore Hope. I didn't draw any conclusions as to the irony of it (actually my lieutenant wanted me to stay behind to run the office), but if some sort of pact had been made between me and Him that night, I wanted to fulfill my end of the bargain.

I wasn't sure how Stacey would handle the news so that evening, while sitting in the car in front of her home, I told her I had to go to Somalia.

"Somalia?" she said, as if it were another woman.

I explained what was happening there but she never really seemed to grasp the gravity of the situation. She asked me not to go, but even if I had changed my mind, it was too late my orders were already written. After two or three hours of questioning, she finally accepted it and made me cross my heart that I would write her every day. Since meeting her I never saw Stacey cry and this time was no different. We hugged goodbye, and even though I hoped we would see each other again, I wasn't sure.

Until *Roots* first aired in 1977, at about thirteen I didn't know where the African continent was and don't recall even being referred to as African American. I was either black or Negro, but after that television series, being called African American became common. I, like most blacks, after watching the series hoped to set foot in the motherland at least once.

When I got off the plane, the Mogadishu airport was nothing more than an empty parking lot surrounded by a barbed-wire fence with hundreds of Somalis peeking through it. The children stared at us as if we had landed from another planet. We might as well have.

Ericson met me on the runway and helped put my bags in the back of the Hummer. We drove to camp, which was only a few hundred yards away, between the airfield and the Indian Ocean. Along the side of the road a woman sold fruit that would have been thrown out days ago at any grocery I ever went to. Milk was being sold straight from the cow; the only running water came from a well that they stood in line to use.

"The planes taking off and landing will keep you up at first, but you'll get used to it," Ericson said while I absorbed as much as of the countryside as I could. He was right about the jets. They kept me awake for the first couple of nights.

Part of our daily routine was to go back and forth to the port to pick up supplies. Once we got there, the locals would crowd the vehicle. Our presence made it the unofficial town square. As we made our way through the gauntlet of people we handed out Meals Ready Eat, bottled water, and surplus items from our care packages, such as shampoo, razors, soap, deodorant, and lotion. I was partial to giving out candy and the guys knew it, so they would put all the candy from their MREs in a bag for me to toss to the children.

After returning from the port there wasn't much else to do that didn't involve a working party of some sort, so I would disappear down to the shoreline to see the Navy ships sitting off the coast. The sand was white and the water looked clear enough to drink. Behind me the trees grew together in bunches, like small oases throughout the hillsides. In America it would have been a lavish vacationing spot that I could never afford. I felt fortunate to be there, but my euphoria would only last a couple of weeks.

With the United Nations taking control, we started being shipped back to the States that's when the atmosphere began to change. It went from friendliness to hostility. When we went to the port, the locals would rip anything off the vehicles that wasn't tied down. Our chief was very fond of his Ray Ban sunglasses—I think he thought they made him look like MacArthur—unfortunately some little boy ripped them right off of his face.

For shelter from the hostility, the whole battalion moved into an abandoned soccer stadium in the center of town. The stadium was a cement fortress with two entrances that were barricaded and heavily guarded. I'm not sure who was held up there before us, but there were huge gapping holes in the walls from artillery. The inside wasn't much better. Along the circular hallway that went completely around the stadium were small offices that had been ransacked. We cleaned them out and used them as our sleeping quarters.

Once a day convoys went to the port, with an armored escort. Throughout the day snipers took potshots at the stadium, but we were ordered not to return fire. When we entered and exited the stadium, the Somalis pelted us with rocks and called the black soldiers American niggers. They seemed to have more animosity toward us than anyone else, and I couldn't imagine why. Then again, maybe that was exactly the reason.

I had no idea what it was like to grow up without a school to go to or a house to live in. I didn't know what it was like not to have running water or electricity. Even when there was absolutely nothing in the house to eat, Mom could always send one of the boys down to the corner store to get a bag of cornmeal and a quart of milk for Cush-Cush. What was considered poverty back home was living in luxury here. To be fair, their leaders didn't ride around in limos and dine at the finest restaurants, but it made me reconsider my definition of poverty. I was humbled by the experience and left there feeling privileged.

When we returned to the States they gave us a few days off. As much as I tried not to get my hopes up, I wanted to see Stacey. I didn't call but just went over unannounced. I parked in front of her home and sat there for about five minutes wondering whether she was there or not. *It doesn't really matter. She ain't your woman*, I kept telling myself, but that didn't stop my heart from pounding as I walked up the drive. When I knocked on the door, her mother answered.

"Hello, Mrs. Hughes."

Without even a hello, she replied, "I thought you were gone somewhere."

Trying not to be rude or impatient, I responded, "I was." And if the obvious had escaped her, "I'm back."

She didn't respond immediately, giving me the impression that she doubted something I said. Opening the door completely, she called out for Stacey.

If her mother's reception was a bit cold, Stacey made up for it. She hugged and kissed me on the mouth and wouldn't stop telling me how much she missed me. Grudgingly, I missed her too. We went back to the base and spent the weekend there. That Sunday night when I brought her back home she hugged me tight and said, "I love you, Mr. Braxton."

I wasn't sure what I felt for Stacey. If I was in love, it was for who I thought she could be instead of who she was, and that's never a good way to start a relationship.

She fought as long as she could, but the evening did come when her mother answered the door; I could see it in her face that Stacey was gone. She didn't have to tell me, but she did anyway.

As usual, she popped up more than a week later; I was indifferent towards her. Going to Somalia had put me behind, and doubling my class load was the only way for me to finish by the time I was discharged. I placed all my focus on that. She sent letters and cards to the base expressing how sorry she was for disappearing again and that she knew she needed help. Never once did I believe that Stacey was in denial. She knew she was an addict, but like Leon, she was addicted to the lifestyle as much as she was to the dope.

I never let on that secretly I still hoped she would clean up her life. The brief moments when I saw who she truly was, were encouraging, but only hints of who she was, weren't enough.

My last night on base, Newman came to my room. He shook my hand and wished me luck. To avoid any emotional outbursts we made it short and simple, but I felt that I owed him a great debt. At about seven the next morning, I went down to the shop to collect my personal effects. It was cloudy and cool; I could hear drizzling rain tapping on the tin roof.

I took my pictures off the wall and collected all of my personal effects and stuffed them into a box. I tried calling Stacey; I'm not sure how long I let it ring before hanging up. Ericson showed up spit-polished, as always, to help load the last few items into my car. We promised to stay in touch, but as with so many other friends before him, I wondered if we really would. We stood in front of each other not knowing whether to shake hands or hug, and I noticed his eyes glazing over. "I know you're not about to cry, Eric?"

"Fuck you, Braxton!" he said, punching me in the gut. We laughed and hugged each other goodbye. At the time we had no idea that a few years later he would be the first casualty in the war in Iraq. He survived, but a road side bomb would take one of his legs and leave one of his hands partially paralyzed.

He told me about a shortcut I could take through the national park, bypassing Palm Springs, which would save an hour or more of driving. But Palm Springs held some good memories for me, and I didn't know if I would ever have the opportunity to go back, so I decided to forgo the shortcut.

It was about nine in the morning and still drizzling as I started down the strip. I don't know what the odds were, but Palm Springs was a small city, so when I saw Stacey walking along the sidewalk, I can't say I was very surprised. That was before I got close enough to see that she was cruising for a trick. She looked unkept, a day shy of filthy. I pulled alongside of her and when she realized who it was, she looked mortified and abruptly ran away. I threw the car in park and ran to catch up with her.

Grabbing her by the arm and spinning her around, I said, "What are you doing, Stacey?"

"Oh, Gary," she whined. "I know. I know." I was the last person she wanted to see at that moment.

"What are you doing out here? Go home!" I pleaded.

"I can't," she said, brushing her hair back and wiping her eyes. "Mom and Dad went on vacation for two weeks. They locked me out."

Without thinking, I began, "So what are you going to do . . . ." then I caught myself. It was pretty obvious what she was doing about it. I glanced back at my car running, and told her, "I'm on my way home."

Her eyes grew wide and she awoke from her stupor.

"Today. Right now."

I'd reminded Stacey of my discharge date every chance I got but each time she acted as if it were her first time hearing it. I wrote down the number and address where I could be reached. Standing in the drizzling rain, neither of us knew what else to say, so I gave her a twenty dollar bill. Before then I had never given her money out of fear she would use it for crack.

"I know what you're going to use that for," I said, "but go somewhere and get a donut or something."

We laughed at my half joke and maybe a little at her wretchedness. I kissed her on the forehead and drove off. Through the rear view mirror, I watched her step off the curb to see me drive away.

I didn't regret our relationship but valued our friendship. She helped me to understand myself better; what more can you ask of anyone?

I watched her reflection get smaller and smaller, and when she was no longer in view, with my shirt sleeve I wiped my lips and my mind of Stacey.

CHAPTER TWENTY-THREE

CORPORATE LADDER

I got to Houston about six in the morning. I had a key to my mother's apartment and while she slept, quietly I began making coffee. The creaking of her bedroom door or the smell of freshly brewed coffee woke her. She rolled over and her eyes grew so wide I thought she was about to have a heart attack. She rubbed them to see if I would go away, but I was still there.

"I'm home," I said, placing her coffee on the nightstand.

Her lips curled down, as if she was about to cry, so I leaned into her and she hugged me tightly. I was thirty years old and her grip around my neck made me feel like I was three.

At the dining table over a second cup of coffee we talked. By her glistening eyes I could tell she hadn't gotten used to the idea of my being home in one piece. She thought Bill Clinton was our best president since John F. Kennedy. Some of the images of the old days came back to her with the riots in Los Angeles. Working in a hospital, she didn't understand why pagers were not just for doctors anymore or how CDs could be better than tape if you couldn't record over them.

She brought me up-to-date on all nine of my siblings then it finally came down to me. "So what's going on with you," she asked, and before I could feed her a standard line she said, "Really, honey. How are you?"

Before enlisting I had barely left Texas. Now I had gone to or through countries that I never knew existed. I became a war veteran, a college graduate, and a divorcee all in a span of four years, but she knew that and was looking for something more, something deeper.

Was she ready to know that I saw life as nothing more than a random sequence of events, where relationships bloomed like spring flowers and died just as inconsequentially? That life was a riddle that couldn't be answered by the living? So I fed her a line, just as she expected, then changed the subject.

"I've talked to Human Resources and I go back to work next week. When I get my first check, I can get my own place."

"There's no rush," she said, looking for any trace of the little boy that used to sit at the bus stop waiting for her to come home from work. She had changed too. Her hair was white and her beauty was now hidden beneath deep wrinkles and psoriasis. But her hands were always freshly moisturized and her polished nails were always immaculate. I loved her girlish voice and that childish grin she displayed when she was happy. If there had been a single incident that sent her on the path that would inevitably affect all our lives, it was the death of her father. "It was the times we lived in," she would justify to herself.

There was always this gleam in her eye when she talked about him. She might have been looking at me, but she was seeing his long khaki legs sticking out from underneath one of the cars he was working on. She would say that she could still hear the clanging of steel tools and the cursing he used to do when he smashed a finger. When he called out for a tool, his huge oily hand would appear from underneath the vehicle and wearing her homemade cotton dress, eventually she would hand him the right tool. Afterward, no matter how many times he washed his calloused hands it seemed that there was never a time she could remember when he didn't have grease under his nails.

He was always there whenever she found herself in a jam, like the time he saved her from that ornery cow and all she got for her disobedience was a swat on the backside. She was his spoiled little princess, and overnight his untimely death made her into a pauper. I could still hear the naiveté in her voice of not understanding why her mistakes cost her no more than a swat on the backside.

I moved into a studio apartment on the southwest side of town and got my fieldsman job back. We had a departmental meeting where one of the vice presidents spoke. Introducing him was a district manager, and I was surprised to see that he was a black man. That was a rare occurrence at the company. Clean shaven, he wore a dark blue suit with barely noticeable pin stripes, a pressed white shirt, and a yellow and blue paisley tie. He congratulated us on the good job we were doing and eventually got around to introducing the VP. After the meeting I asked about the manager and one of the guys said he had a good reputation and was being considered for a VP spot.

After doing a little research I found that the corporate ladder was not just an analogy. Most of the company's officials had been promoted from district managers, and before that they were supervisors, and before that they were project managers.

It was a couple of weeks before I was able to catch up with Mr. Davis again. I'd sent him my resume and wanted him to connect the face with it. When I stopped him in the hallway he didn't seem interested in whatever I was about to say, but put on a fake smile anyway. I introduced myself and asked about becoming a project manager.

His expression was one of surprise, as if it were a secret club that I wasn't supposed to know about. "Well, first you have to have a degree."

"I do," I said, realizing that he must have just glanced over my resume.

After a moment it must have come to him and he said, "Thank you for your service to our country, Gary."

"Thanks," I said, wondering if that was sincere or just one of those things you say when you're a manager.

Looking at his watch to let me know he was giving up precious time, he said, "Those positions are difficult to get. Usually there's someone already chosen to fill the spot when one does come available."

"How do I become that someone?"

"You need exposure." That was the first time I heard the term in that context. "To get that you probably need to be downtown in the tower." Before I could ask my next question, he said, "I'll make some phone calls and get back with you," and he rushed off.

Another week went by, and when I came in from the field one afternoon, the guys looked at me with a distrustful glare. There was a message on my desk to call Mr. Davis. It was unusual for someone on our level to have a message from a manager. If they needed anything, it usually came through the immediate supervisor. I returned his call and he told me that the only positions available in the tower were in the call center of our customer service department. It was an entry-level position, but if I still wanted it he could set up a meeting for me with the manager.

I was virtually starting over.

In the interview the manager was cordial, but not very personable. She looked down at my resume and began telling me that I would be glued to a seat seven hours and ten minutes a day, taking calls from angry customers complaining about their bills. I had one hour for lunch and two twenty-minute breaks; outside of that I was expected to be on the phones. And if I still wanted to be in her department, she would not approve a transfer for at least a year. I shook her hand and began work the next week.

Summer came and it was drudgery putting up with the constant bombardment of complaints every day, but as soon as I set foot inside the doors, I brought a smile to my face and acted as chipper as the very first morning. I was eager to learn and always found a way to do whatever someone asked of me.

It was a year and half before another opportunity arose. My supervisor walked up to my cubicle and stood next to me while I was on a call. She silently asked me to put the customer on hold.

"Gary, you've been recommended for a position in Field Services, if you want to accept it."

I wanted to jump on the desk and scream my acceptance at the top of my lungs. The position was more public relations than anything else. I had to visit customers with bill complaints. Speaking to such a vast customer base was a confidence builder. It was also a professional position, the first rung on the corporate ladder.

After work one evening I flopped down on the sofa and the phone rang. It was my mother, upset about Leon again. Although Paulette was on her own in Los Angeles, Mom's greatest worry was still Leon. He had been holding onto that title since she left A.J.

After a binge he had come by to take a shower and get

something to eat, but he got into an argument with Resa, who kicked him out of the house. Each time he left, my mother always worried whether it would be the last time she would ever see him. Out of all of her children, she hurt for Leon the most. He'd told her to her face that he blamed her for leaving his father and that his life would have been better if she hadn't brought Daddy Jerome into it.

I disagreed with that and never blamed my mother for it, but being older I did see things a little differently than before. Her faults were more visible, especially her choices in men and how that affected us. Despite my own promiscuity, internally I hated seeing my mother compromised by men other than Daddy Jerome, including my own father, but I can't honestly say that our lives would have been any better without him. Either way, Mom still felt responsible for how Leon's life was turning out.

A few Sundays earlier we had all been at Mom's for dinner, and Leon and I got into a discussion that had been simmering for years. With all my brothers standing in the backyard discussing current affairs and solving all the world's problems, Leon zeroed in on me. He began with me and Paulette having it easier than he and the others did. I'd heard that was how he felt—and he was not alone.

Listening, I watched him intently. He was articulate and handsome, with his salt and pepper hair. Though virtually homeless, he chose to buy his clothes at resale shops along Westheimer Blvd, which ran through the richest parts of Houston. With his ostrich boots, black slacks, and a nice dress shirt, he dressed better than I did. He always considered himself a better class of addict.

I agreed that Paulette and I had it easier, with our older siblings getting jobs and contributing to the house, but I reminded him that he hadn't been one of the contributors. He looked baffled that I had my own version of how things were, growing up. I added, "If your life isn't turning out the way you want, that's your fault."

He shot back, "My father was an alcoholic. That's a disease, and you don't—"

"So was Henry Lee," I pointed out before he could finish. I reminded him that I chose the Marines because he had; the company I was working for, he had once worked for. His eyes fell to the side as though he'd never recognized the parallels of our lives. To make my point crystal clear I added, "It's not Mom's bad choices, it's your own."

That left an uncomfortable silence, which Ambus broke by reminding us of Mom's chocolate cake sitting on the dining table.

In the house Leon slipped away unnoticed. I found him sitting on my mother's bed, watching television alone. He had his back to me, and I wanted to apologize if I'd hurt his feelings, but chose not to and left him in the room alone. He was the embodiment of a big brother to me, ever since the night he stole the rope, but I didn't want our mother to suffer because of him any more.

When she called me that evening after Resa had kicked him out of the house, it was clearer to me how deeply he could hurt her. She lived a hard life and it seemed that most of it was worrying over him. It looked as though she would be doing that for the remainder of her life, as well. I knew all she wanted from me was consoling, but I decided to tell her how I felt.

"Why are you still crying over Leon? When are you going to stop letting him tear you down like this?" I should have left it there, but I added spitefully, "He's just one of your sons; you have five others."

She stopped her sniffling and looked at me with cold eyes.

"Son's aren't interchangeable, Gary. You don't have children. You don't know what it's like."

She was right, I did not know. I didn't regret much of anything I did in my life. I saw it as living and learning; except the decision to have the abortion with Metra. Leslie wanted it, but deep inside I knew Metra did not and that guilt stayed with me.

Stacey called from time to time and was up to her old "tricks." She spoke of coming to Houston for a visit when she was clean again, and I played along, as I always did. I believed eventually she would get herself together, but we probably wouldn't know each other by then. Leslie called also and wanted to know if I was interested in having lunch. She and Kevin were married and I hadn't seen her since the night I almost choked the life out of her.

We met at a restaurant downtown and it was awkward, at best. She was wearing tight jeans, a blouse that accentuated her breasts, but I pretended not to notice. Over lunch we talked about old times, but after awhile even that started to get stale.

The more I listened, the further I felt from her. Either she had changed or I had, I'm sure it was a little of both. Ultimately we hugged our goodbyes. On the way back to the office I couldn't see how a friendship between us would be able to sustain itself. She was doing well and so was I; we didn't owe each other anything, and I was at peace with that.

Mom was in her mid-sixties and her clubbing days were over,

but occasionally she and Jo went dancing when they could find a live zydeco band. They coaxed me into going with them one evening and as soon as I walked in, I saw a young lady getting up from the table. When our eyes met, everything around me ceased to move. I don't remember hearing music or even seeing anyone other than her. Each second felt like a minute, and without a nod or even a hint of a smile we broke the trance. I found Jo and Mom at an open table and sat where I could steal peeks at her without it being too noticeable.

She seemed to be having a good time, so I decided to ask her to dance. She looked Puerto Rican, with her bushy hair, fair complexion, and full lips, but I didn't ask because I knew most guys probably did. After dancing we went to the bar. Her name was Rachel; she was twenty-two and from Louisiana. She was living in Houston with her father, who happened to be the guitar player in the band.

We spoke for a few minutes before she stuck her hand out and said, "It was nice meeting you, Gary." And while shaking hands she disclosed, "I'm supposed to be meeting someone tonight."

I didn't know how to respond to that. I appreciated her honesty and directness, so I replied politely, "Good luck."

"Thanks, but I got a feeling it's not going to work out."

"Why is that?"

"I already met someone," she said, leaving me at the bar with a smile.

A few moments later her date showed up and I watched them go outside. She returned and he did not. We spent the rest of the night together and she never asked me what I did for a living or hinted around to find out what kind of car I drove, which was usually covered within the first five minutes. More than anything I liked her directness and her sincerity.

On our first date we went to the movies and afterward to dinner. I learned that her parents were divorced when she was sixteen. She stayed with her mother along with her three younger siblings, and when she was old enough to get married, she did. It lasted only a year then she came to Houston to live with her father. Her candor was refreshing. Whatever connection we'd felt when we first laid eyes on one another was not only mutual, but still there.

On our third date I invited her over for some Hamburger Helper. The only table in the apartment was my coffee table, so we sat there on the floor in the living room with our backs against the sofa and watched music videos. It surprised me how comfortable I felt with her. She was unlike any woman I had ever met. She had zero tolerance for pretentious game-playing, and yet she didn't take life too seriously. She was free-spirited, but unlike Stacey, it was not drug-induced. Her no-nonsense personality and her beauty made her overly self-confident, but her hardened exterior was only a defense mechanism. Underneath she was insecure and desperate for stability.

It was easy for me to see what she needed. Apparently I was just as transparent. We had a connection that neither of us could deny. She was looking for a serious relationship and making love meant something to her, even if it didn't to me. That night I asked her to stay . . . and she never left.

She liked calling us soulmates and I liked calling us cellmates; either way, our bond was deeper than boyfriend, girlfriend—maybe even deeper than marriage. Our companionship was of the type reserved for siblings or best friends. We were comrades of the opposite sex who hung out as much as we made out. We were buddies as much as we were lovers. It was almost the perfect relationship.

That's not to say we didn't have our growing pains, the generation gap was evident. She grew up watching the *Cosby Show* and I grew up watching *Good Times*. Jimmy Carter was the first president she could remember; Vietnam and Civil Rights were only paragraphs in a history book to her, as the Korean War and Prohibition were to me. She was into video games like Street Fighter and Top Gear, but the last video game I played was Ms. Pac Man, circa 1984.

None of that actually mattered, though. We were an inseparable pair. On New Year's Eve we bought all the makings for a party, including a couple of bottles of champagne, and got dressed to go out, but did not. She wanted to stay home and have a party of our own. It was a quick courtship, that summer I asked her to marry me.

CHAPTER TWENTY-FOUR
THE SMELL OF INNOCENCE

It took three years before another project manager's position would become available. After several interviews that seemed more like interrogations I was asked to return to the office. Usually you got a call from Human Resources, but my manager wanted to notify me personally that I had been selected.

That Sunday at my mother's, I told her about the promotion. Not until I heard the dishes being pulled out of the cabinet did I know there was someone else in the house. It was Leon; he was in the kitchen making a plate for dinner.

"Go fix you a plate," my mother insisted.

While waiting patiently for him to finish pouring gravy over his mashed potatoes, I asked, "How's it going, Bro?"

"I should be asking you, little brother. You da man."

We smiled it off like there was nothing underneath the comment.

He had a talent for writing and singing, and he excelled academically when he wanted. But eventually he did come to that fork in the road that most addicts come to—if they live long enough.

One morning, after stealing a bike and selling it for a rock, he began walking down the sidewalk and had an epiphany. Proud of his writing ability, he figured he would write an article on the different types of trees in the neighborhood and send it to the Audubon Society. It wasn't for the money; he just wanted the recognition, to see his name in print. He walked through the old neighborhood, hitting his pipe and counting trees. About every other tree he would stop to jot down anything of special interest. Between tokes, he even collected samples of bark and stuffed them into his backpack to support his findings. Unbeknownst to him, at the end of the block a couple of cops watched from their squad car.

After so many hits and so many trees, he finally noticed the cops and ditched the pipe, but it was too late. They arrested him, and though he had been arrested numerous times, this time was different. As he was being cuffed, he remembered looking forward to being off the street. He spent a year in a state jail; inside, he joined a group called the Therapeutic Community. It was a group designed to instill discipline in inmates with drug addictions. They marched to chow as a unit and their assigned guards acted more like Marine drill instructors.

When he got out, my mother and Resa were there to pick him up. Instead of free-loading off my mother and sister as he had in the past, he made arrangements to stay in a rehabilitation center, sort of a halfway house for recovering addicts. For a year and a half he mentored other addicts and because he was so inspirational after graduating from the program they hired him as a counselor. There he met a lady and he started going to church regularly. After a brief courtship of his own they got married a year later.

My mother had been legally married to A.J. for more than thirty years and never sought a divorce. My sister Jo was the only sibling who openly held a grudge against A.J. and when she was married she refused to allow him to walk her down the aisle. My mother had always filled those shoes and would be the one to give her away, with A.J. trailing behind them like an afterthought.

All ten of Mom's children were now doing well, and she took pride in that. Without our fathers, she raised us, and despite the parasites we met along the way, somehow we all managed to get through it. Our fathers were old and docile and wanted us to be in their lives as we'd once wanted them in ours. They were an intricate part of our lives, but we didn't need them anymore—and neither did our mother.

Jo's wedding was the last time A.J. would see all of his children in one room. A year later, at the age of seventy he would die peacefully in his sleep. Adrian and Resa took it hard, but my mother and Leon took it the hardest. She believed he was her one true love, and as for Leon, he never felt that he measured up. To what, I'm not sure.

No matter what A.J. did, they loved him dearly and that sort of confused me. When the time came, maybe I'd feel the same, so I searched for ways to connect with my own father. Being a simple man, he had many, but it was still difficult for me.

What I liked most about my father was that he was an emotional man and genuinely cared about people. When I looked at him I saw so much of myself, even though for years I rejected that. All his weaknesses, all his strengths, it seemed that I was nothing more than a new and improved Henry Lee.

I bought a home in Richmond, a quaint little town outside of Houston, hidden underneath enormous pecan trees. The colonial style homes and the golf course were a far cry from the Fourth Ward; however, I was continuously drawn back to where I grew up on Cleveland Street.

It was now a vacant lot with waist-high grass. I remember vividly when my Uncle Charlie had me and my brothers tear it down because he was too cheap to pay to have it done. With sledge hammers and crowbars I enjoyed ripping each infested board from its rickety frame until it was a pile of rubble. The cement drive was the only evidence that a house had even been there. It looked too short and narrow to have accommodated the long brown Buick that Daddy Jerome used to park there. The tree that Jo fell out of and broke her wrist was not so menacing anymore; even the lot itself looked too small to accommodate all the memories it had to bear. My entire world had once existed on that fifty-by-one-hundred-square-foot lot.

I longed to walk through that house one more time. I wanted to stand in the kitchen where I stole private moments with my mother at four-thirty in the morning. I wanted to see the living room where my siblings and I used to sing the lyrics to *Jesus Christ Superstar* and watched *Soul Train* to learn the latest dances. Oddly enough, most of all I wanted to stand in the room where Daddy Jerome and I held our sessions.

I held nothing against Daddy Jerome. I met with attorneys, city officials and million dollar real estate developers who hung on my every word. My career was dependent upon how effective I communicated and I was making a very good living at it. There was a time when I thought all that was in spite of Hotshot, but now I know it is not. He is among many threads that make up the fabric of my being.

We were all grown. My sister Renee' was happily married and taking care of my Aunt Rita. Riley was married and Madison was in Connecticut with his partner of ten years. Paulette had traveled the country with an off-Broadway production of Will Rogers Follies. She went to England for vacation and brought our mother along. Living in

Los Angeles, she landed guest parts on television shows and small roles in film. She was fulfilling her dreams and beaming with pride.

Adrian was married, with three sons, and though they were not his own, I could tell he loved them as if they were. He was a gentle and loving father, nothing like he had experienced, although like our mother he could put the fear of God in them with just a stare.

Ambus was now the manager of the restaurant he once bartended for and became the family's computer wiz. He made his own music, set up web pages, and designed graphics without ever taking a single class. One of his high school teachers told our mother that he was a potential genius, and I think he probably is.

Jo began teaching the fifth grade, because she felt she could make a bigger impact on that age group. She'd always wanted to teach. Locked arm in arm with her husband, she seemed to be the happiest one of us all.

Leon was always in a jovial mood, and if asked, didn't mind talking openly about his addiction and the suffering and degradation it caused. He carried an air about him as if he had conquered the greatest evil known to man.

Resa, the eldest, was our surrogate mother and got that kind of respect. Even as adults we rarely cursed around her; when the boys came to visit, my mother always got a kiss on the cheek and so did Resa. She believed her place was to remain close to Mom and said it was because our mother wanted it that way, but we knew better. Either way, our mother was approaching her seventieth birthday and Resa her fiftieth, so we were grateful that neither one of them had to live alone.

Even though so much had changed for us, I could see tiny bits of who they had been thirty years ago. I guess that meant they would always see a little of Hotshot in me too. I can't change that and don't think I would, even if I could. That was a vulnerable time for us all. More than blood, it was those times that bonded us for life.

I began to rethink my decision about having children, although Rachel and I had agreed early on not to. She saw herself as the cool aunt who let you play video games before homework and eat junk food before dinner. With only ourselves to consider, a typical weekend was putting a pork roast—or anything else that would cook for an hour—in the oven, then popping the cork on a bottle of champagne and staying in bed until the food was done.

It was more than giving up that kind of freedom, though.

Raised in the country, Rachel felt she was expected to get married, have children, and be this meek and mild wife who cooked and cleaned. She despised cooking and admitted to burning things on purpose to keep from being asked. She was opinionated and her rough edges caused problems with her boyfriends. None of that bothered me and loving her for who she was, made her more receptive to cooking and having children. It still took another year, but once she was convinced I was not going through a phase or an early midlife crisis, she agreed.

Within five weeks she was pregnant. It happened so quickly, neither of us was prepared for it.

My mother's excitement was about as great as if we were adopting a puppy dog from the pound. She had always discouraged us from having children and never really warmed up to the idea, no matter how old we got. She wanted to be the most important thing in our lives, as we were in hers. I only wondered when she was going to realize, that she already was.

The void a father leaves behind can never be filled, but my mother was good at bridging the gap.

Having a son, I thought more of Henry Lee than I did of Daddy Jerome, probably because the things that Daddy Jerome had left behind were mostly controllable, but the things my father had, were not. When I told him his voice swelled with pride. He got along great with Rachel and thought she was perfect for me. They had much in common; loved being from Louisiana, hated being alone, and never had a loss for words. She thought he was going to make a wonderful grandfather, and I thought so too.

He was a custodian who could not read or write, but by appearances you would never know. He was extremely street smart and knew how to make the most of a dollar. One summer when I was about ten years old he called the house on a Saturday morning to ask my mother if I could go fishing with him. Usually when I saw him, he was in one of his new cars and cleanly dressed. This time he picked me up in an old beat-up truck he used to haul scrap metal in. As we drove out to the country, I ran my mouth the whole way telling him about school, Diane the bully, and anything else that came to mind.

We got to the fishing spot, which was nothing more than a narrow wood bridge over a shallow creek or ditch, I couldn't tell which. At one time our fishing poles were probably among the junk he hauled in the back of his truck, because the line was tangled and the reels didn't work. I have no idea where we were or whose property we were on, but as he baited my hook, across the dry field of tall weeds I could see a truck kicking up dust on a dirt road not far away. No vehicle traveled down the road we were on, for which I was thankful, because there was no place to go except in the water if one did.

Being born the day President Kennedy was laid to rest and having seen footage of the funeral every year since the day I was born, became a fascination of mine. I had interrogated my mother for every bit of personal information she could remember about that day; now it was my father's turn. When I asked, I could tell he had no idea what day or month I was born. That may have made him feel uncomfortable, judging by the long drag he took from his Marlborough cigarette. I didn't ask any more questions, but settled for enjoying the moment. Neither of us caught anything that day, and although I was a little disappointed, he didn't seem to mind. He was taking time to relax and just wanted me to be there. He didn't say anything profound or try to teach me the meaning of life. He was just there. That was all I ever really wanted from Henry Lee anyway.

I never really looked up to my father as sons usually do. When it comes to a father figure I took the Frankenstein approach, you might say. I took different things from different people, whether they were boyfriends, teachers, coaches or drunks like Otis. I searched for any redeeming value and tried holding onto that. I hoped when the time came it would make me a better man; a better father.

With that being said, holding you in my arms, my life has come full circle once again, as I speak to you, my son.

By the time I got here your mother was already in the delivery room. I've never felt so helpless in my life. All I could do was hold her hand and wipe the sweat from her forehead, while the doctor and a small army of nurses helped to bring you into this world.

That was a little while ago. The room is nearly empty now, except for the nurse, who has cleaned everything at least twice. She has glanced over at us several times, patiently waiting for me to end our conversation.

You see, your heart stopped beating hours ago and it's time for the nurse to take you away. I've put that off as long as I could. Long enough for you to know that for me evil is a dark arm grappling at my mother through a rickety screen door or Papa being left on the side of the road to bleed to death. Also that faith is believing that right does prevail, friends are to the very end and although virtuousity is rarely sustainable, parenthood is forever.

More importantly, Myles I needed to steal this private moment with you to commit to memory your dimples, your black hair, and the curvature of your lips that resemble my own. You leave me knowing the taste of purity and the smell of innocence. And that God takes those we love, because He needs another angel in Heaven.

ACKNOWLEDGEMENTS

Rebecca N. Braxton

LaVerne Harris

Amberesa Braxton

Leon & Doris Braxton

Riley & Linda McGuire

Ambus J. Braxton

Jarvis & Jo Braxton-Trimbel

Leonard Adrian & Ursula Braxton

Madison McGuire & Brian Heston

Melvin & Rita Renee' Middleton

E. Paulette Braxton

Rita Babineaux

Henry Lee & Mary Lee Malbrough

Anthony Malbrough

Christian Braxton

Patrick McGuire

Metra Liggins

Florida Dotson

Melissa Slade

Nicole Tarver

Kasey Haynes

Tesslyn Gibbs

Mona Navy

Willie Clyde Jackson

Albert Powell Sr.

Delta Sigma Theta Sorority

And most of all thanks to my wonderful mother Mary Joyce Braxton